THE KENNETH WILLIAMS LETTERS

The
KENNETH
WILLIAMS
LETTERS

Edited by Russell Davies

9/3 93223

HarperCollins*Publishers*

HarperCollins*Publishers*
77–85 Fulham Palace Road,
Hammersmith, London W6 8JB

Published by HarperCollins*Publishers* 1994

1 3 5 7 9 8 6 4 2

A catalogue record for this book
is available from the British Library

ISBN 0 00 255024 5

Photoset in Linotron Meridien by
Rowland Phototypesetting Ltd
Bury St Edmunds, Suffolk

Printed in Great Britain by
HarperCollinsManufacturing Glasgow

CONTENTS

ILLUSTRATIONS

ACKNOWLEDGEMENTS

I am grateful once again to the Estate of Kenneth Williams for entrusting to me both the task of editing Williams's collected papers, and the papers themselves. Both the legatees with whom I have had personal dealings, Paul Richardson and Michael Whittaker, have been unfailingly helpful. The complete Williams diaries, available to me throughout the editing process, have proved an indispensable source of cross-references, explaining much that might otherwise have remained obscure in the letters. For further clarification, and in some cases for letters which illuminate odd corners of Kenneth Williams's life, I am grateful to several of his friends. Annette Kerr's kindly help with the early years has been invaluable; the young KW was fortunate in having such a devoted friend and colleague. Stanley Baxter, Sheila Hancock, and Michael Codron all made vital contributions; and the later years, when KW seems to have put less energy into his correspondence, were illuminated by materials kindly passed on by Paul Richardson, Michael Whittaker, Jeffery Kemp, Nick Lewis, and Peter Cadley. My thanks also go to the BBC's Written Archive at Caversham, and Rhoda Cousins, lately retired as Manager, BBC Records Management Services, for stretching their rules and allowing me access to the complete files of Williams/BBC correspondence. Many readers of the published *Diaries* have written to me, and I am particularly grateful to Michell Raper, Dr David Delvin and Mrs Betty Ince for information received. Philip Speight, Roy Oakshott, Professor Hugh Mellor and several readers of the *Telegraph Magazine* have gone out of their way to help me with the minutiae of certain footnotes. The passage from Isaiah Berlin's 'On Historical Inevitability', in *Four Essays on Liberty* (Oxford University Press, 1969), is reproduced by kind permission of Oxford University Press. I have found useful (and also enjoyed) the personal impressions of KW provided by Jonathan James-Moore, Simon Brett and David Hatch.

Richard Johnson, Editorial Director at HarperCollins, and Robert Lacey, the ever-patient editor of the text, have again been delightful to work with, as has Melanie Haselden, the Managing Picture Editor, assisted by Anna Grapes. I am thankful as always for the support of Pat Kavanagh at Peters, Fraser & Dunlop, and my enduring gratitude goes to Caroline Dawnay at Peters for encouraging me to involve myself with the fascinating story of Kenneth Williams in the first place. To all these, to my stoical family, and to an army of unsatisfied correspondents, I apologise for being as neglectful as Williams was diligent in the writing of letters.

R.D.

INTRODUCTION

'No mail. It is disgraceful,' wrote Kenneth Williams in his diary on Monday morning, 10 July 1972. Few days brought him no letters at all, but when such blanks occurred he was disgusted, and almost hurt. He saw the implied neglect as a poor return for the energy he habitually put into his own correspondence, and he was right. Whether judged by the quantity or the quality of his production, Williams was one of the great letter-writers of modern times.

The early poem which serves as an epigraph to this book shows how strongly he felt, even at the age of twenty, about the power of correspondence to keep friendship – and at this stage, perhaps, love – alive and growing. Indeed, some of his friendships were inaugurated and maintained, and occasionally terminated, solely by letter. Kenneth Williams acquired pen-pals of all ages, and several nationalities. These epistolary acquaintances often turned out to be more reliable correspondents than his close personal friends, which caused him real distress at times. He would often complain to certain 'old chums' that they failed to write regularly, or even at all. In his younger days, such complaints could be forceful. Later they took on a more resigned and regretful tone. It seems to have been his aim to reply to all letters – the welcome ones, at least – by return of post, which is a habit that can become tyrannous. Just occasionally, he would ask a correspondent to slow the eager rhythm of his dispatches, and give him a rest.

The content of Williams's letters reflected in its variety the wide range of his acquaintanceship. To Erich Heller, the distinguished Germanist, he wrote seriously, inquiringly, argumentatively in an intellectual sense, but always with affection and respect. To the Stokers' Mess of HMS *Leverton*, he naturally presented himself as all mateyness, lecherous jokes and 'performance'. To many younger correspondents, he acted as, in his own phrase, 'an avuncular mentor'. He would patiently explain English institutions to Andrew Hathaway, a correspondent from New Jersey, yet would come down hard on the young man for what he saw as naïvetés and misconceptions. Members of the public, sensing that Williams was a natural source of pungently expressed advice, wrote asking for his guidance; one friend asked for help over sexual blackmail at work. He always replied, and at the appropriate level of seriousness. As for his fellow professionals, he wrote promptly and appreciatively to those whose work he had admired: 'potent little notes', Sheila Hancock calls them.

And he also wrote from time to time to the proprietors of products or services he had found more than usually satisfactory. I much regret being unable to produce the letter which prompted the Brand Manager of Jeyes UK Limited to thank Kenneth Williams, in December 1971, for 'taking the time and trouble to compliment us on Sanilav'. It would have been interesting to see in what terms this celebrated obsessive in matters lavatorial had expressed his appreciation. Alas, too much water has flowed round the bend since then, and Jeyes now tell me that their correspondence file for 1971 is no longer extant. 'Naturally we share your views on the efficiency of this product,' the Brand Manager had remarked. Perhaps that says enough.

Williams's impulse to 'write in' like this virtually replicates the cast of mind satirised so well by his friend Joe Orton, in Orton's epistolary persona 'Edna Welthorpe'. Parcelling out unsolicited praise and blame in just the same way, Edna's letters were complicatedly hilarious. Her attempts at moral loftiness were constantly subverted by the house-wifely fussiness both of her stated preoccupations, and of her prose itself, which mixed the worst clichés of newspaper critic-speak with undigested advertising motifs, and wrapped it all up in the lordliness of the consumer, the Customer Who Is Always Right. And through all that, again, there sometimes poked an unmistakable desire to impress the letter's recipients by speaking to them in their own language. All in all, it is an idiom that takes a lot of reproducing: yet Kenneth Williams, on occasion, almost managed it – quite unconsciously, of course. A part of him was very like Edna. His exclamatory letter to the *Daily Mail* in July 1971 needs only the addition of the odd absurdist detail to resemble quite closely one of Orton's pseudonymous concoctions.

Some of Williams's letters were merely chatty recitals of his own doings, variously embroidered. Entertaining as they are, these auto-biographical gossips tend to overlap with his diary entries, so I have tended to suppress them, except in cases where an interesting new slant is offered on known events. It should be noted, however, that the diary is a good deal more trustworthy as a record of fact than the letters are. In correspondence, Williams's usual purpose was to keep his friends amused and interested, and he considered himself entitled to veer off into fantasy if necessary. There are passages in his letters which closely resemble the monologues he co-wrote (and later wrote alone) for his introductory stints on BBC2 cabaret shows, where disconnected and surreal nonsense, strung along a tenuous autobiographical thread, was unspooled with a remarkable appearance of fluency.

The selection of letters presented in this book is drawn very largely from Kenneth Williams's private archive. Early in his adult life, he acquired the habit of typing his more important or considered letters, and keeping carbons – enough, in total, to fill a book perhaps three times the size of the present one. Even though calligraphy was his hobby, the pen somehow didn't encourage him to write anything longer than a note, he said; and besides, he found it easier to 'compose' a letter on the typewriter. He certainly made an extraordinarily neat job of this compositional typing. His errors were amazingly few, and since he corrected them by repetition rather than alteration ('lesg I mean legs' and so on), he was able to preserve the immaculate appearance of every page. He seldom bothered with paragraphing, which wasted space ('I get a lot on these air mail forms don't I?'), so the reader must prepare for some disconcerting changes of subject here and there.

I have asked Williams's close friends to fill a few obvious gaps with items of correspondence they have kept – on the whole, his friends do not seem to have treasured his letters as he treasured theirs – but one serious lacuna remains. Looking back over his files in 1971 in order to satisfy an enquiry from an academic, he was puzzled to discover that nothing survived from the years 1957 to 1963. This mystery was never solved. It would appear that during one of his moves from flat to flat in search of peace and quiet, a file of correspondence was left behind. (1974 seems also to have gone missing, possibly during the transfer of the material from place to place after his death.) Since it has not been possible to find enough correspondence to maintain a worthwhile continuum between the late fifties and early sixties – the time of Kenneth Williams's maximum activity as a performer, but possibly not so productive of letters – I have used this as a convenient break with which to divide off his early adulthood from his years of fame.

Some of his early letters are, in their original versions, immensely long. He was 'resting' for extended periods, and it is clear from these communications that when he was not writing, he was reading. That he was able to engage so eminent an intellectual as Erich Heller in meaningful debate about Heller's own literary and philosophical specialism shows that Williams possessed a naturally speculative mind which positively relished dealing with abstracts, and deserved far better training than it ever received. No doubt he was proud of mastering the arguments of certain writers, and sometimes quoted them with intent to impress, for he liked to be thought intelligent; but one cannot accuse him of picking out the easy bits. The syntax alone of some passages he cited, from Rilke, or Proust, or Isaiah Berlin, might defeat some readers. Later, more set in his ways, Williams tended to the moralistic and dogmatic, particularly in his stubbornly monolithic defence of religious faith, though he was not changeless even there. The notion of eternal life, for example, suddenly came in for a powerful drubbing in the very last weeks of his time on earth.

Kenneth Williams was always in search of control over his own life. He was destined never to achieve it, but he discovered palliatives along the way. Letters were one of them. He detested the telephone, he admitted, 'pathologically'. Its use was restricted to the tiny circle of close friends who knew his 'ringing code', and to the barest professional necessities. The ring of the telephone vividly expressed the world's desire to control *him*. But a letter was written in his own time, he could regulate the frequency of the correspondence if necessary, and the exchange of writings brought him much of the pleasure of human intercourse without the intrusion of its objectionable in-person disappointments (such as cigarette ash, body odour, and the intolerable desire of visitors to use his lavatory).

Perhaps this sounds bleak, but for the solitary Kenneth Williams in his bare, monastic flat, it was one of life's major pleasures. On a good day for mail, he enjoyed the morning routine: 'coffee and a fag' at breakfast time, to accompany the reading of his letters. And then the replies – sometimes, after one of his radio features or a prominent chat-show appearance, a great many replies. In 1971, in a letter to his friend George Borwick, he mentions having sent off fifty-nine of them that morning. Even if they were 'all notes', as he explained, this would have taken some doing – yet I think Kenneth was not exaggerating on this occasion. He was at the height of his fame, had just been on holiday, and probably expected to face a task such as this on his return. He was as willing to engage with his public by mail as he was reluctant to meet them in person. Anything that counted as proper correspondence commanded his attention. Christmas and birthday cards he mostly threw away.

The signs are that the old enthusiasm for the 'composed' letter deserted him in the last decade of his life. He kept far less of his correspondence than before, and sent off, for the most part, hand-written notes. He no longer enjoyed using the 'machine'. Perhaps his journalistic stints, at the *Tatler* and *Radio Times* among others, had made typing seem more like work. He was still capable of writing a pungent letter, and of revealing the odd autobiographical detail (see 12 January 1988) which occurs nowhere else in his writings.

These letters confirm, in a more outgoing way, what Kenneth Williams's diaries have already suggested: that this was a man with an extraordinary desire, and talent, for self-expression, which was by no means fully contented by his work. Much of the left-over energy and thwarted sociability went into the writings reproduced here. It is unusual for a man of so many remarkable voices to be completely confident of his own voice, and indeed to prove just as compelling a communicator on the silent page as in the flesh. Kenneth Williams had no problems in this line. He always sounded exactly like himself, and still does.

The Text

Especially when written in batches, the preserved letters overlap considerably in content. For different recipients, amusingly different interpretations are sometimes offered of the same events, but this is small reward for a long repetition, so I have felt free to cut all letters back to that minimum which advances the story and enhances our view of Kenneth Williams. The early letters, had they been reproduced as written, would have overrun the book. The letter of 5 September 1951 gives some idea of the size of the problem, though even that example is considerably cut. Many later letters, because they were typed on airletter forms, single-spaced, without paragraphing, reached a standard length; but they were often padded towards the end, and I have cut them freely, too. As with the published *Diaries*, some cuts were enforced by discretion. Williams seldom held back in his private assessments of others, but in public, one must sometimes do so on his behalf.

His habit of breaking into capital letters, familiar to me from the diaries but suppressed in the published version, is maintained in the letters, and this time I have decided to keep them in, so that readers of this book may share in the amusement, and feel the emphasis, which Kenneth Williams intended to create for his original reader. An appendix briefly describes his favourite correspondents. Occasional recipients, where known, are characterised in footnotes.

Chronology

The fullest guide to the life and career of Kenneth Williams is supplied by *The Kenneth Williams Diaries*, but he offered the following useful summary in a letter to his American penfriend Andrew Hathaway.

15 January 1972

Dear Andrew,

Thank you for your letter of January 7th, must admit I found the Groucho lines which you quoted very diverting indeed. I saw 'Night At The Opera' on Friday, and it was a joy from start to finish . . . As to your question about why did I take up acting, well I don't know a short answer to that one. I suppose it must have been a combination of ego and circumstances. I was an apprentice draughtsman, and when it came to being conscripted I went into the Army as a Sapper in the Engineers Survey section doing much the same work (albeit in an Army drawing office) that I did as a civilian. When the war finished, I was in Singapore & we were allowed to transfer out of regiments if we felt we had a talent for something else. I applied for an Entertainments branch of the Army, and got into an outfit called C.S.E. (which stood for Combined Services Entertainment) by virtue of an audition at the Victoria Theatre in Singapore. In that unit, I met Stanley Baxter who is now a well-known comedian over here, and we have been friends ever since. Others in the unit were John Schlesinger (he directed 'Midnight Cowboy' & 'Sunday Bloody Sunday' etc.) and Peter Nichols (he has written several successful plays – 'Day in the Death of Joe Egg' and 'The National Health' and 'Forget-Me-Not Lane' etc.) and a lot of other very talented people. They all went their different ways on being demobbed. I still see Stanley quite regularly, and John irregularly, and Peter not at all. The sort of shows we did in C S E would be loosely described as 'revue' and were designed for army audiences. I don't think any of us were terribly subtle performers but we had a lot of energy and a considerable amount of arrogance and these are the qualities that make for good performers in the long run. When I came out of the army, I went into repertory companies where we did a play a week & I learned about stage confidence and technique empirically. Making a hell of a lot of mistakes, and trying it all out on provincial audiences. My first London role was the Dauphin in Shaw's S A I N T J O A N and then I went into Orson Welles' production of M O B Y D I C K at the Duke of York's Theatre, and then . . . Oh so many shows, so many theatres, right up to 1963 when I had my first flop. It was a play called GENTLE JACK by Robert Bolt which starred Edith Evans, and the critics really knifed it. It was murder. To me, it was a bitter experience indeed, because I KNEW that it was a work of consequence and that it did not deserve to be dismissed in such an insolent fashion. I started to hate newspaper critics from then on. They are a pack of parasites who specialise in the sort of treachery that is unspeakable. So, after that, I steered clear of the footlights and all that kind of hurt. I did films and television instead. (I had always done radio, being in the cast of HANCOCK'S HALF HOUR from its inception, where I initially enjoyed working with Tony Hancock, but later found him too difficult, and joined Kenneth Horne instead in ROUND THE HORNE and stayed with that lovely man right to the end.) The films have been mainly Carry Ons and the television series things like INTERNATIONAL CABARET in which I was link man with the anecdotage. I was persuaded to return to the theatre in 1970 when Ingrid Bergman decided to come over and do CAPTAIN BRASSBOUND'S CONVERSION at the Cambridge Theatre. I thought it was a happy choice, since it was a play by Bernard Shaw, and it was in another of his plays that I had first had a London success. It was an enormous success commercially and made a lot of money cos it was packed every night, but I didn't enjoy it because I don't really like institutional work CONTINUOUSLY. It becomes such a grind night after night. This would doubtless be redeemed with the right sort of company – actors who really cared about getting the SCENE over and not THEMSELVES – but for the most part, the acting profession is like all the other professions: some of the practitioners are dedicated and professional, but the majority are either irresponsible or untalented. Either way, it is DIRE to work with them for any great length of time. It becomes completely dispiriting. If I had the chance all over again (ah! how many have started such a sentence!) I would go for a regular job in something which you can leave at the place of work. With acting, you can't ever LEAVE it. It is with you all the time. The face gets known, and you lose the anonymity that enabled you once to walk abroad unnoticed. Now, all the time I get the moron's nudge and the cretin's wink & there is no privacy anywhere. But it's too late to change. I can't start another job NOW.

yours,
Kenneth

KW never regained his former trust in theatre work, but continued after this time to concentrate on broadcasting. He made only a few more films. His direction of two Joe Orton plays proved successful, but he found the life of a theatre director uncongenial. Towards the end of his life he was busiest in chat and game shows, and his most lucrative work came from voice-overs in advertising. He lived, from mid-1972 onwards, in a flat adjacent to his mother's, and during the 1980s her welfare became increasingly his concern. His own health began to fail in 1986, and in April 1988, at the age of sixty-two, he died of an overdose of alcohol and barbiturates. The Coroner's court returned an open verdict.

THREAD

The scrap of paper flying
'Twixt you and me
Both hands stretched out to grasp:
We cannot see,
We are as two friends blinded,
On either side a sea.
But the blind have touch.

And all our little world now,
Imagining,
Is waiting its eager
Unravelling
From the muddle. Friends parted,
Platitudes singing,
But not with the tongue.

The blackness and despair
Chain and fetter:
Mental prisons for both
'Hope for better' –
Ol maddening long delay!
And at last – the letter!
A word, and a thought,
A hope,
From you.

KENNETH WILLIAMS,
April 1946

1

THE EARLY YEARS

1947–1956

To VAL GIELGUD[1]

57 Marchmont Street,
London WC1[2]
n.d. [BBC date-stamped 16 December 1947]

Dear Sir,
I have recently been demobilised from the Army, and am anxious to obtain work in the field of broadcasting.

Whilst in the service, I worked entirely under Combined Services Entertainment, and through them, the opportunity presented itself to me of broadcasting over the forces network of the B.B.S. in Rangoon, Radio Malaya in Singapore, and latterly 2BW Hongkong, in various dramatic features and etc.

This experience has served to make me eager to devote my career to it – in England – if possible, and I should be terribly grateful if you could offer me any advice or help on the subject in any shape or form – (or, if this is impossible – pass on my letter to anyone who might be interested).

Meanwhile, I am –

Sincerely yours,
Kenneth C. Williams

[1] But redirected by the BBC to 'Mr [David] Manderson'. Gielgud was Head of Sound Drama.
[2] Unless otherwise shown, all letters in this section of the book bear this address.

1

To DAVID H. GODFREY (BBC)

4 April 1949

Dear Sir,

Mr Scott-Johnston has suggested to me that I might write to you, asking for an interview, with a view to your using me in any future production you may be planning.

As far as voice is concerned, I have a remarkable range, and can play juveniles and mature men with equal success. Am able to handle all types of English dialect (my best being Welsh), a good French accent, and a working knowledge of German. Also sing very well. (Baritone). I am twenty three years old.

At the moment I am playing at the New Theatre, Bromley, but am free during the day. My telephone number is TERminus 4870. If there is any chance of your seeing me and you will name a time, I shall be there.

> Yours Sincerely,
> Ken Williams

To STANLEY BAXTER

11 January 1950

My Dear Stanley,

It was wonderful to read about the terrific reception given to the 'Tintock Cup'[1] – and especially gratifying to know that the hit number's all yours! And the newspapers serialising the script! What marvellous publicity for you! The whole thing is really exhilarating: makes you feel that all the misery of the 'other days' in the theatre have all been worthwhile. My sincere congratulations on this big achievement. How nice to have you say that you wouldn't dare to exult about it to anyone but myself. It is in sentences like these that I get to know you and like you more, as time goes by. Of course, I can't wait to see the news cuttings, the show, and hear all about it from your own lips.

Grieved to hear that you have laryngitis. Such a bore, that sort of thing. Not even what I call an interesting complaint. I mean you can't

---

[1] Stanley Baxter describes 'The Tintock Cup' as 'a repertory theatre's Christmas romp', based on James Bridie's 'book', much of which Baxter himself, as assistant director, replaced with contributions from the company. 'It led eventually to Duncan Macrae and me going "illegit" in the big Scottish pantos and summer shows.'

SHOW it to anyone, can you? Still, it sounds as though you're getting plenty of commisseration. (Well you know I can't spell).

My swan song at Wycombe is *Eliza Comes To Stay*. A terribly dated farce which was first produced at the Criterion in 1913! Written by Henry Esmond, and played by Henry Esmond, you know the sort of thing. Personality vehicle, with the other parts written in for friends. Girl comes in out of the rain – 'I'm all wet' with the reply 'You should be more careful' – big laugh, if you're lucky. Ugh. It's gruelling.

Heard this wonderful story from a girl in the company here – a young actress playing in the middle east with Ensa during the war. A fervent Catholic, she was determined to visit the famous Grotto in the Holy City, and eventually persuaded an American pilot to take her on the trip. Eventually she got there, and was kneeling in profound and deep meditation in the place of peace and stillness. Suddenly she heard a voice full of exaggerated sibilants cutting across the silence with 'Well, of course, Harbord's all right, but Binkie Beaumont pays better.'[1]

> Love,
> [K][2]

To DAVID H. GODFREY

20 June 1950

Dear Sir,
I don't suppose you will remember, but I wrote you in April 49, asking if there was any possibility of your using me in any of your productions. I wrote on the advice of Mr Scott Johnston, for whom I worked in the series 'Gordon Grantley K.C.'[3] I have also worked in radio for Mr Hugh Stewart.

I have not written again to you, for I have been working in repertory in Eastbourne, at the Devonshire Park Theatre, and have just finished my seasonal contract with them.

---

[1] Gordon Harbord and Hugh (Binkie) Beaumont (of H.M. Tennent): London theatrical managements.
[2] Where signed original letters are available, I have reproduced KW's signature in the form he gave it (Ken, Kenneth, etc.). The form [K] designates carbon copies of letters, which he naturally did not sign, and where the precise form of his signature on the original is not known.
[3] A radio serial by John P. Wynn, to which KW had contributed character-cameo roles in early 1949.

You said in your reply that you could not help me at that time, owing to the fact that you were very much engaged on a serial programme. If the circumstances are at all easier now, I should really appreciate it if you would see me please.

Sincerely yours,
Kenneth Williams

To ANNETTE KERR

Swansea
17 August 1950

My Darling Adored Annette,
Forgive my not writing sooner, but I haven't had a minute to call my own. C[lifford] E[vans] rehearses us *every* minute he's able and it's just GRUELLING. Of course he's quite a wonderful and fascinating man, but where *does* he get all the ENERGY from? – I mean!!! Just to make it all a little *more* bloody, we have that awful old Tchehov now!!![1] – with me understudying Richard Burton (which is just sheer ballyhoo! 'cos he only wants a stand-in!!) fascinating to watch though. And Lydia Sherwood!![2] terribly Grande Dame act. My dear the LOT!! – sheer NYLONS, and hat veil. Gawd. Me beads! *Wish* you were her. You are the only actress who really gets LOVED in a company. You have exquisite poise – beautiful movement – and a lovely face, everything you do is tempered with good taste. So right theatrically. *And* you've a delicious sense of humour. In fact you're unique. Congratulations. Needless to say I never realised all those things *fully* till I left you after the Margate fracas.[3] Heigh ho. Gorgeous. I understand from R. that he has definitely got C.E. to agree to your coming here immediately after St Joan. That means I'll see you in Sept. CAN'T WAIT. I'll roll down every bleedin' carpet in the place!! Of course I feel terribly sorry for John. He should get *out* of that dreadful set up. I mean, even if you do get worn out up here, it is in a good cause. I mean you do die in Tchekov . . . Digs are OK. By the sea. Lav. outside

---

[1] *The Seagull,* in which KW had 'only one line, as the cook'. (The spelling of Chekhov's name had not yet become standardised; KW gives two possible versions in this letter.)
[2] Actress (1906–89), later Vice-Principal of RADA.
[3] KW and Annette Kerr had worked for Margate and Eastbourne Reps in the early months of 1950. It was a turbulent engagement, and KW, among many others, was given his notice, effective from 3 June.

though. COLD and draughty for passing motions, but it's an ill wind that blows nobody . . . etc. etc. Write to me soon, and love to John,

Ken

To RICHARD AND SYBIL BURTON

Grand Theatre,
Swansea, Glam.
10 December 1950

Dear Richard, and Sybil,
If sincerity ever meant anything, believe that I use it now, when I say that I was delighted to receive your charming letter yesterday. It was doubly appreciated because I know you must be inundated with work, and all the various tasks that go with appearances abroad, that time becomes fleeting, invaluable, and precious, and therefore it was singularly kind of you to find time to send me – not the conventional few lines, but a long and interesting letter. Actually, it came at the end of an acutely depressing day, like a rainbow in the pouring rain of Swansea, and sent my morale soaring, just before I went on to play Feste in the current production of *Twelfth Night*. It also gave me an added sense of importance, for members of the company saw the airletter with New York postmark in the rack, with your name on the flap, and were all inquisitive to know about your activities in America. I passed on your good wishes – especially to Judy Mannock[1] who was very thrilled, and obviously secretly adores you. (She still says it was mean of me to stand behind the dressing room door on a certain night . . . !!) They all send you their best wishes in return, and hope you are having a wonderful time in NY. Your film came here last week (*Waterfront*[2]) and we all went to see it. I thought yours was a lovely performance, and the line, to the girl just before you went on board ship at the end – 'it will have to be a quick goodbye' – was incredibly moving. Somehow you got all the culminating emotions of the film into that one sentence. You enjoyed making it, didn't you? I am grieved to hear the sad news about Sybil's sister. Grieved because it is such a blow to lose someone so near to her, and she was so infectiously happy and sunny when I saw her last. When does she come back to England? – it's a remote possibility I know, but tell her

---

[1] Assistant stage manager in the Swansea company.
[2] *Waterfront*, directed by Michael Anderson with Burton as Ben Satterthwaite.

that if there IS anything I can do – any help I can offer – I shall be her servant. Really.

Thank you for all the nice things you said about my work. You have no idea what heart it gives me. I know exactly what you mean about the pitfalls of repertory, and will try to do something worth while about it. My home address is 57 Marchmont Street, London WC1 (TERminus 4870) and that is where I shall be after the 16th of this month. Your account of the wonderful party, where you met such fabulous personalities as Mary Pickford, and Lillian Gish, sounds like a dream come true. What a glorious experience! I hope you will tell me some stories about them when you come back to this country. How is *The Lady* going? Is J G still as magical as ever in that fascinating role?[1] Forgive the untidiness of my composition, but I want to get in as much as I can, so I'm not bothering about paragraphs. Judy Mannock says she has prompted this play so much now that it dwells on her mind. When her landlady called her yesterday morning, she sprang out of bed crying, 'Cesario, by all the roses of the spring'. The landlady was furious about the whole thing, and says she will never take 'theatricals' again, because she 'just gets taken advantage of'. I hope you spend a memorably happy Christmas – all my good wishes should make it so – bless you both.

Love,
[K]

To MISS M. HOPE-ALLEN (BBC)

n.d. [BBC stamped 10 January 1951]

Dear Madam,
Miss Lydia Sherwood has suggested to me that I write to you, with a view to your using me in any future productions which you may be planning. I have just returned from a repertory season with Clifford Evans company at Swansea, for Arts Council. I am twenty four years old . . .

Trouble is, it takes an age for anyone to have any faith in my ability, because I look so young. No one believes I could possibly have

---

[1] John Gielgud played Thomas Mendip in Christopher Fry's *The Lady's Not For Burning*. Burton played Richard.

experienced anything! Still – if you could do anything at all – I shall
be eternally grateful –

>Sincerely yours,
>Kenneth C. Williams

To DAVID MANDERSON (BBC)

20 March 1951

Dear Mr Manderson,
This is to confirm that I should like all negotiations and monies for
future BBC engagements to go through my agent – Peter Eade. Perhaps you would be kind enough to notify the departments concerned.

>Yours sincerely,
>Kenneth Williams

To STANLEY BAXTER

29 May 1951

My Dear Stanley,
Up we went last night, with our opening of 'Venus Observed'[1] at
Guildford. Out of the chaotic fortnight's rehearsal – the temperaments
of leading actors – the inevitable shortcomings of repertory – a
wonderful magic came over the theatre, and all of us were thrilled to
discover that it had come off, after all. A packed house – electric
excitement throughout, and a terrific reception after, when the curtains went up and down to handclapping and floor banging. The kind
of evening when everything seems worth while, and all the nagging
little bitternesses are vanquished for a wonderful short space.
    I read 'The City and the Pillar'[2] and enjoyed every page. I am
intensely grateful to you for pointing it out to me; it is a book I should
not care to have missed. For the first time I read about queerness in
what seemed to be a thoroughly truthful light – there was a strange
wholesome quality about the character of Jim which no other writer
has made me believe before. I can't help feeling that much of it is
autobiography, what do you think? Please comment on this in your
next letter.

---

[1] By Christopher Fry.
[2] By Gore Vidal.

Peter Nichol[s][1] left Guildford after the production of 'Richard of Bordeaux'. As I believe I told you in my last letter, he wasn't very good in it. I suppose he isn't a clever actor really. He certainly didn't suggest an English nobleman in Richard II's court, to me. But I didn't care about it terribly. I had no scenes with him, and when I was off in the dressing room we used to sit and yarn the whole time about Singapore and Malaya and Hongkong. It was lovely to go back over it all with him, for I realised then, how little I knew of him during our Service days. Like discovering a personality all over again. He remains exactly the same as ever. Still faintly common, and rather uncouth. He had flatulence a lot of the time. But so amusing. He went to a cleaner's shop in Guildford to collect some trousers and came back with the story of the assistant on the telephone to some customer ... 'Yes, Mrs Booth ... no, Mrs Booth! that was ... I say that was ... but Mrs Booth, I ... You had Squash and Press, Mrs Booth, seven and six Mrs Booth. No ... It's always been seven and s– ... .but Mrs Booth! ... yes, the red costume and the cerise ... ? Yes I know. Yes. We had trouble with that stain Mrs Booth ... couldn't make out what it was ... OH? – well of course ... I see, Mrs Booth ... then we'll say no more about it Mrs Booth ... seven and six, Mrs Booth ... squash and press ... yes ... I'll tell Mr Nest ... yes ... squash and press ...' etc. ad infinitum. The way he told it to me, with the Tulse Hill sibilants, was unutterably funny. As you say, he should write, that boy. He only rings me up when he wants some contacts for work, though ... I have put him on to someone doing a pageant about Dickens at Rochester. It sounds terrible to me, but he may make some money out of it. Haven't seen him since. Met several of his girl friends, though ... charming young things of the usual ASM in Rep calibre. They obviously offer him solace and massage his ego ...

Love,
[K]

To ANNETTE KERR

23 August 1951

My dear Annette,
Feeling terribly decadent and unhealthy which comes of gadding round bars in town with the Baxters who are on holiday from the Citizens, and doing everything. We traipse up and er down Bond St.

---

[1]   KW habitually referred to the future playwright as 'Nichol' in his early writings.

looking for bloses O dear, that was supposed to be blouses! – and things, for his future wife, Moira, who is with him – that's why I said 'the Baxters' instead of just him, cos already I regard them as unutterably 'spliced' and can see that my relationship with Stan has become or is rapidly becoming bifurcated. I think she is rather boring which is a pity for she is terribly sweet, but it's just that most women do bore me, as you very well know – you being the exception that proves the rule, up down in my ladies . . . gents . . . or what you will, thanks very much goodnight. So everything is a little bit dully wully and tarnished as it were; being out of work makes me nervy and restless. Peter[1] said the other day that I was staccato and that's always one of the first signs . . . Believe me darling, fortnightly rep is better than the depression of out of workness. It does us no good. It is better for us to be employed on ANYTHING. I think the indolence is killing. I know that most of my unhappiness is due to inaction. The West end will-o'-the-wisp will just have to catch up with us some time in the future that's all. I think auditions are sickmaking and nothing ever seems to come of them as far as I am concerned. London should only be used as a stop gap.

　　　Love,
　　　Ken

To 'JAN' (probably JOHN HUSSEY)

5 September 1951

My dear Jan,
Just finished painting the downstairs lav and I flatter myself it looks rather gay. The walls in a sort of erotic dirty yellow, and the woodwork in a completely negative, but very clean-making cream. It all ended up rather streaky, I'm afraid, revealing the amateur hand beneath all the bluff mountebank stuff . . . 'just you leave this to me – I'll show you how to slap a bit of paint on the wall old boy' and etc. You know only too well. (Viz our extraordinary whitewashing of the first floor front.) Needless to say, I thought of you continually, and sang all the old melodies, in between the business of cleaning myself with evil smelling turpentine rags. I am terribly pleased with the result; in truth, I have become really conceited about it, and sit in the place for hours on end being fugged with smugness.

　　Absolutely nothing happens in the way of work; but then, if work

---

[1]　Probably Peter Eade, his agent.

does nothing for me, I must admit, I do nothing for *it*. One (being me) just sits around the telephone, looking vaguely hopeful, and behaves rudely in a quite reckless fashion when some utterly inane voice half laughs nervously foolish 'wrong number' over the wire. Thank you for all the charming observations concluding my er 'déclassé' friendship. Ex. Re the Baxter. Being constructed as I am, it's true I overestimate the importance of such a relationship: in reality it is no more than the readjustment of friendship from service life to civilian. Something which was definitely born of adversity, and which supplied a very real need at the time. Nothing more than that. The bubble was bound to explode sooner or later, I suppose.

What a great comfort it is to be able to read a paragraph like this – 'Morality is the mob instinct working in the individual. To be customary is to be moral: to be individual is to be wicked. Every kind of originality involves a bad conscience, and every good gift that has been given to man, put a bad conscience into the heart of the giver. Every good thing that was once new, unaccustomed, im-moral, gnawed at the vitals of the finder like a worm. Primitive men live in hordes, and must obey the horde voice within them. Every new doctrine is wicked. No man can be disobedient to custom, and NOT BE IMMORAL, and feel that he is immoral. The artist, the actor, the freethinker, the discoverer, were once all criminals and were persecuted. Thus they were rendered morbid, as all persons must be, when their virtues are not the virtues idealised by the community. The whole phenomena of morals are animal-like, and have their origin in the search for prey, and the avoidance of pursuit.'

When I say 'comfort', I mean in the sense of enlightened minds like this existing in the world. It is an extract from Havelock Ellis on Nietzsche. Don't you think this cold, penetrating logic of a reasoning mind is fascinating? It's prodigiously refreshing to me. Nietzsche compared himself to a mole, boring down into the ground and undermining what philosophers have for a couple of thousand years considered the very surest ground to build on – the trust in morals. One of his favourite methods of attack is by the analysis of the 'conscience'. He points out that whatever we were regularly required to do in youth by those we honoured and feared created our 'good conscience'. The dictates of conscience, however urgent, thus have no validity as regards the person who experiences them. 'But,' someone protests, 'must we not trust our feelings?' 'Yes,' replies Nietzsche, 'trust your feelings but still remember that the inspiration which springs from feelings is the grandchild of an opinion, often a false one, and in any case – not your own. To trust one's feelings – that means to yield more obedience to one's grandfather and grandmother and their grandparents, than to the gods within our own breasts; our own reason and our own experience.' Thus he points out – how expertly! – that Faith in authority is really the source of conscience: it's not the voice of God in the human heart, but the voice of man. The sphere of the MORAL is the sphere of TRADITION, and a man is moral because he is dependent on a tradition and not on himself. Another interesting point he makes is that men must become better and wickeder. He compares Man with the Tree. To climb higher, he must dig his roots down into the depths, into the wicked. Man must be really capable of wickedness, in order to be capable of real goodness. Without this depth, everything is a shallow affair of mediocrity. It gives one much to ponder upon does it not? – tell me how it strikes you.

As to the thousand natural shocks that flesh is heir to. Oh my dear fellow! What tablets, lethal or otherwise, are there to recommend? Perhaps at best, everything is a drug! I am resolved that heaven and hell is of our own making – ergo – let us fashion it well. As well, that is, as circumstances will allow. Faith is the important thing . . .

Now then, be honest! You know very well that life is NOT dreary. It is the charm of charms, this exciting, changing, dangerous, gloomy, yet sometimes sun-filled existence. It is an adventure to live – take this side or that – it will always be the same. Cause is revealed ultimately to be nothing more than effect. The world presents to us a dazzling wealth of types, a prodigious play of forms and metamorphoses. Yet up comes some poor devil of a moralist who says 'No! men ought to be something quite different' and straightway draws a picture of himself on the wall and explains 'Ecce homo'. BUT ONE THING IS NEEDFUL – THAT A MAN SHOULD ATTAIN THE FULLEST SATISFACTION. Every man must be his own moralist. It is pointless to say that life is dreary because it has made you dreary. Life is this great colossal variety of things. If you say 'life has made me dreary' you are saying that the only facet of life which you have imbibed is the dreary facet: this is a ridiculous insult to Ego. Besides that, you know it to be untruthful. You are a civilised man. You have witnessed absolute beauty in ALL ARTS and been continually breathless with surprise. You have discovered great pathos in the face of a thousand braying asses, you have known great moments of elation. Why give way to the temporary nature of the moment and say that LIFE is drear. Why not feel that you haven't really BEGUN it yet? That's much nicer. We're gay. We've sweated blood to be gay, and by thunder we've just bloody well G O T to be G A Y. 'He took his friends running along with him through blissful lanes of magical laughter; and the best that can be said of him is that he left them, to cry.' That's the epitaph. No friends to see the crying. We do that alone. The virgin soil which Virginia Woolf talked of so eloquently . . . 'Where even the print of a bird's foot is unknown . . . there we walk alone and like it better . . .'[1]

I think it is truthful to say that I am by nature a coward. And I suppose that most of my latter development has consisted, psychologically, in the bettering, or manufacturing, of personality 'defence mechanisms'. The weapons one fashions, with which to combat the world as one knows it. All the hard varnish – the veneer with which I have covered the O so vulnerable M E – has become increasingly thick through the years. It has even succeeded in shocking myself at times. Like building such a formidable series of Maginot lines, that to come upon them in later years is to wonder. I stand, as it were, to look upon the great, vast barricades of my psychological retrospect, and slowly recognise them all, and say – 'yes, they were all necessary once. There was a war then.' Now I want to able to say 'There isn't a war any longer. The bitterness was allowed to grow, excused on the grounds of "frustration" – and now, really, that isn't good enough. Isn't Honest. Frustration is no excuse for bitterness – and anyway, bitterness is such a negative and unrewarding quality.' That's what I want to be able to say. Only the future will show the merit, or otherwise, of the desire – effort – or what you will.

Now the evening is wearing on, and it is almost ten o'clock. I reach for a cigarette, and withdraw my hand from the packet disappointed: poverty necessitating abstinence. I don't go out to the flicks cos there just isn't the money. It's books, and letters, and painting the lav for me. That's what it is, and no use kidding myself it's anything else. There is a tear staining the page even as I write. O yes there is a tear. A tear for the year . . .

A lyric is running through my head, if I stop for a minute . . . yes, I believe it has come . . .

> A tear on the page of my letter
> To tell me my thinking's effete:
> But O that the tear

[1] Virginia Woolf, 'On Being Ill' (1926): 'We do not know our own souls, let alone the souls of others. Human beings do not go hand in hand the whole stretch of the way. There is a virgin forest in each; a snowfield where even the print of birds' feet is unknown. Here we go alone, and like it better so.'

> For the year
> Of defeat
> On the breast that I beat,
> Wasn't sweet!

To be entitled 'Self Masochism' (unnecessary 'Self') or 'A Fear of Self Pity'. Ho. Yes. How very clever we all are. My, but it's nice to be clever. And where does it get you? I should like to know, where does it get you hey? – you'd be better off in the gutter, yes, that's where you'd be better off. I said you'd be better off in the gutter, I said . . . Yes. We heard you the first time. You must excuse us if we don't seem to act on your very honest, well meant, and down to earth advice, but you see, we're IDEALISTS. Yes. We're quaint I suppose. Quaint if that's the way you look at it, and I suppose we must be grateful that you are looking at all. Or should we tell you to mind your own bloody stinking business?

Think no evil of us,

much love,
[K]

To ANNETTE KERR

12 September 1951

My Dearest Annette,
An exciting morning here, with real thunder and lightning, stage management up there must be working overtime – Heaven does these things so well; I thought there had been a bit of skimping lately, but this morning rescinds all former verdicts. The skies boomed, the lightning flashed with a year's vengeance, and the rain streamed down like everlasting tears on the world.

And now to tell you about a wonderful poem I have just found:

> 'Full of life now, compact, visible,
> I, forty years old, the eighty-third year of the States,
> To one a century hence, or any number of centuries hence,
> To you, yet unborn, these seeking you.
> When you read these, I, that was visible am become invisible;
> Now it is you, compact, visible, realising my poems, seeking me;
> Fancying how happy you were, if I could be with you,
> And become your loving comrade;

Be it as if I were with you. Be not too certain but I am
Now with you.'[1]

I like it very much. Tell me your reactions. You probably know it
already, so perhaps it's an impertinence to say it belongs to Whitman.
I know a lot of critics maintain that his wasn't poetry at all. I can't
help feeling they're wrong. One must believe poetry of a man who
could write 'The art of art, the glory of expression, the sunshine of
the light of letters, is simplicity. Nothing is better than simplicity. To
carry on the heave of impulse, and pierce intellectual depths, and give
all subjects their articulations, are powers neither common, nor very
uncommon. But to speak in literature with the perfect rectitude and
insouciance of the movements of animals, and the unimpeachableness
of the sentiment of trees in a wood and grass by the roadside, is the
flawless triumph of Art . . . What I experience or portray shall go
from my composition without a shred of my composition. You shall
stand by my side, and look in the mirror with me . . . A heroic person
walks at his ease through or out of that custom or precedent or authority that suits him not . . . The cleanest expression is that which finds
no sphere worthy of itself, and makes one.'[2]

This last expression of Whitman's philosophy could almost be an
echo of Nietzsche! In *Zarathustra* one finds: 'Morality is the mob
instinct working in the individual. To be customary is to be moral. To
be individual is to be wicked. Every good gift that has been given to
man, put a bad conscience into the heart of the giver . . .' etc. 'They
were rendered morbid, as all persons must be, when their virtues are
not the virtues idealised by the community . . .'

On reference to the copy of my last letter to you (23rd August)
I am reminded of the fact that you have taken ages to reply to me.
In addition to that (insulting enough in itself, God knows!) you have
not dwelled on any of the points I touched on. This makes correspondence absurd. Nothing is more exasperating than receiving a reply
containing no real answer to one's letter. It's obvious you didn't keep
the thing by you, when answering. And legibility should be excellent
as far as I am concerned. None of your Richard West[3] calligraphy with

---

[1] 'Full of Life Now' from the 1871 edition of Walt Whitman's *Leaves of Grass*.
'Loving', in the third from last line, is a variant not always included in reprints of this
poem, while its last statement comes often in brackets.
[2] From the Preface (1855) to *Leaves of Grass*.
[3] Actor/producer son of the actress Gladys Young, and at this time the leader of
the group of young performers with which KW was associated. They had first acted
together during KW's first repertory engagement at Newquay.

me. Well, I think the whole thing is quite livid making I don't mind telling you. Don't look surprised, when I tell you I loathe you . . .

All my love,
[K]

To Dr ERICH HELLER

The Opera House,
Scarborough, Yorks.[1]
20 October 1951

My dear Erich,
No, you are quite wrong. The book is entitled 'The Modern Theatre' and it is by Eric Bentley: not, as you maintain, 'The Modern Author'. In the American edition, it was called 'The Playwright as Thinker' — but I can only assume you are confusing it with something else. For me, the outcome of Bentley has been an interest in many of the German dramatists, with whom he is so absorbed, and as a consequence, I have been studying a fascinating book on Hebbel,[2] by Edna Purdie.

From this, it would appear that Hebbel's conception of tragedy lies in his belief in the fundamental truth that Excess of whatever kind incurs retribution. His characters in relation to their age and type determine their own doom, because they represent a source of danger to the whole.

The individual is irresistibly driven to assert those qualities which make him individual, but this emphasis, this self-assertion, is incompatible with the preservation of a general balance. Herein lies the necessity for tragedy. I understand the theory of this, but don't think I can subscribe to it.

Incidentally, I should be grateful if you would give me the English of: 'Die Helden stürzen, weil sie sich überheben' and 'Masslosigkeit',[3] by which I presume he infers the inevitable guilt incurred by the tragic individual in relation to the whole.

I don't know that I care for this line of reasoning. The idea that the Universe always wins. Surely it is the poet's eye which sees the real victory, and reduces the material issue to relative unimportance? That

---

[1] But actually written at York: see last paragraph of letter.
[2] Friedrich Hebbel (1813—63), playwright.
[3] Respectively: 'Heroes fall because they overreach themselves' (or 'presume too much'); and 'lack of moderation' (or 'proportion').

reminds me of our conversation regarding the Epilogue of the play *Crime Passionel*[1] which we had at Swansea. The unimportance of Hugo's death, compared with the superb victory of his belief. I mean I do not regard that kind of end as Great Tragedy.

Hebbel reinforces his Individual-v-Universe argument by likening man to the autumn leaves that fall and wither, but fertilise the products of a new year. 'Das Gute selbst kann Feind des Guten seyn, die Rose kann die Lilie verdrängen wollen, Beide sind Existenzberechtigt, aber nur Eins hat Existenz.'[2] The idea that, as the leaf that falls is of little account in the total sum, so too is the man that suffers. Somehow, it is all too plausible and logical. Nonetheless, it is horribly fascinating: the idea of guilt that is not sin, of flaw that is not fault.

How very charming of you to compliment me upon the tidiness of my typing. But wait! – you make it sound as if the idea of secretaryship belonged to you! – whereas it was entirely mine in the first place. Ho ho. Yes.[3]

I thank you for what you say about Love 'at whatever distance' – and I think you know how much I value your words on this subject. You know that I reciprocate that love insofar as complete friendship is concerned. But when I spoke of it as a destructive force, I was thinking of a different kind of love. I suppose it is basically lust, certainly it is of the flesh. More and more lately, with the coming of darkness, I experience peculiar sex urges, which are directed in a mental attraction to the symbolic antithesis of what I feel myself to represent. Perhaps it is wrong to call this feeling Love. But you will understand what I mean about its destructiveness. Put into practice in my own life, these mental experiences would – I am sure – become destructive. In the material sense, it would necessitate a Jekyll and Hyde existence, an automatic deterrent to my work. And in the mental sense it would be a constant fight between my feeling of 'moral conscience' (simply the outcome of upbringing, Non-conformist background, and the conventions of a society I am forced to respect – if only because of the place it gives ME) and my instinctive knowledge of what is right or wrong for me, according to natural impulses which are certainly truthful.

The dreadfulness of it all is that physical attraction can only lie, for me, in that which is devoid of culture, gentleness, or any degree of

---

[1] By Jean-Paul Sartre. K W had played Hugo in Swansea, November 1951.
[2] 'Good itself can be the enemy of good, the rose may require the ousting of the lily, both have a right to existence, but only the one has it.'
[3] There had evidently been a proposal that K W join Heller in a secretarial capacity.

sophistication: in fact, any of those qualities which are an automatic requisite to a mental affinity with me! It is seemingly impossible anyway. Will HOT and COLD (for want of better terms) retain their individual attractions when put together. If the very fact of separation makes them what they are, then it would appear that physical abstinence is the only way, as far as I am concerned.

Still another week of this dreary play *September Tide*.[1] My nasty little midshipman gets all the laughs the author intended, and (I'm afraid) many more besides. Unfortunately this has not been so much the result of playing in the clever tradition of Comedy, so much as the audience's desire to laugh, after the tedium of listening to two acts of dull sentimentality which the actors seem to absorb, rather than combat.

I must finish now – it is late at night, and I still have the packing to do, in readiness for the journey to Scarborough tomorrow. We play there for two weeks, and it is a pleasant change to be by the sea. The evenings grow cold now, and it is the time for sitting round the glowing fire, with the curtains drawn, thinking wistfully of the past, and hopefully of the future, a time for intimate conversations with the real friend . . . pouring it all out, chaff and grain together; knowing that a faithful hand will take the thoughts and sift them, keep what is worth keeping, and with a breath of kindness, blow the rest away.[2] Goodnight now, think no evil of us,

> Love,
> [K]

To VALENTINE ORFORD[3]

Theatre Royal, York.
12 November 1951

Dear Val,
In between learning the script of 'The New Will', our current production of the Guitry play,[4] I have been profoundly moved and

---

[1] By Daphne Du Maurier.
[2] Probably K W's favourite quotation, from the Victorian novelist Mrs Craik. He refers to it many times in his letters, in more or less shortened forms.
[3] K W's oldest friend, from his pre-Army stint as a lithographic draughtsman with the cartographers Edward Stanford, of Long Acre, London. Orford remained a faithful correspondent of K W's into old age, but often had quite cuttingly critical things to say about K W's performances and choice of material. Mr Orford died in January 1993.
[4] A translation of *Le Nouveau testament*, first produced in Paris in 1934.

tremendously influenced by a wonderful book — THE CAGE[1] — by two officers in a prisoner of war camp; it was written during their period in prison by mutual collaboration, and some of the dialogue is so incredibly vivid that it almost lends itself to being read aloud in the dramatic medium. Undoubtedly this is the best book of its kind that I have ever read, and the heterodox theme is treated with such soul-searing truthfulness that it is brought home to any and everyone, with a poignancy which is heartrending. The tragedy is ironically completed by the fact that both the authors were shot while trying to escape; the manuscript was forwarded to the parents by a friendly Italian farmer, when hostilities had ceased.

Now that this part of the year has come round again, I am automatically reminded of the early days of our friendship — falling leaves in the parks, and wet pavements along the deserted embankment, and the heart's ease through confidence shared — the trust established. There will always be that part of the one of us, in the other — bound, as Meynell expressed it so beautifully — in the tissue of time; and truly 'one cannot untouch that touch' which remains for ever, consciously or unconsciously embedded through all the years, in the heart's core. I sometimes feel that our real tragedy in this world is mutability — an inability to transfer our thoughts, untarnished and whole, from mind to mind with absolute understanding. So many of the innermost thoughts are unspeakable, and one finds oneself slipping into worn clichés through the stumbling effort of articulation. I am just trying to say thanks, dear friend, for all that we ever shared together.

Yours, as always,
[K]

---

[1] By Dan Billany, with the collaboration of David Dowie, the original manuscript being in the handwriting of both men. A note in the original issue stated: 'The War Office has presumed that they were recaptured and lost their lives while attempting to escape from Italy to Germany.' *The Trap*, another book by Billany (1913–44), was published in 1950.

To MICHAEL HITCHMAN or MICHAEL HARALD[1]

Theatre Royal, York [headed notepaper]
4 December 1951

My dear Michael,
. . . I believe that people like yourself and Richard and me are
unfinished products, and therefore capable of progress in theatre –
and I believe that a philosophy such as we have evolved must in the
end yield fruit in the material sense. The idea of that group where a
wealth of variety is bound by the thread of spiritual sameness, the
desire for continual betterment, the shared excitement of experiment,
and loyalty born of unity of purpose. Everywhere, people are asking
for explanations. Man continually seeks some answer to the problem
of existence. Science ignores the 'why' and fulsomely illustrates the
'how' – religion retains the dogma of the Jewish Commandments
and blithely disregards their meaninglessness to a generation which is
hopelessly bewildered by the speciality fashion of a civilisation which
becomes better and better at less and less. The ritual remains, but the
original meaning is gone. Christ is lost in the miasma of organised
Churches. There is no one to point the way for adolescents, nothing
to inspire . . . only a host of meaningless creeds . . . the whole world
seems to be waiting for spiritual re-awakening . . . and the repertory
theatres . . . ? . . . Rookery Nook dear.[2]

> my love to you,
> [K]

To MICHAEL HITCHMAN or MICHAEL HARALD

9 December 1951

Mon cher Michel,
Sunday morning in York; Bootham Bar almost obscured in the steadily
falling rain, and it is very nearly dark – because of the overclouded
sky – in the attic of the White Horse where I sit tapping the keys of
the typewriter dejectedly. You're bound to be dejected if you're as

[1] Internal evidence does not quite settle the problem of identification. Both
Hitchman and Harald (né Cotton) were part of the same 'group' as KW, and both
had experience of York Rep. It may be that the lack of salutation to Harald's partner
of the time, Susan Sylvester, makes Hitchman fractionally the more likely recipient
of this and the following letter.
[2] *Rookery Nook*, farce (1926) by Ben Travers.

allergic to cold feet and cold rooms as I am. The walls are patterned
with graph-like differing heights of dampness; my cigarettes are
always unsmokable if left out on the table overnight, and I myself am
beginning to show the inevitable signs of wear and tear on the morale
system. As always, when situations like this are forced upon me, I
begin to long with all my heart for a place of my own; somewhere
with only reasonable convenience, where I could plan the decor, fix
the bookshelves, and nail a worthless picture to the wall for the sake
of pure sentiment; and the lovely feeling I would have, when I closed
my own front door! Even as the thoughts go whirling round my head
on the damp pillow at night-time, I know that it has all happened
before. In Singapore it was always damp, and lying in bed there,
I used to daydream in the same way: the gentle sound of a
mosquito-net was the only real difference; planning what I should
do within the confines of those O so precious walls which would
keep out, in some vague symbolic way, the hurts of the world.
Just now, I feel it would be worth anything! – even the mundanity
of a civil service existence, if only I could come back in the evenings
to something like it.

This will be my last letter to you from here. I am hoping to catch
the night train on Station, about midnight Saturday, probably arriving
home approx 5 on Sunday morning, the sixteenth. The thought of
coming home is joyous, though paradoxically mixed with an inward
feeling of utter futility; the knowledge that it is not really home, that
the inability to behave freely as I want will automatically frustrate
and irritate me in a hundred different ways, that I will want to be
away from it all almost as soon as I have arrived, that the lack of
professional work will send me down into those black depths
of depression where nothing seems to make any sense, and the idea
of God is a hell of a joke.

See you very soon –

Love,
[K]

To JOHN HUSSEY

9 January 1952

My dear John,
There was a brilliant and wonderful plan afoot last week. Richard
[West] was to take over the Artistic direction of the Theatre Royal at
Stratford Bow. It would have been our wonderful opportunity to

present all those new plays which we have been reading for so long, and wondering how on earth we could get them on to a stage. Everything was planned. Michael Harald producing the first play, Hitchman the second, and Richard the third. You were to be in the Harald play, which he says you read so brilliantly at 57 [Marchmont Street] ages ago, and everything was going to be fantastic. The landlord has now been removed by the LCC who have condemned it. Unless one can find several thousand pounds with which to do rebuilding and renovations the theatre is to become a boxing ring. Oh shocking disappointment, because needless to say, we could not find the couple of thousand. It is all very sad though Peter Eade seems delighted. He did not like the set up from the very beginning. Said it was the wrong kind of theatre for try-outs, and that it would prejudice the entire venture. Probably quite right too – after all, it IS the east end, and one can't pretend to be playing to intelligent audiences.[1] Still.

When Susan Sylvester heard that Richard needed a lot of money, she rang up Noël Coward, whom she knows rather well, and intended to ask him to help! However, he was out, and blessedly, there the entire affair might have died a natural, and much wished-for, death. But NO, she left a message saying 'Ring Richard West, at KENsington 8868 as soon as possible. Urgent.' Later on in the day, the unsuspecting Richard was sitting quietly at Thurloe Close when Noël rang, and demanded in outraged tones to know what the devil it was all about!

'Why have I been asked to ring you in such a peremptory manner?'

'I'm terribly sorry, Mr Coward, but I . . . well, er, you see, we needed some money to launch a repertory theatre . . . to do some new plays by young and interesting young attractive young er playwrights and er . . .'

'What plays?'

'Oh, er well, the "Bonny Ivy Tree".'

'Never heard of it. Who wrote it?'

'Michael Harald.'

'Never heard of him either. Look here young man, is this some kind of a joke?'

'Oh, no sir! I do assure you, we are absolutely sincere in our desire to raise the money for something which we believe in . . .'

---

[1] Under the regime of Joan Littlewood, which began the following year, the Theatre Royal did manage to attract the kind of audience KW preferred.

'WE have not got that kind of money. Ask Prince Littler.[1] Good afternoon.'

And that, as they say in the 3 act dramas, was THAT. The line was dead. The great manner was gone, the inimitable voice had ceased its indignant tones, the wire was quite, quite dead. Richard was furious and rang Mike Harald and said Sue must have been RAVING. Ticked off everyone rotten, and then rang me up for commiseration. Of course I simply fell about laughing, and in the end, he laughed too.

Love,
[K]

To ERICH HELLER

Arts Theatre,
Salisbury, Wilts.
30 April 1952

My dear Erich,
The other juvenile in the company here is called Denis Goacher. He is a clever young actor of German extraction, taller than me, but with much the same colouring, and blond. It seems he is very unpopular in the company; he is very aloof, not any kind of mixer, and obviously has no intention of meeting anyone half-way. He is twentysix. Everyone warned me against him! 'Oh! – you won't like him! – just because he's appeared in London so much, he looks down upon Salisbury; thinks we're all tats, and not worthy to act in his company!' and so on, ad infinitum. Unfortunately, I felt in complete agreement with him. He was the only actor in the company whom I felt any kind of 'theatre' with. The only one who evinced any kind of quality.

Your idea of strolling through the world for one year is quite beautiful. It would be enchanting. The great thing is to pretend that it IS like that anyway. To believe in a beautiful idea in spite of the 'slings and arrows of outrageous fortune'. To realise that everything has to be experienced, that we *have* to die, before we can live; that cause is, after all, nothing more than effect, and for you – and your love, there is an end.

Salisbury is very tranquil now, after all the thunderstorms and rain

---

[1] Theatre proprietor, manager and producer (1901–73). Chairman of Stoll Theatres etc. A specialist in musicals and American imports.

which we have been having of late. It is late afternoon and the sun is shining. I am thinking of a poem of Blunden's, which ends –

> '. . . and hope that they may leave their little room,
> Some bell-like evening when the may's in bloom . . .'[1]

Love,
[K]

To TERENCE TILLER? (BBC Features)[2]

21 June 1952

Dear Sir,
The echoes of so many begging letters are in my ears, that I hardly know what phrase to fashion next; and it's tortuous writing an unprovoked letter anyway. For me it is.

I can't embarrass you with an account of my work etc & parts – it will have to suffice that I have some little experience in radio acting, and for commendation of my talents I would name Mr Norman Wright, Mr Hugh Stewart, Mr Scott-Johnston,[3] Miss Gladys Young. My voice age is somewhat mature – about 30 to 40ish, though I am myself 24 – and at the moment I am desperately in need of some work.

While I know I've no right to burden you with worries of a purely personal nature, you must believe that I am a young man of unusual talent & belong in the theatre. I won't tell you about stage experience because it wouldn't help at this juncture. But really – I assure you I shall not be wasting your time if you see me – and you'll hurt me terribly if you don't.

> Hopefully –
> Kenneth Williams

[1] From Edmund Blunden's 'Almswomen'.
[2] The identity of the recipient here is deduced from the fact that Tiller replied to KW on 26 June, mentioning his letter of the twenty-first. KW also sent letters to the producers Norman Wright, Peter Watts and Miss M. Hope-Allen on this date, and the above sounds like the last one on his writing-list.
[3] Other BBC producers with whom KW had worked.

To MICHAEL HITCHMAN?

3 July 1952

My dear Michael,
I refused the TV offer when I read the script.[1] It was no more than
ten lines, and rubbish at that. I felt it just did not warrant precious
time and energy; also it would be bad for me to be seen playing such
a ridiculous walk-on, after my initial television appearance[2] – from
the monetary and prestige point of view.

To the Palladium to see this superb man Jack Benny yesterday. He
stands, indulgent and aloof, looking down upon his audience with an
expression of kind and gentle surprise, he seems to be vaguely calcu-
lating just how many more moronic faces could possibly have been
gathered about him. You feel that he senses the irony of it all, and
you know that he knows he is much too subtle at times for so many
people; he is aware, as it were, of all this suffering, of the littleness
of human beings, but you feel that he himself – well, he'd just gotten
over it some time ago, and was standing outside it all, looking in . . .
and giving you a comment now and again. Now and then he gives
you the feeling that a wise and elderly psychiatrist (who started off
by analysing you) has taken you by the elbow, led you away into a
corner, and whispered something startlingly intimate to you about
his own sex problem. You're just about to make some serious rejoinder
when you realise that his eyes are full of laughter; you find yourself
laughing too. Then he gives your arm another 'look after yourself'
kind of squeeze, says goodbye and bids you 'have a good trip'. You
go upstairs, and are halfway through packing your suitcase before
you realise that you weren't going anywhere.

And there you are at Carlisle, spinning your incredible web. Not
catching any little flies, and shrinking from the bluebottles. You will
be free about mid-August. Free as the air, no doubt. O what hopes
are there? – what remains to be sought after? I am playing one line
in 'Twelfth Night' – sound radio with Peter Watts, after a grovelling
letter. Of course it isn't good enough, but youth and humiliation seem
to go together in Portland Place; how I hate them all. Self conscious
little gnats smarming around microphones and producers, and talking
about their domestic fetishes a la Kensington. As the American youth

[1] K W went to Lime Grove (25 June) to read 'small part of Hitler youth' for the
director Rudolph Cartier. '2 speeches!' he recorded in his diary; 'ridiculous, I turned
it down.' Two days later he also turned down Peter Watts's offer of Curio in *Twelfth
Night* on radio: 'One can do nothing with one line. It's absurd and meaningless.'
[2] As the Angel in H.G. Wells's *The Wonderful Visit* the previous February.

remarked to a co-educational school-teacher − 'I know crap from shineola'. It's the kind of statement which renders him inviolate.

My moods alternate with alarming rapidity, from blithesome gaiety and optimism to dark and frightening melancholia. I have lived so long with fear − I mean fear of some kind or another − that I sometimes feel I should be lost without it. Fear, like a rat crawling over my stomach, leaving my pounding heart banging like a skin-drum all over my body; I feel myself all over to make sure the ribs aren't cracked by the strain of it. Smoke a cigarette and deliberately bring myself back to reality by saying that everything is terribly ordinary. So ordinary that it is ridiculous. That cause is, after all, no more than effect, and that, when every reservoir of secret spiritual energy has been entirely used up, Death will kiss it goodbye for you. And then − O! sublime peace, when every man made hurt, anguish, trouble will rain slowly out of the tortured mind and body, and leave a serene emanence to smile about the night, and smooth the troubled brows of poor living, restless souls.

Saw Larry Queen of Bohemia,[1] in Verona. Thought he was very sibilant and high shouldery. Priss'ish. Not a very good performance. I thought the entire thing was pleasant enough, despite the self consciousness of voice minded people like [John] Neville. He should be told to forget all about John Gielgud, and start acting. Revolting creature. Michael Aldridge and his dog were absolutely enchanting I thought. Of course I deplore animals on the stage. They are always far better actors than the human beings, and the competition is terrible. Most unfair . . .

all my love,
[K]

---

[1] Laurence Payne, with whom KW had acted in rep at Guildford (1951). 'Mr Lawrence [sic] Payne and Mr John Neville repeat their nicely contrasted sketches of Proteus and Valentine' (*The Times*, 1 July 1952).

To ANNETTE KERR

2 December 1952

My dearest Annette,
Rehearsals for this epic[1] are the end; chaotic to say the least. James Donald[2] condescending and saturnine: Brenda Bruce[3] rather helpless and 'I am no wiser than you dear but I insist on having the number one dressing room' and all the awful Conti kids behaving like darling little bastards the whole time . . . Poor old Cecil[4] (and old indeed it is, for he is reputed to be nearly eighty, and it is very believable) apparently holds the rights of production direct from the dying hands of Barrie who seems to have moaned some stuff about 'Don't let them alter all the lovely traditional Biz in the production, Cecil'. The latter dutifully promised and the result is that we are being produced by someone who knows the thing backwards but cannot articulate himself not for love nor money not for money nor love. The Children are all horribly clever, and frighteningly shrewd. 'He hasn't a clue about the geography of this scene,' remarked one little fellow of eleven to me, during the underground scene. 'Er – no, er – yes of course,' one remonstrates feebly, and then gives up in the face of such ruthless analytical truth. Children are alarmingly truthful . . . I tried to make some kind of a stand about ribbons in my hair. 'I just don't feel it's in my character,' and all that old stuff, but it didn't work. 'My dear! all the Slightly's play it with ribbons, it is the traditional biz' – and you either have hysterics or give in to utter defeat. The entire thing is DEFEAT really. That the play can still go on DEFEATS me, that people can be so fearfully insulted by its dreadful immorality is DEFEATING, and that actors should try to bring a little reality to it is completely DEFEATING. You just don't stand a chance. Once you're in, you're in. And after a few weeks I suppose you start to accept the fantastic stupidity, and inconsistencies, and start saying things like 'well, it is rather CHARMING' etc., and rubbish like that . . .

---

[1]   *Peter Pan*, at the Scala Theatre.
[2]   Actor (1917–93), prominent in fifties films in fatherly or dignified soldierly roles. According to KW's diary, Donald left the show on 2 April 1953 (at the Alhambra, Bradford) 'after smashing the windows of the theatre in protest against lack of fresh air'.
[3]   Actress (b.1918), equally at home in sensitive or outspoken roles, here playing Peter.
[4]   Cecil King (d.1958), veteran director, especially of *Peter Pan*; this was his thirtieth production of the Barrie play.

I have left the Rationalist philosophy for a bit, and am now in the middle of the Stuart period with Pakenham's biography of CHARLES THE FIRST. I have read the letters from him of that period, and also Carola Oman's HENRIETTE, so this more or less completes the Trilogy. It was a terribly significant historical period you know. I SHOULD LOVE TO PRODUCE CHARLES THE KING – the episodic drama of the reign by Colbourne. Of course it is rather odd because

1) this has always been my favourite period

2) Maurice Colbourne was in KING JOHN on TV in which I was cast for the English Herald

3) I got out of that to play in WONDERFUL VISIT with BARRY JONES WHO PLAYED CHARLES THE KING for Colbourne at the Lyric in 1936!

I am sorry to hear about your cold. My dear, but HOW AWFUL. Of course you got it from PETER EADE that awful charlatan! He must have given it to you! I know he was infectious. I dosed myself SILLY with QUININE BISULPHATE on that evening. I must have been raving but I was so frightened of catching the germs that I went much too far and took TWENTY FIVE GRAINS! – when I got back home, after leaving your place, I could hardly STAND! My ears were singing so loud (one of the principal symptoms of overdosing of Quinine – I know from Burma) that I was completely oblivious to ordinary noises, and the giddiness made it well nigh impossible to stand upright. I fell into bed, and went off into the most ghastly stupor. But in the morning I knew that I had not got the Eade Germs. Thank the powers, I cried! – the plague has passed me by. And it came to pass that I rose again in the morning WHOLE and UNDEFILED, and they cried out in wonder, saying Blessed is he that puts QUININE in his lamp for he shall not be a foolish Virgin . . . Peter Eade says that I am HYPO-CHONDRIAC which is ridiculous – just because I take proper precautions and don't go through all his sneezy wheezy phases he tries to make out that there is something ELSE wrong with me. I got my feelings I says 'Shouldn't have feelings at your age,' he says, 'T'isn't normal' – 'Well!' I says, 'that's the most terrible rubbish I ever heard in my life there now' I says. 'Ave a cup o' tea Duchess . . .'

    all my love,
    Kenneth

To ANNETTE KERR

Alhambra Theatre,
Bradford,
Yorks.
29 March 1953

My dearest Mentor,
To find your letter awaiting me this morning was both a blessing and a
surprise. I had underrated you. You boomerang back so promptly – I
practically bruised myself. Happy making to have more news of you but
you don't say if you are actually rehearsing, and if so – where? Obviously there have been readings of something at R's. All that stuff you're
having to do at Watford must be driving you as daft as I am! I bleed
artistically & metaphorically for you. There is only comfort in other
people's minds. Those minds, that is, which we respect. And they can
be our stimulus – escape from immediacy – and our inspiration. That
Frost novel[1] puts an entirely new pair of spectacles on my nose – and I
rejoice to see through them . . . I have also acquired 3 of the Firbank
novels. These are delicious. Homosexuality is almost the last word in
'chic' in these witty pages. He (Firbank) was almost the last representa-
tive of his period, and the echoes are still enchanting.

My dear, touching what you say about sympathy. You do more
than that. Your letters are wholly empathetic, for you know me AND
the situation only too well, and this goes straight to my heart. I think
our relationship has been one strangely – yet ideally – mixed with
peace AND impetus. You have provided so much motive (of which
you are probably unconscious) and your presence has always held for
me a great calming influence – a relaxing, if you will. A feeling of
complete ease. This is born of trust. I shall never cease to be grateful
for it: and the years seem to bring us always closer together.

I think we're both much too GOOD for the theatre. Good in the
moral AND artistic sense: we are better suited to the contemplative
life, for that is where our interests become wholly identical and true.
That is where we REALISE ourselves. We should be able to WATCH
so much more, for it is in the greatest sense our natural birthright.
It's absurd the economics forbid us that kind of existence, but life may
be kinder yet.

>   all my love,
>   Kenneth

---

[1] Unidentified. Several Frosts had written novels in recent years.

To ANNETTE KERR

Birmingham Rep.
Station Street
Birmingham 5
24 June 1953

My dearest Annette,
Well, fundamentally I agree with everything you say. Like most other
things it is only in outward form that we differ. But you've obviously
taken my written words far too literally. I tend to write as I speak –
IMPULSIVELY – and you must indulge me, over what appear to
be ridiculous statements. Mentally, I'm comparable to a mosquito: it's
a sort of Buzz around OTHER PEOPLE'S brains. The reaction is
really the ONLY thing that matters. The fact that it inspires any kind
of rejoinder is justifying its existence – the mosquito's I mean. Yes.
Well! Your letter was certainly a bibful! I felt quite absurdly YOUNG
and immature after perusing it. Made me feel that half the stuff I put
on paper is otiose. It is something I shall have to take up with you at
some future juncture. At the moment, to write anything is to cheat
the clock. We have 3 dress rehearsals this week, quite apart from the
usual 8 performances! O! tis fatiguing and unrewarding: and of course
we're all made to stay in it. You would be WONDERFUL and
SUPERB as Queen Margaret.[1] The girl they've got is amateur and
horrid. She sounds like a Menotti aria, badly off-key and everyone
despairs. Big rows, and FACTIONS in this company. Thank god I'm
not a member of the permanent rep. It's all too schizo-making. Say
one thing to ONE and another thing to TWO. And be O! so bloody
careful that never the twain shall meet. Freddie Treves is quite suicidal
and says he never wants to see the wretched place ever again. Neither
do I, for that matter. Only came for the prestige, and natural curiosity
about this rep . . .

> all my love,
> Ken

---

[1] In *Henry VI*, Parts I and II, which were presented by Birmingham Rep during a
long series of Shakespeare's histories.

To JOHN HUSSEY

14 October 1953

Mon cher John,
Still no reply to my last letter, so I assume that things are going to
fall back into the old pattern despite those rash promises you made
to write at least one letter per week! O how are the mighty fallen! O
how pointless words and promises are made to seem! How corrupted
and distorted are all the effigies of speech. O let us sit upon the ground
and tell sad stories of the death of Kings . . . You will be interested
to know that as the result of a film test along with about 20 other
dreary juveniles I have been given the part of the boy – Wishart – in
a film called *The Seekers* with Jack Hawkins and Glynis Johns, to be
done by Rank at Pinewood. It is a sort of psycho neurotic coward on
the brink of adulthood and all that sort of stuff, the kind of script that
falls into every conventional pattern with stock situations and cliché
dialogue which is sometimes full of revolting sentimentality, but one
cannot help oneself. One is at the mercy of these kind of employers
and one wants the money. I start filming during the week of the 26th.
Peter Ashby Bailey[1] writes offering me a special week with a possible
permanency at Redcar in Yorkshire at six pounds a week. He also says
that the company is full of 'poppets' and that they are 'altogether a
very happy crowd' etc and etc. I suppose there was a time when this
kind of thing would have rendered me a child of spleen indeed. This
time, however, I wrote a sad letter in reply saying that if only I had
known sooner and so on and so forth. It was not the Redcar place
that put me off; and it wasn't the awful salary; it was the poppets bit.
It's the kind of thing that is calculated to rile me. How anyone in their
right mind could apply epithets like 'poppets' to repertory actors, I
shall never know. It's as bad as the Birmingham Rep. There, everyone
that was sufficiently innocuous to assure a complete lack of competition, was referred to as a 'sweetie'. The latest madcap plan from
Richard West is that we all go to a rep theatre which he wants to
open in Newport, Monmouthshire. Of course I agreed with the plan
and roared my assent into the telephone, raving passionately about
the wonders and the advantages of working in Monmouthshire. As
there are no advantages or wonders, this was no easy feat of eulogis-
ing. I felt the curtain coming down throughout . . . London is very
miserable at the moment, the leaves falling in the parks, the evenings

---

[1] Another actor/director whose acquaintance KW first made at Newquay. He
acquired KW's services for Bridgwater rep in 1954.

becoming colder and foggy and everywhere, the depression wrought by a Conservative government – O to be out of England, now that Winston's in. I hope that you will send me some word about yourself soon . . .

>   love,
>   [K]

To JOHN HUSSEY

1 November 1953

Mon cher John,
As I believe I mentioned in my last communication of Oct 14th, I have noted that your erstwhile promises to write letters was short lived, to say the least. Why are you such a straw in the wind over these matters where you give your word? It's really rather awful. A sort of flouting of your friends, because you just KNOW that they will TAKE it, all the bloody time. You might send me some South African presents – you know – people do. Things that you can only get in South Africa and people send them to their friends in England and say that it's a sort of souvenir. It's really too much to ask me to wait until you get back here. I should have thought you would have been delighted to send me some little thing that I could show around to the few friends I have got left. It's really all too misery making.

   My first week on this film *The Seekers* began last week. It was all night shooting and absolute HELL. The shots were all taken in a downpour of rain, and I had about five hoses playing on me and I was soaked to the skin. Please comment on this when you reply. Of course I promptly got influenza and had to go to bed . . .

>   yours,
>   [K]

To ANNETTE KERR

11 November 1953

My very dear Annette,
We really must keep this thing in proportion. You know quite well how to rate Maugham, both as novelist and dramatist; neither would bring one into terms of profundity. Go back to what you first con-

ceived in the part,[1] and play it for all you're worth. The first thing is nearly always the right thing, and what is more important, it gives you enormous trust in yourself. A sort of lovely inverted outside effect.

The reason I am not enjoying the film here is purely because I don't like acting mechanically. After twelve takes on the same old bit I begin to lose all sense of whatever it is I am supposed to be interpreting in the dramatic sense. People peering at you through lenses and muttering esoteric undertones about 'crack up the dolly' and 'take the lily' – it all makes me feel excessively bored. The business of acting is not CONNECTED with anything COINCIDENTAL to the picture. This is damning for any actor. Of course, in millions of cases the DIREC-TOR should be able to bridge this gap and spur one over the rougher passages. In my case there is no director. Peter Brook[2] was wonderful compared with this creature. And Benthall[3] a genius! However, I am aware of what I am SICK about, and therefore I don't get any worse, and each day finds me working out some new kind of remedial action with which to combat my surroundings. I sit alone in odd corners reading the Literary supplement, and Heller on Symbolism. This tends to make the Studio world rather like a comic strip, and one can cope with it on that plane.

I don't know if this will get to you in time to say that I shall be delighted to see you on Wednesday, but I am hoping it will, and shall post it as soon as I have licked the envelope so to speak. It carries all

> my love,
> [K]

To ANNETTE KERR

22 January 1954

My dear Annette,
A moment of quiet in which to write to you properly. All I seem to have done is send you scrappy little notes recently. Anyway, I believe that I informed you, in my last one, that I had seen Richard? He went on at considerable length about the necessity of getting you for his

---

[1] Of the mother in Maugham's *The Sacred Flame*, directed by Richard West at Aldershot.
[2] Brook had directed KW in the film of *The Beggar's Opera* (1952), with Laurence Olivier.
[3] Michael Benthall (1919–74), Director (1953–61) of the Old Vic, where KW had briefly worked in the summer of 1953, resigning on 22 July.

Aldershot season. We walked through the wintry desolation of Kensington Gardens with its children, nannies, sailing boats, and J.M. Barrie everywhere; even one or two fairies: though it's hard to tell nowadays . . .

I went to see *Hamlet* last night. After the second act I said to myself I shall never come to the Vic again. And then I realised that that was what I had said the last time I was at the Vic. But I always go again, somehow or other. I thought it was all so awful. Richard Burton of course was much too strong for the part. No indecision here. One felt that such a young man would have had no doubts at all about killing Claudius, or indeed of killing anybody. Strapping great forthright youth. No indecision. No sign of the poet, scholar, doubter . . . Michael Hordern got loads of laughs from all the young girls in the audience. All the typists KNOW A JOKE WHEN THEY SEE ONE and they roared with laughter at this wonderful send up of an OLD MAN. Not my idea of Polonius at all. A funny walk, lots of business, and old senile grimacing which amused everyone no end. Claire Bloom just bored me. Fay Compton looked like an advertisement for KEEP DEATH OFF THE ROADS. She had a make up which was dead white and dark blue over and below the eyes. It was shocking. No producer with any sense would have allowed an actress to appear in such a ridiculous make up. Claudius was dull and heavy in a costume which made him look like the Mikado. The rest were plain amateur. Except the Gravedigger. Very good. Cockney. But then, since Stanley Holloway in the film,[1] it always has been.

Hope that *Anastasia*[2] is not proving too much of a strain. It must be sheer hell knocking back all those scripts in weekly [rep] and I feel for you. But what can one do? I envisage myself going back to it I am afraid. Aldershot or bust. And none of us can really face Busting, can we? Don't bother about writing. I know that you have little or no time,

think no evil of us,

> your loving,
> [K]

---

[1] Olivier's 1948 film.
[2] The play by Marcelle Mourette, English adaptation by Guy Bolton, filmed in 1956 with Ingrid Bergman.

To ANNETTE KERR

17 February 1954

My dear Miss Kerr,
Of course we're not in any wrong grooves. It's a long playing record
and contains one or two discordant passages. Good Gracious! you
don't expect the music to be sugar sweet the whole time!! It's the
WHOLE that matters. If I were seeing you I would disagree sometimes, and have a good old barney with you, and that goes for correspondence too! Besides I like to disagree sometimes, out of sheer
maliciousness. I am malicious. I cut your head off last week. Really.
But this week I have stuck it on again. The plaster doesn't show . . .
Don't forget my birthday is on the 22nd. I don't want any cards or
gifts, but THOUGHTS and silent concentration at 12 midday.

> Somnambulantly,
> Ken

To STANLEY BAXTER

16 March 1954

My dear Stanley,
Hugh[1] invited me to tea at Hampstead on Monday, with the suggestion
that if I arrived suitably early, we might walk on the Heath for a bit.
Ever since Hugh has moved to Parliament Hill he becomes consumed
with guilt about remaining indoors on a fine day; he has taken to
castigating his friends heavily on the subject, and grows eloquently
Whitmanesque on the virtues of the 'open air' life in general. He says
that the birds have 'got to know him' on his flat roof, and there is a lot
of talk about breathing in through the nose and out through the mouth.
One feels that very soon, the whole thing will assume giant proportions
with shorts, bare knees, knobbly sticks, and Hallelujah! I'm a bum!

In the evening we went to one of the suburban Empires to see a
riotous drag show, *Call Me Mister*. The house was packed with obviously sympathetic (and I suspect empathetic) spivs who roared their
approval in no uncertain fashion. There was the usual sketch about
two drags arriving at the Holiday Camp, and the hearty young man
in a sports vest assuring them that he would be available for anything,
during their stay, with the continual repetition of the line 'if there is
anything you want, just let me know' and you can guess the innuendo

[1] Hugh Manning (b.1920), actor.

and variation made on that. The two pieces playing in this were contrasting. One very thin, and the other enormously fat. The first one had to say to the other 'I never forget a face. But in your case I am willing to make an exception', whereupon Hugh laughed so singly and loudly that she turned to where he was sitting in the stalls and said 'thanks dear' – and Hugh was tickled pink.

Thank you for your letter which I received today. Quite understand what you say about the restlessness following your arrival back in Scotland. Only to be expected reely. Another facet of our discussion apropos living on twin levels of consciousness. Am beginning to feel that a Henry Miller, sit-on-your-arse sort of attitude is the only one to take. There is a lot to be said for an enlightened kind of passivism. If one *is* going to fiddle while Rome burns, there is no reason why one shouldn't *face* the flames. Like that Shavianism – if you feel that Life is one of God's jokes, there is still no reason why we shouldn't make it a good joke. I think you're doing very well.

Dinner on Sunday with George.[1] Rudi was there. Also two young Germans. Very UFA Clang.[2] They have invited us to their place on Friday. Lots of records of German songs sung by everyone from Askel [sic] Schiøltz[3] to Marlene Dietrich. And some nice pictures. If you'll come this way, I'll show you the Original score of the Bohemian Girl.[4] If it's all the same to you lady, I'll have a cup of tea. Didn't finish till 2 o'c. and I had to get a taxi with the Germans and they kept falling asleep and repeating Es ist nach Chelsea . . .

> your old nabob,
> [K]

To MICHAEL HITCHMAN

25 March 1954

My dear Michael,
Delighted to have your letter of the 19th, also the lovely card which you enclosed. Another superb addition to my collection. The situation

---

[1] George Rose (1920–88), unobtrusive but widely employed actor in feature films; much stage work in the US.
[2] UFA Klang: Universum Film AktienGesellschaft, the chief German film production agency from 1917 until 1945 (*Klang* = sound).
[3] Aksel Schiøltz (1906–?), baritone, interpreter of Lieder (Schubert, Wolf etc.).
[4] The idea of seeing the 'original score of *The Bohemian Girl*' (by Michael W. Balfe, 1808–70) became a lifelong joke with KW, whenever a meaningless (and non-existent) treat needed to be evoked, see e.g. letter of 9 September 1987.

grows steadily worse here. I have still not done a stroke of work since
December, and am now in a quandary. John Hussey writes that there
is an opening for me in the company out there. But it means giving
my assent now! – though I don't actually get taken on until August
which means that if something turns up in the meantime I am unable
to do anything about it. One has got to agree to remain virtually
unemployed until such time as you sail for South Africa. Of course,
as you can imagine, Eade is dead against it, and keeps making baleful
remarks about never speaking to me again if I leave the country.

I hesitate to say 'well you haven't got me any work so there is little
else I can do' because I know that he tries to do things but it seems I
am devilish difficult to sell to anybody. I come under the 'unorthodox'
category of actors, and no one will know what to do with me until I
am forty. Then I shall be invited to many offices where producers sit
and are amicable. 'Well now, Mr Williams,' they will say, 'I hear that
you are a very promising young soprano, and I would like to do
something for you.' 'Ah, that is good of you,' I answer, 'but I am not
a soprano any more.' 'You're not?' they echo incredulously, 'well
how is that?' 'You see, I waited underneath your files and memor-
andums for so long that the dust got into my throat, then into my
lungs, and now it is in the very fibres of my being. In fact, I am rather
dusty. So now I can't be called soprano any longer. I am afraid I am
contralto now.'

And they will hum and har and say that is just too bad because
they have already got Mary Ellis for the contralto role and of course
they can't possibly sack Miss Ellis because she is quite a name and
frankly you don't mean a thing on the bills. I point out that I may
not mean a thing on their bills, but I mean a considerable amount on
my own bills, and they have got to be paid and how can I pay my
bills if no one will let me earn my living? And they say that it is my
own baby.

George [Rose] has left town now, to go filming on location in
Felixstowe or Lowestoft or somewhere where there are boats and
things. The film is called *The Sea Shall Not Have Them* and lends itself
to all kinds of rudenesses, so George says.[1] As you can doubtless
imagine.

Sylvester is leaving Harald at last. She is moving to Hampstead and
he is going to stay on in Marchmont Street until he finds somewhere
else. Things had reached a stalemate with those two, and they have

---

[1] True: the editor of the present volume once participated in a television spoof of
the film entitled 'The Sea Does Not Want Them'.

mutually agreed that it is better to say goodbye now. And leave it alone. All round us, edifices are toppling.

Denis Goacher is working with Harald in the Competitions racket, which you will recall Harald doing last year? They both sit in this office in the Strand and judge competition entries, and roar with laughter and send everything up, and put on different expressions when the boss is about and say yes sir no sir three bags full sir as the occasion demands.

I really don't know what I am going to do. I seem to have reached rock bottom in more ways than one, and know that this everlasting insecurity and drifting CANNOT go on forever. I am not the kind of person that wants to drift and waste my life away, but if the theatre doesn't employ me, what else is there to do? I am waiting for a sign.

> love,
> [K]

To ANNETTE KERR

Repertory Theatre
Bridgwater
Somerset
6 Juin [sic] 1954

My dear Annette,
We played a lunatic asylum last week at Tonevale, and it was enchanting. Beautifully set in a delightful valley, the audience was wonderfully attentive, & laughed in all the right places. It was all so civilised and sane. One felt one should have stayed there. You know.

> 'They are not long, the weeping and the laughter
> Love and desire and hate:
> I think they have no portion in us, after
> We pass the gate . . .'[1]

We must take comfort my love – never despair while there is one soul that understands one sympathy that leans towards you – one empathy that makes it durable. As it is all a prelude to death, it rally has no great importance in so far as achievement is concerned. It's the method. Yes. That's the thing. Mind out for a Lark. Up on the comic cone. Peep at ourselves in passing. You couldn't get any lower than Bridgwater. Compared with this – you're on Broadway my dear.

---

[1] From *Vitae Summa Brevis* by Ernest Dowson.

People can't even LEARN lines! It is fantastic. They dry up several times a night! I had a letter from Peter Nichols.[1] Rep at Yarmouth. He says he hasn't been young since he got there. Grey hair every week! Says he is 70 next week! The depression is very understandable is it not? We have got to get out of the theatre. There is no point in drearing on like this . . .

It has rained for the past 2 weeks here. So even the countryside has been no consolation. There is a young ASM with lots of handsomeness and no talent who follows me around and keeps pestering me to 'teach' him how to act! After 2 years at RADA. Constricts the throat every time he walks on! It's so ridiculous. Wants to impersonate everything that impresses him! Layers of inhibition – can't even fart without blushing. And I want to be alone. I'm like Garbo in the Gobi desert – with a few bits of crepe hair and no chance of a rep. It's so awful. I used to be interested in PEOPLE. Now, I wish I could care. All sexual desire has vanished so I can't even moan about that old thing! The landlady is stinking neurotic and feels my toes through the bedclothes when she comes in with the morning tea. She sings a snatch of something – then 'Shall I raise the blind dear . . . ?' 'No, don't bother please . . .' I'm so weary of the view – rain falling on the dreary bit of garden – but she presses on. 'It will let in a bit of light dear . . .' And in my head I plan a murder.

> all my love,
> Kenneth

To MISS M. HOPE-ALLEN (BBC)

24 June 1954

Dear Madam,
I don't like writing an unprovoked letter, and I suspect you dislike receiving them, but I have just returned from rep in the provinces, and you did once say that you would look out for something for me. I was commended to you by Miss Lydia Sherwood, with whom I worked at Swansea. You saw me after we had corresponded and I told you something of myself. You said you would see what could be done.

I have done very little in radio, but I feel sure that Mr Norman

---

[1] The future playwright was at this time a jobbing character actor. See letter to Andrew Hathaway, p. xvi.

Wright would tell you of my vocal facility, and if there is any possibility
of your seeing me I should be greatly obliged indeed.

> sincerely yours,
> Kenneth Williams

To PETER ETON (BBC Variety)

24 June 1954

Dear Sir,
I wonder if there is any possibility of meeting you with a view to your
using me in a future broadcast . . .
   If you would see me, I should be very grateful.

> sincerely yours,
> Kenneth Williams[1]

To DOUGLAS ALLEN (BBC Television)

28 July 1954

Dear Douglas,
I enjoyed 'Misalliance'[2] enormously.
   My unspeakable thanks for giving me such an opportunity.

> Sincerely,
> Kenneth

To PETER NICHOLS

10 August 1954

Dear Peter,
The television play had a very good reception, and considering how
utterly mediocre it was, it seems right that Douglas Allen should have
been fulsomely congratulated. There is a kind of justice in this somewhere. As a result of this play, indirect or otherwise, I was asked to

---

[1] Letter annotated by Peter Eton: 'This bloke appears to want a job!' Similar letters
were sent to the producers R.D. Smith and Archie Campbell on this date, showing
that KW was still active in self-promotion after three years on the books of Peter
Eade.
[2] By George Bernard Shaw. KW had played Bentley Summerhays in Allen's TV
production.

go and see John Fernald at the Arts. He asked me to play the part of the Dauphin in *Saint Joan* for him, and I said yes and it rehearses about the end of this month. Siobhan McKenna is to play Joan I am told – Irish you see. Hm. Well I think it will sound national, rather than regional – Lorraine v Ireland, but what the hell. Peter Eade says it will be a 'wonderful shop window' and hopes Fernald will dress us all properly and that people will come in and buy something. 'Don't bother to wrap it up – Wyndham's is just round the corner . . .' Some hopes. Ha!

John Hussey has written to say that he has now been appointed producer of this Durban Theatre, and that the erstwhile director has been dismissed for incompetence. He says he will be in a position to sack this awful crew, and engage people about Christmas. Of course I like the idea of going out to Durban – all those beaches and sunshine – but all that racial discrimination frightens me soppy. I remember the terrible feeling of guilt which that kind of thing engendered in India.

You in drag in one theatre, and Stanley in drag at another. Yes. Well it is CSE turned full circle. The irony should appeal to you. Please tell me how long you are in Scotland for, and the dates of where you will be during the period 15 to 21st August. Because I may get together some odds and ends, put them into a bag, and travel up to Caledonia, to see all this hysteria for myself.

> love,
> [K]

To ANNETTE KERR

17 August 1954

My dear Annette,
Calligraphy now, instead of cacography; perpendicular thickness nicely offset by horizontal fineness: a conspectus at once pleasing to the eye and succinct to the mind. All praise, then, to Parker and let us hope that your acquaintanceship with 23/4[1] will resolve itself into wedlock. After my three enquiries, I am thankful at last to receive acknowledgement of my news cuttings, but any chagrin I might have felt over this belated regard has been utterly vanquished by your elegant satirical remarks concerning Phyllis McGinley[2] with which [I]

---

[1] Her new pen.
[2] Oregon-born author (1905–78) of best-selling light and topical verse.

heartily concur. It is interesting to note the obvious esteem in which she is held by such a brash magazine as Time. I am afraid that I am totally ignorant about Runyan – or Runyon[1] – whichever it may be: I gather that he is a clever depicter of comic characters in the American lower classes – the 'Bronx' area etcetera – but it is a kind of writing I have never felt impelled to investigate. I did read some of Thurber (James) at one time, but as I recall, it was somewhat laborious, and I did not persist with it. However on the subject of American humour, I must perforce admit to being vastly amused by the ironies of Leo Perelman.[2] He possesses a limited style, but there is a genuine self-perception in his work, and some of his stories are truly comical. Penguin published a volume of his entitled 'Crazy Like A Fox' which I stupidly lent to someone, and cannot recover. It is now out of print. I don't know whether I have mentioned her before, but Mary McCarthy is a contemporary American satirist greatly to be com-mended. Her analytical brilliance and shrewd perception of the intel-lectual dilemma in the current American university scene is excellently shewn in her novel 'Groves of Academe'. I have just finished reading Hortense Powdermaker's 'Dream Factory' – which is an anthropologist's view of Hollywood, and the result of much careful research. It is mildly interesting, but the conclusions are overstated and there is a considerable amount of needless repetition. She begins on the self-conscious high-note of the transatlantic specialist – 'My interest in American society is both as an anthropologist and as a citizen. The interpretation in this book is based on a way of thinking conditioned by twenty years of anthropological training and experi-ence and the particular orientation of my personality . . . it is the anthropologist's job not only to describe but to say also what he thinks his data mean.' In this passage I have quoted you may see how the inability to write properly has led the author into overstating her case. This ignorance of words and their proper concise usage results in continual prolixity throughout the book. She is technologically partial, and revels in such words as 'physiological' – 'anthropological' – 'socio-logical' – with which her pages are liberally bespattered, yet when she wishes to say that people unconnected with the cinema in Holly-wood are labelled 'Private People' disparagingly, she says 'the people who are not connected with the making of movies are referred to as "Private People", the implication being that such individuals are unimportant'. After a mass of verbiage, including many five and six

[1] Damon Runyon (1884–1946).
[2] Not Leo, but Sidney Joseph Perelman (1904–79).

syllabled words we find her using five or six WORDS instead of one, and instead of saying that an actor may fall into the narcissistic category, she says 'Even the most pronounced type of "Look at me – look at my body" type of actor has a desire to exhibit what he can do' – and later she goes all round the bush to say that the camera technique of so many studios is calculatedly masturbatory.

There are many printing errors – '. . . what he thinks his data mean' should obviously read 'what he thinks his data means'.[1] And alas! Margaret Lockwood is referred to as 'the English actress Marjorie Lockwood'!!! It doesn't hold a candle to Lillian Ross's *Picture*, which is infinitely superior in style, content, readability and factual accuracy, and which only sets out to be reportage!

I don't really think it is peccable for actors to indulge in what you so aptly refer to as 'complaint and grumble, eternal dissatisfaction and endless talk of inactivity'. Conditioned as we are by current condition and environment, that is roughly as it should be. Actors should be in a continual state of temperamental flux; that is the quintessence surely, of the acting spirit. The fact that the actor possesses no identity makes him naturally inconsistent, and paradoxical. Thus the true comic is so often fundamentally serious. And the man who cannot change his mind is indeed in danger of losing it altogether.

If you know that you are definitely returning to London in September I think that you should write and tell Eade and ask if he has any suggestions for you. Say you want to do something quite definite like TV – or films – or something, and ask if he has any ideas. But decide on something definite. That's the only way with these philistines. Specialisation. It's the ONLY thing they understand. The actor that says 'mitteleuropean only' is always being offered mitteleuropean work. Of course it is dreadful, but it is the only way.

The Everyman dictionary is a very good one, for its size, and I am sure you will be pleased with your choice. Otherwise I shall feel it incumbent upon me to pay for it! Ha. My mother sends you her love, and warm good wishes. She is very much sold on you.

      and now goodnight and bless you,
      [K]

---

[1] No, Miss Powdermaker was right. 'Data' is a plural noun.

To ANNETTE KERR

1 October 1954

My dear Annette,
I suppose I asked for that crack about churches![1] – Miss Kerr of Norwich comes back on me with a vengeance! Nonetheless, I am tempted to pursue . . . a wee bit . . . ? You see, there are churches and churches . . . (I know this is going to be tricky) and in Norwich I found the entire atmosphere stuffy and ex cathedra. The town literally reeked not with religion, but with the business of religion; business which seems to have grown a little slack in this present vacuum of mammonism. I feel that religious business is very often bogus business. Too often its perpetrators are guilty of the sin they preach against. The sin of self pride. However, if you will answer for Norwich, I will answer for Ely.

I did not go to King's whilst I was in Cambridge. I disliked the town. Only went to Ely Cathedral during my stay in the vicinity. I dislike most regional towns, especially University ones, and Cambridge proved no exception. The snobbery of them all seems so much more obvious because of their smallness. In London, the University area in Bloomsbury is just a charming drop in an interesting ocean. In these other places it becomes a monopoly and beauty can be so boring. All lumped together. So to speak.

The notices have been very good as far as Siobhan is concerned and it should put her on the London map. I think she is good. But not Wonderful. Not very good. Not as good as Hermione.[2] I think that Hermione is probably the Best Joan ever. Obviously better than that silly old cow Thorndike.

       all my love,
       Kenneth

To JOHN HUSSEY

26 January 1955

My dear John,
When the production of *Saint Joan* came to an end at the Arts Theatre in November of last year, I 'filled in' so to speak on radio. Got a job

---

[1] Miss Kerr's admonition is now lost.
[2] Clifford Evans's wife Hermione Hannen, to whose Joan KW had already played the Dauphin.

with the variety half hour for Tony Hancock with Moira Lister, Bill Kerr – the Australian comedian – and Sidney James. It was a very pleasant little group, working only at the week ends, so I was left with plenty of time to seek something else in legit. There was all kinds of talk at the Arts, prior to the end of *Joan*, about the possibility of it continuing. There was even a rumour about it being presented in New York, because Gilbert Miller was so thrilled with Siobhan McKenna as Joan. But I regarded all this speculation with scepticism. One has had so many hopes in this profession. I was therefore very surprised indeed when I read in the Telegraph recently that the Arts Theatre production of *Joan* was to be presented again! – and later I received a telephone call from Sherek asking me if I should like to play the Dauphin again. I accepted of course. It was unfortunate that it clashed with an offer from TV to play Marchbanks in *Candida*, but stage must come before mechanical camera work, and I had to forgo the television. We have almost the same cast as before, except for Tremoille, Courcelles, Dunois and Poulengy. These actors had since got other work and were not available, so replacements have been found. The substitutes are not good. Really, we are continually being told that London is full of good actors. Well, all I can say is, I never see them! It's the same old constipated self-conscious delivery that so many English actors seem to suffer from. The fault of course lying in the fundamental approach to the part. The stress is on form; instead of on truth. These actors are primarily concerned with HOW they are going to act, instead of WHAT they are going to act. This may sound so childish as to be unmentionable, but it's a fact. And it is this cart before the horse stuff that is so prominent in English acting today. They should be taken aside, and told to THINK. Think first about WHAT they are playing, how they would react if they were identified with it, and then decide how best to project the IDEA of it. Of course the intuitive actor often does this automatically, and I know that they are often accused of doing too much. But I prefer this kind of wrongness to the other. What accounts for this kind of behaviour in actors? – this over stressing of FORM at the expense of CONTENT?

I think that the real reason is LACK OF IDENTITY. For various reasons, an actor decides – subconsciously or otherwise – that his own identity is not the right one. Always assuming that he has got one. This may be through genuine thought, or through sheer lack of faith in his own ability. So, he decides to identify himself with someone else – or something else. It may be Gielgud, it may be Olivier, it may be Guinness. Whatever it is, the accent is on purloining. The result is imitative, derivative acting – patchwork personalities – woolliness –

uncertainty – and a complete lack of INDIVIDUALITY. This in turn leads to the over-valuation of PRODUCTION. More and more, the actor relies upon the producer to find ideas for him – business etc. More and more the producer is blamed if the actor fails to get at the part. But the producer is very often worse off than the actor. He is generally poverty stricken imaginatively, having failed as an actor, and possesses an intricate knowledge of lighting and technical detail, but no idea of the simple business of ACTING. Or, he is a clever scholar, knowing a colossal amount about the Drama, but he has little or no ability to transmit ideas. No ability to CREATE AN ATMOS-PHERE in which actors may work without feeling inhibited. I think this last ability is the most important one for any kind of leadership in the theatre.

Still, *Joan* is a great play, and it takes a lot of vandalism to bash down the fabric of it. It stands up to the worst producers in the world. And if you have a good Joan, it can even redeem itself through sheer good acting. Siobhan certainly pulls it through some dreadful moments. I hope for her sake that it is a success at the St Martins, for she deserves it.

> Love,
> [K]

To ANNETTE KERR

13 April 1955

My dear Annette,
Enclosed, some of my ideas, in reply to your interesting notes on the subject of the play.[1] I suppose our *real* interest in discussing them lies at the core of what we consider the theatre to be. I know intuitively that this kind of play is unhealthy . . .

I did enjoy the evening with you enormously. Indeed I always enjoy your company, for I find your views invigorating, and discussion profitable. But in you, there is always the danger of compassion without discipline, where error lies all in the 'not done . . . all in the resolution that faltered . . .'

> Love,
> Kenneth

In reply to you:

---

[1] *South*, by Julian Green, at the Arts Theatre.

You write: 'If, as you say, there is a preponderance of queer novels with similar endings, then Mr Green is unoriginal . . .'

My reply: Well this is logic indeed. And we arrive at the fact that Mr Green is unoriginal. Not too awful an accusation to be levelled against anyone! *Except that* I did not mention the fact that his play follows closely the pattern of many homosexual novels MERELY to show that Green was unoriginal. I mentioned the fact AS A SIG-NIFICANT FEATURE of practically ALL contemporary writing in the homosexual vein. We have to look for a reason for this, and as always we find more than one reason: but let's enumerate the ones that spring to mind.

1) The author may have his homosexual commit suicide (or cause himself to be killed) because –

a) he wishes to show that the man decides that his position as abnormal is incompatible with his position in society, and therefore takes his own life.

b) he wishes to show that the frustration involved with abnormality is so great that the human spirit cannot bear the strain, & so kills himself.

c) he wishes to show that the homosexual believes his desire to be wicked, and decides to kill his own wicked self.

d) he wishes to show that the homosexual, believing his desires would horrify those he loves, sacrifices himself in order to spare their feelings.

Well, there's a few reasons to start with. And most of them are lousy. But still, let's try to see the validity of the case for homosexual suicide – with which so many writers seem obsessed.

Now I believe that the reasons these writers have their homosexual characters kill themselves is because they wish to make their homosexual characters HEROIC: and for some extraordinary reason, novelists & playwrights (Graham Greene is an excellent example) seem today to regard suicide as heroic.

They wish to make their homosexual characters heroic because they wish to engage our sympathy: because their writing is motivated by the desire to bring about a more tolerant attitude – or a condoning attitude – to what has hitherto been regarded as 'perversion' and which is now being referred to as 'sexual diversion'.

Needless to say, these writers are themselves abnormal and the appeal is therefore direct. It is they that are killing themselves artistic-ally, in every third Act.

So we are forced to examine the position of the homosexual in society. FORCED to try to understand WHY homosexual writing has such a self-pitying Masochistic flavour, all the worst of the Oscar Wildean 'each man kills the thing he loves' philosophy so adolescent and fatuous, in itself.

And the reasons are not hard to find. We have created a situation in society where more & more homosexuals are encouraged to regard themselves as persecuted. They band together and become gregarious as a result, and create freemasonries of their own, in countless industries & organisations. Automatically this leads to a falsification of ALL values. The corruption is obvious. Of course the creative homosexual SEES the trap & tries to avoid it. If he succeeds he often only becomes a lonely, bitter person, pouring his frustration into his writing. Seeing himself as the proud, tortured soul, who is unable to declare his love for the beautiful, but alas, normal young man, and killing himself as the result.

Which brings us to Mr Julian Green . . .[1]

To JOHN HUSSEY

26 September 1955

My dear John,
I have just returned from the Cable Office in Whitehall, from where I sent an immediate reply to your long, eagerly awaited, and very interesting letter. Before I begin to reply properly however I would like to make one point quite emphatically – PLEASE do not allow these lapses in correspondence to ever occur again – I mean this J. It is dreadfully important. Lack of news can do ghastly things to people, mentally and physically. I think it can be really evil. There is never any need to spend masses of time on letters. Postcards by landmail are excellent for keeping in touch. You simply go out to the Post Office and buy a dozen appropriate stamps, stick them on a dozen cards, put them in your wallet, and scribble a message on one of them every week and post it. That means 12 weeks taken care of. It is NO TROUBLE. It is something that has GOT TO BE DONE. I don't care if I do sound carping. And this applies to your Mum. Just two lots of important channels which must be kept open. The fact that you have neglected them is shocking and wrong.

I was more than interested to read all your interesting news about developments out there. I think that you were right to leave Durban

---

[1] There followed eight more pages of biographically-based analysis of Green's play.

when you did. The accomplishment was complete. I cannot applaud the aftermath holiday of self indulgence which you enjoyed, but I suppose I must not indulge in recrimination about an experience which I cannot know first hand. Over here, I am doing all that I can to create something we can build on together, and I don't waste a penny. I have not had a decent holiday in years! Certainly not since the Army. We shall need every penny if we are ever to get a place to live in.

I think it is rather silly of you to say that you hope you will still be the same to me and all that – and 'more vital'. Our friendship came about because of the ESSENTIAL YOU and the ESSENTIAL ME. The result has been an important relationship. You are my best friend, alter ego, what you will, BECAUSE of the essential you. NOT BECAUSE OF THE POTENTIAL YOU. NOT for what you may become, or possible alteration etc.

It is always dreadfully difficult to analyse a human relationship – it's such a tenuous and delicate business. So it's generally best just to take the facts. And the fact is that we generally get a kick out of life, do some work, and have a lot of laughs. That's the great thing – humour. I still laugh about the Chepstow and Dolly Gwynne and Swansea and Mumbles and Eastbourne and Margate and painting rooms at 57 – laying lino, having terrible rows and arguments with you. Let's face it lovey! it's LIFE – it's the THEATRE! (remember Barri Chatt![1]) O! the gaiety of it all.

Well, after *Saint Joan* at the Arts and the St Martins, I joined Orson Welles and his band of assorted morphinomaniacs at the Duke of York's, where we did Orson's own version of *Moby Dick*. Then I went into this musical play *The Buccaneer* at the Lyric Hammersmith, so I am working for Binkie now.

Annette is in rep at Bromley, so it's near to town and she is a bit happier. Michael Harald is still as unresolved as ever. He had this job as Courier to Bluecars Travel Ltd. and escorted parties of drears on holiday over the continent, but he wasted all his money and now he is back here in the same old dreary frame of mind, not knowing where to live – or what to do. Richard West is now producing for the BBC Television service – a serial called *The Grove Family*.[2] I believe it is dreadful – but I never watch TV myself.

Yesterday I walked in the country in Buckinghamshire with Mike

[1] Dancer and drag artiste with whom KW had shared stages in the CSE troupe. Peter Nichols recreated a version of him in his play *Privates on Parade*.
[2] The BBC's first successful serial or proto-soap opera.

Hitchman – poor unemployed Michael, sad and depressed – but the day was beautiful. We went through the fields and woods across country from Missenden to Wendover. Everything was quiet and autumnal, the trees starting russet, and only the occasional flurry of birds in hedgerows – England can be so lovely. We talked about you, and argued why no letters came.

> Love,
> [K]

To ANNETTE KERR

Wintergarden Theatre
20 July 1956

My dear Annette,
I have just come back after my first entrance.[1] Not a thingle laugh. Charming! The girl and I were practically hysterical. The being of the play is *always* in the auditorium. It's *their* lives we are rehearsing, and their tears we cry. So when they're too lethargic to enter into it, there's really nothing the actor can do. Those actors who say a dull audience is a challenge and all that crap know nothing about the theatre. They're only voicing their own inadequacy. A real actor responds to a good house – he is only a behaviourist with a bad one. Anyway, the matinee is the kiss of death, unless you're playing asylums or schools, and then you're greeted with the joy specially reserved for interruptors of monotonous routines. My back is agony. I really must do something about it – apart from these daft pills. What good are pills? I ask you. When I'm ill, I always get the feeling I'm going to have it forever. When it's all over, it's easy to smile and say 'fancy me worrying so much over that – it's all gone now'. But at the time, it seems it will never end – and I get terrible ideas about literally limping to the grave – well, into the box anyway. Not that I like boxes. You can't see the whole of the stage, but there is a certain snob appeal in being actually seen in one. I would prefer a sail cloth . . .

> 'Sunset, and evening star, and one clear call for me
> And may there be no moaning at the bar
> When I put out to sea . . .'[2]

---

[1] In *Hotel Paradiso* by Feydeau, with Alec Guinness and Irene Worth. It ran until 3 November.
[2] From Tennyson's 'Crossing the Bar'. 'No moaning *of* the bar' is the correct line.

Louie and Charles saw you on the television screen. It sounded as if you were flitting, but they said it was comforting to know you were around. A reminder of civilisation, so to speak.

Well there's no reason why we shouldn't take tea together or something, at any time, you can always contact me at the theatre, or in the flat in the morning. Or you could call on me at Endsleigh Court[1] at 10.30 for coffee or something – I could show you the original score of 'The Bohemian Girl' . . .

Love,
Kenneth

[1] KW had moved to 817 Endsleigh Court, Upper Woburn Place, London WC1, on 24 March 1956.

2

LATER YEARS

1964–1988

To JOHN[1]

62 Farley Court,
Allsop Place,
London NW1[2]
4 May 1964

Dear John,
Thank you so much for your delightfully long letter. It sounds like
you had a marvellous holiday; you certainly pack a lot into a few
days! I had heard all about the success of Bea Lillie in 'High Spirits'
– but that sort of thing is not really my cup of tea, and she doesn't
really amuse me. Looks like a man and the comedy is always rather
private, as far as I can see. I was furious that you didn't linger on
the baths. The whole thing is dismissed in one sentence as 'filthy,
depressing, iniquitous' etc. You sound like an outraged puritan. No,
I know there is no reason why you shouldn't; it's just that this is
supposed to be my role. Well usually. You are supposed to be a good
all-round guy and well integrated. That is the impression you're supposed to give. Don't you know that. I sit here dispatching my neurotic
doodlings, and you're supposed to return with generous, warm, North
American, well composed panaceas for all ills. Well you know what
I mean. This is what the New World is for. This is the cure for the
European decadent. And what happens? – one look at these baths
and you fly off like a scalded chicken, screaming about filthy dens of
iniquity. And you leave it at that! – I mean, you don't say what in
particular was iniquitous. It's the particulars I am interested in. I like

---

[1] Probably John Wood in Toronto, with whom KW's diary shows him to have been
corresponding at this time.
[2] His new address since 12 October 1963.

to get it all down. I like to get down to the particulars. How can I say
I love you, when I can hardly breathe down here. With the particulars
. . . Funny about you getting the book shelves fixed in your apartment. That is what I have been doing. Last week I went chasing all
over the town, and eventually I found some 35 inch units which
exactly fit a recess I have got, and I am going to have them right up
the wall. They will accommodate loads of books. I am fed up with
having them lie about getting dusty. Books dress a room very well
too. Of course I have got very little fiction. It's mainly reference and
biographical and historical stuff I am interested in. Though I did get
Radcliffe[1] because I read such a superb review of it in the newspaper.
I was not disappointed. I thought he used a very wide canvas. Heavy
with symbols. And most of it came off. This idea of equating the
sexlessness of Christ with the invalidation of modern man is a fascinating idea, and the dichotomy of Law and man's need for man's love
was brilliantly expressed. And HOW he understands the puritan conscience! – I have never seen it done so well. Of course I lent my copy
to John H and I haven't got it back. O no. They never return books.
It doesn't do to lend them in the first place. I should not let anything
out of my sight I should not. Your handwriting was so bad I thought
you had written – The National Bank of Canada is doing 'Romeo and
Juliet' – but eventually I deciphered it as the National Ballet. I thought
it was funny at the time.

   I had this telegram last week asking me to telephone a Kensington
number and signed 'Sybil BURTON not THORNDIKE' which I
thought v. amusing. So I rang her and she asked me to accompany
her on the opening night of SHE LOVES ME[2] at the Lyric. So on
the next morning I went over to collect her. She has rented Peter
Glenville's house in Brompton Square, and there were oil paintings
of him everywhere. Gave the whole thing a glowering sort of heavi-
ness. We sat there with fags and glasses of sherry, grimacing and
giggling for hours, gossiping about the divorce and Taylor and Richard.
The marvellous thing about Sybil is that she never loses that sense of
perspective, or her ability to send everything up, including herself. So
nothing is tragic. And in an age like ours this is very sane making.
Then we went to this musical She Loves Me. Well I cannot describe
the utter vacuousness of it all. It is unbelievably boring, and the sentiment so incredibly arch and cloying that you really can't believe the
first curtain. It left me stunned. The sheer banality of it is crippling.

---

[1] 1963 novel by David Storey (b.1933).
[2] Book by Joe Masteroff, music Jerry Bock, lyrics Sheldon Harnick.

If you know what I mean. And there isn't a decent tune anywhere. Not anywhere. I was looking under the seat. Nothing. The auditorium was full of sycophants and they received it rapturously. It got quite a decent press too. Some were bad notices, but some were really quite good. Which is really amazing. Well, after the performance Sybil and me went on to the Pickwick for dinner, where we met two friends of hers who joined us for a meal – Donald Macleary and Graham Usher – both with the Royal Ballet and both very charming. We were all standing at the bar chatting when I felt someone shoving his finger up my bum. I just went on chatting – I thought I am not going to turn round because anyone that behaves like this must be awful – and then it happened again; this time it was pushed up so far that one really couldn't ignore it. It was Peter O'Toole. I said 'Oh it's you!' rather sheepishly and he started all that hugging stuff and saying 'How are you me old darling?' as though one was a Border Collie, and ruffling the hair and everything. And I said to Sybil that it was him who had been putting his hand up my bum and she laughed so much she choked over her drink and said 'O Peter you are A W F U L, you really are' and laughed all over again. I seem to be typing like mad and yet the page never seems to grow. I used to think that when one typed a letter, it always improved the quality of one's writing. Now I don't think so any more. And it shakes one's faith too. I used to think I could spell but when you actually see the words coming up in type, it all looks so strange and alien and you think that it can't possibly be correct. You think. You type so beautifully; and on such imposing stationery. It's all so grand. And I am green with envy. With envy I am green. But then you do everything so well. You are so successful. All these people you are always meeting. Always fresh fields to conquer. The field behind you strewn with the corpses of your ruthless conquests. It's the ruthlessness of you that appeals to everyone. They K N O W you are ruthless and they are frightened and attracted at the same time. That's the secret of it all. Everything about success is contained in that. You have to give an impression of absolute mastery. Mastery in whatever field – personal or professional. That is what always impresses people. 'He knows exactly what he is doing!:' they all think, with admiration. Because we live among such tottering standards, and values are being so constantly eroded, then when someone comes along and says 'this is how it should be done' it wins immediate respect. All the world loves a lover . . .

love,
[K]

To JOHN

29 June 1964

My dear John,

. . . What a marvellous city you live in. The bars and the parties and
the excitement. Everything seems colourless here by comparison. Did
I tell you that I went to see *Othello* at the National? – Maggie [Smith]
got me two seats and I was v. curious to see what she did with Desdemona and I am here to tell you that it is quite stunning. It must be
the best Desdemona in the history of the English theatre. She has
increased in stature so much, she astonished me. The performance is
superb vocally and physically. Not one of her gestures comes from
the elbow; when an arm is raised, it is raised totally, and with an
authority that is classic. The costumes are wonderfully authentic, and
richly Venetian; when she appears, with yards and yards of heavy
silk brocade trailing behind her, and that magnificent red hair braided,
she walks downstage for the first part of the speech and then turns
in a great sweeping movement, so every fold in the umber and gold
material undulates under the lights; the rest of the court are in those
heavy long velvets, and the entrance of Olivier in a simple white linen
tunic is in perfect juxtaposition. He gives a performance of soaring
grandeur. He goes from simple dignity and gentleness into vexation
and terrible anger, and then – heartrending despair. I think it will be
a milestone in my theatre going. The performance stayed with me for
days afterwards. I wrote him a fan letter. I told him that twentieth
century spontaneity was out of place: that one needed eighteenth
century precision and formality to convey one's thanks. He is a giant,
John, really, and I think he is the last of a breed that is almost extinct
in this country. Who else has got this hugeness in all the senses? –
this fantastic generosity of spirit that comes pouring over the footlights
and envelops you – and encompasses you in a world where the artist's
vision is complete, and leaves you richer for seeing him. I would work
for him ANY day. I can tell you that. The rest of the company does
not match these two. The Iago of Frank Finlay is simply too ordinary
for poetic drama. He is hewn out of OUR world, not the world of
poetic drama. He splits the speeches into 'points' which make a kind
of sense, but the sense is one of prosody. You are never swept into
the iambic pentameter, and it is strangely worthy and dull.

   Last week end there were eight shows closed in the London theatre.
Audiences are dwindling to the merest trickle. The Phoenix had eleven
people out front on Saturday night, and Eli Wallach at the Globe had
five for one matinee. It is all so frightening that the London Theatre

Managers have appealed to the owners to reduce the theatre rents. I predict the closing of a lot of theatres. Soon there will only be a coterie audience for the serious play – and theatres will house only musicals and light stuff.

> love,
> [K]

To NOEL WILLMAN

8 July 1964

Mon cher Noel,
Well you know, these notes you're sending are a bit measly I mean, well, aren't they? – they give one no idea of what you are doing, who you are meeting, conversations you are having, etc. Letter from my old friend John Hussey who is at Stratford with the Wars of the Roses saying that his mother was very ill, so I went to Portsmouth and got the boat across to the Isle of Wight, to visit her in hospital. The boat was crowded. Absolutely suffocating, and the sun relentless. No shade. I could feel me skin going up in smoke. I was ablaze when we stepped ashore. Going down the gangplank, a drear in Bermuda shorts confided to me 'There is a new ferry service from the other pier that does the crossing in 5 minutes by Hovercraft, but it costs twice as much.' I was furious. I thought to hell with the cost, if only I had known one could actually avoid all that stifling mass of inanity. Eventually I got to the hospital at Shanklin. In the foyer there was a huge notice 'Will visitors remove stiletto heels before entering?' which I thought was very sensible. I had prudently left mine in London. When I got in to the ward, I found the old lady quite cheerful, and full of malicious gossip about fellow patients who peed the bed, exposed themselves, and generally behaved badly in the cottage hospital. By the time I got back to Portsmouth I was exhausted. The train up to Waterloo was packed with sailors who drank beer out of the bottle and played cards, their fingers yellow at the tips with nicotine. On Wednesday I took Sybil Burton to see the trade show of my latest 'Carry On Spying'. She sat there, speechless. There was hardly a laugh. At one point in the picture I have to come out of a cubicle lavatory and say to a man who is waiting to use it, 'I should give it a minute if I were you . . .' and Syb said, 'O Ken – that is really terrible!' and I said yes but we've all got to earn a living, and we argued all the way to the Corner House. Lunch at the Grill and Cheese, you see. Everybody goes there. There was John Perry, and Anna Massey and John Schlesinger and

O just everyone was there, and you get people going round the tables waving at everybody else. It is a riot. The Eli Wallach plays[1] at the Globe came off after a fortnight. And I was told that Binkie had said 'they are the American equivalent of the Shaffer plays but they are chic'er.' But I think they misheard him. He must have said 'cheaper'. On Thursday a costume fitting for all my clothes in this next Carry On.[2] I am playing Caesar. In the script, everyone calls me 'Julie'. On Friday in the evening to the Royal Ballet who are temporarily at Drury Lane, where we had a box for 'Marguerite and Armand' danced by Fonteyn and Nureyev. It was superbly theatrical, and the applause went on ridiculously long. After twenty minutes of it, I went off to the bar and had an iced sherry. As I was sipping a voice behind me said 'How's your asp?' which rather shook me. It was Judy Garland. She was referring to that record I made about the Asp in the revue. I said to her 'You must have some marvellous elixir you keep under the bed, to look like you do' and I meant it. She looked like she had just come off the set of 'Wizard of Oz', absolutely marvellous, and of course I was very flattered she remembered me so I got hold of my party and blithely said 'You must all meet Miss Garland' with a tremendous air. It was all Belle of the Ball stuff, I can tell you.

Our lovely weather has all gone now. It is overcast and raining today. I have treated meself to a new recording of the Bach Double Violin Concerto. And a copy of the Penguin New Poets. Fantastic buy at only four and sixpence! – came home with them both under me arm and had a mad lunch of cream cheese and celery. I went out to see Gordon Jackson in the evening, and on the bus I heard this dialogue behind me. Honestly.

'What sort of affair is it then?'

'My dear young girl, it is a select and private little dinner party.'

'What sort of dinner?'

'Cold consommé, ribs of beef, and strawberries.'

'Will there be wine?'

'My dear young girl, of course there will be wine!'

'Mm. Yes. I hope it is Tia Maria.'

'A Y?'

'Tia Maria.'

'My dear young girl, that is not a table wine. It is a liqueur.'

'Well I hope we have it after.'

---

[1] *The Tiger* and *The Typists*, double bill by Murray Schisgal.
[2] *Carry On Cleo*, intended at the time partly as a pastiche of the Burton/Taylor *Cleopatra*.

'Of course we shan't. They will serve port, after.'

'Oo . . . I've never drunk port.'

'Port, my dear young girl, is the drink of a gentleman.'

When I got up to go at Heath Drive, I had a good look at these two I can tell you. I was v. curious to see the faces that had made these remarks. He was school tie and flannel suited, she had a woolly over a print dress. He looked about seventeen. She looked slightly younger. I assure you that I have not embroidered this account. Of course, there was more said, but this was the tale end. Afterwards, they lapsed into silence. I suppose I should have written TAIL END and not the other. But you know I am no scholar.

> love,
> [K]

To STANLEY BAXTER

20 October 1965

My Dear Stanley,

Well, we are in the middle of the last week of our rehearsals,[1] so of course the trepidation is starting to grow, all the worries about the tour, how it will go, whether we shall get a theatre and whether it will be a good one and so on. It has been a very interesting period for me. In fact, if the worst came to the worst, and we were the most awful flop, it would still have been worth while. The cast have all got better and better during the four weeks, and this has been mostly due to Bev.[2] It has been the first time in my life that I have worked with a real director. I know that this is probably not saying very much, because I have met with so many bug-eyed phonies, and I have always tended to dismiss them all as a meretricious bunch of parasites, but B is really good, and not one of the rehearsals has been boring. The girl – Caroline Mortimer – has come on very well, and if she goes on the way she is at the moment, I should think it will make her. It is a marvellous part for any actress. Anyway, we will have our first audience on Monday the 25th when we open in Brighton.

Saturday was really lovely. Warm and balmy afternoon. I walked with Louie to see that new precinct in Victoria they've just opened. It's like another city. Fantastic. Then we walked down Victoria Street, and as we approached Parliament Square, L said 'What is that building

---

[1] For *The Platinum Cat*, by Roger Longrigg.

[2] Beverley Cross (see appendix, p. 290).

there?' and I said it was Westminster Abbey, and she said 'I've never been in there in my life. I've often wondered what it would be like – it's where the Queen got married, isn't it?' I said yes, and asked her if she'd like to go in, and she said 'How much is it?' and seemed quite surprised to find that it cost nothing. We were just in time for the afternoon service. It was very full, the organ soaring into the great fan vaulting, and the choir was superb. The boy-soprano voices quite magnificent, and incredibly moving. It was all lovely, but I was disappointed with the hymn selection. I am pretty good on hymns as you know, and know many by heart, but their choices were obscure, with indifferent words, and melodies I had never heard before in my life.

Well I hope everything continues to go well for you, and that your reception with the show is all you could wish. There isn't any more to tell you, so this will be a short one, but I felt the urge to keep in touch. I think it's important when you are all those miles away.

> my love to you,
> [K]

To SHIRLEY du BOULAY[1]

3 August 1966

Dear Shirley,
So civilised of you to write – so many people in our profession use the telephone – it is a refreshing change. Well, about this food thing. I'm almost the *last* person really. I can't stand gourmets and wine lovers and all that chi chi rubbish about eating. I'm too much of a puritan I suppose. I will always remember eating wild strawberries in North Burma because they were particularly piquant AND totally unexpected, and I have exotic memories of tasting Heart of the Palm when lunching with a v. ritzy film producer, but retreating from these dizzy heights I have to face the fact that as a bachelor, living alone, and only bothering with simple things, I still find a boiled egg delightful – cut off its head with a sharp whack & feel every bit as satisfied as if I'd learned of a nationalised industry returned to its rightful owner. One looks forward of course to visiting other people's houses and whenever I'm going to Gordon Jackson I always pray that his wife is going to produce a crumble. Apple or peach or whatever. I think a

---

[1] Producer, 'Woman's Hour', BBC Radio. KW had been contributing talks on sundry topics, favourite foods evidently being the latest suggestion.

crumble is utter luxury. The most I'll do MYSELF is v. raw tomatoes with cucumber in oil & vinegar and pepper because it reminds me of Greece – whenever you go there it seems an inevitable accompaniment to the meal whether you order it or not. Indeed cucumber is a constant favourite with me – in between wafer thin slices of bread it is quite perfect – and, as I once found when I played in 'The Importance' – one of the few things you can eat and speak with! If you think any of this might be worth hearing, just let me know –

> yours,
> Kenneth

To SHEILA HANCOCK[1]

15 January 1967

Well darling – I went to see your film[2] tonight and I've just got home, but I can't go to bed without sitting down & writing to tell you my impressions while they're still fresh & the morning hasn't blurred & jaded everything. I have never seen you perform so beautifully in my life before. You did everything with immaculate taste and precision – the throwaway line on the stairs ('About the only thing you'll ever lay') to the great show-down scene, and the culmination from the lines about Terry – 'He's not much, but . . .' etc. to that great 'whoopee', was practically cathartic – the audience LOVED it and WANTED it – that feeling that THEY were speaking thro' you – that sometimes happens superbly in the theatre, but very rarely in the cinema – but you did it tonight & you moved us to tears in the process.

> Love to you,
> Kenneth

---

[1] b.1933, KW's leading lady in the 1961 revue *One Over the Eight*.
[2] *The Anniversary*, starring Bette Davis. Sheila Hancock as Karen Taggart, Jack Hedley as Terry Taggart.

To JOE ORTON & KENNETH HALLIWELL[1]

10 June 1967

Well my dears, I guessed Joe had returned to Morocco, and I had not
been able to see him, or indeed anybody, because I have been up to
my eyes in work on this film.[2] It's an eight week schedule, finishing
[at] the end of June but it seems to be going on for ever! Today I saw
the article in the Evening News about Joe, with the great sexy photo
and all. Quite a spread! – all that stuff about success not affecting Joe
'I will go on living in Islington in my bed sit' he said wryly. Big fucking
deal. I got this filthy letter from Uncle Whuppity.[3] Do you think that
this is a real name? – it sounds assumed to me – or what they used
to call at my finishing school in Paris a nom de plume de ma tante.
Something of that fashion. He must be raving mad. He seems to have
a built-in prejudice against suossantneuf [sic]. Quite ridiculous. The
man has obviously never lived. So different from the home life of our
own dear Queen. Did you see that the Windsors had been over for
the memorial to Mary unveiling?[4] – they've got a nerve I must say!
– I saw the photographs of old Wallis Warfield sucking up to the
Queen Mother and trying it on. Of course she got the bum's rush.
Serve her right. They flew off to Paris the same evening. Disappeared
in a flurry of lavender without so much as a kiss your arse . . . I have
just heard in the BBC that Nasser is out. Apparently resigned. It's all
very melodramatic out there, isn't it? I suppose you are both pooh-
poohing it, but I am right behind Moyshe in this matter.[5] I am all for
the actual LOOK of the thing. And the uncircumcised shall be cast
out and the daughters of the Philistines rejoice. Publish it not in Gath.
You'd never collect a penny in royalties if you did . . . I don't suppose
you would recognise me at the moment. I have had all me hair off.

---

[1] John Kingsley Orton (1933–67), playwright, and his partner (to some extent
editor) Halliwell had discovered the sexual delights of Tangier. Less than two months
after this letter, Halliwell killed Orton with a hammer in their Islington flat and then
committed suicide.
[2] It eventually came to be called *Carry On – Follow That Camel*.
[3] This exceptionally scurrilous document, offering advice to children on how to
catch venereal diseases, survives among KW's received correspondence. 'Whuppity'
is the correct form.
[4] The invitation extended to the Duke of Windsor and his wife, the former Wallis
(Warfield) Simpson, to the unveiling of a plaque in memory of the Duke's mother,
Queen Mary, had been interpreted as a sign of some small rapprochement between
the British royal family and the abdicated King Edward VIII.
[5] Moshe Dayan was Israel's military coordinator in the Six-Day War with Egypt,
then in progress. President Nasser of Egypt resigned on the fifth day of the conflict.

I am playing this Prussian in the film. People just don't recognise me at all! – just walk by me in the streets; considering their conversation, it's probably just as well. I was dismayed at the rushes to see that the monocle is bigger than I am. But me accent is very good. Now that is where I score you see. It is a vocal talent. I went to Sheila Hancock's party. What a posh place she has moved to! – it's all Scandinavia and patio-Spanish. V. mod I must say. I got terribly sloshed. A good job I had ordered the car. Chauffeur practically had to scrape me off the floor. I fell in the lift at Farley and have hurt all me foot. Part of me foot I meant. That twot Jim Dale dropped a rifle on me! – and I have a terrible boil come up and there is no health in us. Tom and Clive[1] telephoned me tonight to ask if I had any news of you and the situation out there. They are getting apprehensive I think. Drop them a line if you can. Like a card or something. Meanwhile don't forget your old pal and the pubic hair of the Matabele. Kept in a tobacco tin they're effective against yellow fever and sock rash. Be reckless and always bold – lots of love,

[K]

To the Hon. GEORGE BORWICK

14 June 1967

Well my old Capting I have missed you and that's a fact! The weather here is fabulous and we have been basking in temperatures of 75 with cloudless blue skies, it has been positively Ionian I can tell you. Regents Park full of the nits in deck chairs smoking fags and everything. Of course the Israeli-Arab war caused a few murmurs, but this country seems firmly on the side of the Jews I'm glad to say. Most cars carry stickers to that effect, and I saw one today which said 'go to work on an Arab' – as you know, it used to be an egg that you went to work on. I heard from Maggie [Smith] at long last. She is being married quietly and with minimum amount of fuss, tomorrow, to Bob Stephens at the Kensington Register Office – ironically same place as Beverley. I am seeing them the following day, in the evening. She said all that stuff in the paper about the National giving her leave of absence for a year was a load of rubbish. 'I got the sack,' she said, and added that Sir L. was having the wife in the company for loads

---

[1] Two young friends from north London with whom KW dined, travelled and variously socialised.

of parts.[1] What a rookery is there. I had tea at the Dorchester on Saturday with Phyllis Silvers[2] and we were joined by Dick Van Dyke and Yul Brynner. I would like to have heard them talk but they didn't get a chance with PS ranting on and on – 'my lovely wife and those five beautiful daughters have left me, and I have had this operation on my eye and believe me fellahs I am only half the man that I was – why even one of the waiters here – who remembers me from way back when I did this USO show with Frank Sinatra – he said that he hardly recognised me from the old days . . .' etc etc. I saw Stanley B. just before he left from Harwich. Moira is going to stay at home and 'do the garden'. I think it's disgraceful don't you? Well goodness knows when I shall see you again, but certainly you are never far from my thoughts, so think of your old pal sometimes,

[K]

To JOE ORTON

19 June 1967

Mon cher Joe mon ami! –
Merci blow through for your letter which I was delighted to receive this morning; very relieved to know that you have experienced no troubles apropos the recent upheavals, but astonished to find no reference to N. in your missive! – not a word of this lovely! – in the old days you were always wont to have her on your lips and now – silence. Is there some sinister reasoning here? – or is it part of the Arab backlash? – is a new propaganda campaign to be launched? – are you going to throw a bomb in her outside loo? – I look forward to your next article in the Tangier Times, I can tell you. Well, I saw John Hussey – with whom I went to Morocco last – on Sunday. It was swelteringly hot, so we emptied ourselves into deckchairs in Hyde Park, and surveyed the scene round the Serpentine. You would have been appalled. The slightest change in the temperature seems to give City dwellers an excuse for filth. Londoners take off their clothes at the drop of a hat. Or a rise in the barometer. They were sprawled everywhere. The queens making NO concessions at all. Lying there in those terrible Vince Man Shop Briefs which are totally indecent, with their clothes piled beside them; the stained underwear on top.

[1]   Joan Plowright married the then Sir Laurence Olivier in 1961.
[2]   Phil Silvers (1912–85), best known as 'Sergeant Bilko', was appearing in *Follow That Camel*.

No wonder Mr B. Graham found our parks disturbing, I find them intolerable.[1] 'I find this place intolerable,' I cried out to my friend, Joan Hoosay. He agreed. So we walked to Hyde Park Corner where we boarded a bus for Piccadilly, and within fifteen minutes we were ensconced in the Grill and Bumhole. It was nice and cool in there and we were just adjusting ourselves to the subdued lighting when I was appalled to see at the next table – W H O? – N!!! I tried to duck my head under those plant-like lights but too late! – her eagle eyes had lighted on us. 'Shall we come and join you?' they shouted. Well what could we say? 'Oh yes – er – do!' finding a face to meet the face.[2] I was all teeth and doing very well, but J H actually began to laugh hysterically. Right in their faces. I was terribly embarrassed as you can imagine. You couldn't pretend it was because of their jokes. They hadn't made any. But I had to join in to keep him company. So there we were laughing uncontrollably and I kept interjecting weakly 'It's something we've just remembered' but it obviously didn't amuse either of them. They had no news of Tangé because they said 'We left before the war broke out' – like some people refer to the second act of a play or something. Or other . . . Delighted to know that Billie Dentie[3] put my picture up at the Windmillee. But fancy them flogging the bar to those 'mental looking queens' as you describe them! – that is a blow I must say! – I mean, B D was quite reasonable really, and most of those Beach places are a terrible swiz. That Pergola is much more expensive, don't you think? Fancy them trying to cut off Peter Pollock's dick. That is dreadful. No one deserves that kind of treatment. I expect passions were involved. That and the temperature I imagine. I miss you and K[enneth Halliwell] not being at Noel Road. I was up that way recently and habit took me as far as the Canal till I realised you would not be there. 'There'll be no haddock for you, my lady,' said a small still voice as I made my way down City Road. I like your expression 'I speak as I find' – I like it very much. And I am sure that it is true, but some of the things you find are best rejected – they do not always B E A R speaking about. I myself was brought up – as you know – in the sensitive and rarefied atmosphere of the Caledonian Road, where very few dropped more than their aitches, and the odd providence cheque was hard to come by.

[1] Billy Graham, the American evangelist, had expressed similar shock at the affectionate intertwinings to be seen in London's parks, and at the dress, or not, of the participants.
[2] cf. T.S. Eliot's 'Love Song of J. Alfred Prufrock': 'There will be time, there will be time/To prepare a face to meet the faces that you meet'.
[3] K W uses the name of the comedian and eccentric dancer Billy Dainty (1927–86) to play upon the name of a Mr Dent.

I am glad that you say you will write to Clive. He is a good lad, and any energy spent in that direction will be amply rewarded. He is looking forward enormously to Maroc. Never stops talking about it. Last time they had a most unfortunate experience. In Athens. They took it into their heads to go to see the Acropolis by moonlight. Don't ask me why. If anyone had suggested it to me I would have thought they had lost their reason, but then I am generally abed by midnight and think those that aren't are scoundrels. Anyway they went up there at this ridiculous hour, and met these two Athenians who seemed very pleasant and apparently offered to show them the way. So up they went – into the labyrinth and suddenly, they round a corner and these boys set upon them and ended up with the wrist watch and the money and there were tears before morning. They said it finished Greece as far as they were concerned. They said they never wanted to go there again. Amazing about you losing an inch on the waistline. I expect you are not eating properly. One banana and a glass of water at the Windmill. You're not going to expand much on that my dear. It says in the paper that Laurence Olivipong has got a tumour come up on the prostate. He is to have radium treatment at St George's Hospital. And they have taken OTHELLO out of the repertoire. I see from my window that it is pouring with rain. So much for our summer spell. I did the last in the series *Round The Horne* today, and sang a song about 'scroping my moulies' which went down fantastically well. Shame it's off the air now till next year. After a bit, I quite start to enjoy it, and then suddenly it's all over. I have got to start writing the TV series next.[1] Soon as the picture finishes. And I am to do another record. This time, entirely devoted to Rambling Syd Rumpo songs. There has been great demand. The other LP 'On Pleasure Bent' is doing very well indeed. Six thousand in the first week, and Decca tell me that is very good. Of course that is only the London area. Well that is what I am told anyway. I went over to see Maggie Smith last week. She is now married to Robert Stephens, and loving it all. She looked very well, and laughed a lot about Edna Welthorpe. Especially the episode at the Ritz. This story was also all the rage at Pinewood. Peter Butterworth is always saying 'Tell us again about Edna at the Ritz' – they love the 'gloves of some sticky vegetable matter' bit.[2] And the Boots folder. The Boots folder is a very nice

---

[1] 'International Cabaret', on which KW introduced the acts, and was featured between them in camply whimsical monologues.

[2] Orton's fake housewife Edna had written to the Ritz claiming to have left a handbag there. It supposedly contained 'a Boots folder with snapshots of members of my family and a pair of gloves made of some hairy material'. See appendix to *The Orton Diaries*, ed. John Lahr.

touch. You have probably read that Dannia Kaye has now refused to appear at Chichester after all, and is going to Israel instead. Fenella Fielding has rushed into print saying 'I feel outraged on behalf of the entire profession' and adds that she is 'awfully sorry for poor John Clements' who is the half-baked nit who is supposed to be running the theatre. But really – in the last analysis – who cares? – it's really as simple as that. I am invited to dinner with Gavin Astor[1] in July. So let me know if there is any subject you want raised with regard to the Observer – or indeed anything else. Love,

[K]

To PETER ROGERS[2]

11 August 1967

Dear Peter,
Thank you for sending the script of 'Carry On Doctor' – but I don't want to play the part of Tinker. To make a success of any role I always feel you must be able to see it in your 'mind's eye' so to speak and I can't do it with this. The only other time I felt this with a role that I DID take on was in Screaming, and I never really got it right. I don't think this Tinker part is at all me. I hate all the physical fitness element in the role, and I've always hated stripping off and showing my body, and it's obvious that a lot of the playing could be physically painful. I know you will think it namby pamby of me, but I really do have a horror of cuts and bruises and I really can't take any more of them. Besides – let's face it, Bigger is the part, and what the film is about; and it will be terribly funny. It made me laugh out loud and you know what an awful audience I am! – the other parts don't compare in size or in content. It would not be possible to do a good job with these sort of misgivings, and as atmosphere and happiness on the set is S O important, I think it best that I decline.[3]

yours ever,
[K]

[1] Hon. Gavin Astor (1918–84), President, Times Newspapers from 1967. KW had in mind Hon. David Astor (b.1912), editor of the *Observer* 1948–75.
[2] Perennial producer of the Carry on pictures, in partnership with director Gerald Thomas.
[3] Frankie Howerd dropped out of the featured role, and KW replaced him, starting filming on 14 September.

To NOEL WILLMAN

13 November 1967

My dear Noel,

Yes – I had this cable from Robert [Bolt] saying 'Sarah[1] gave birth to a very large and ugly son this morning' – and I sent a note of congratulations. I didn't telephone cos I didn't want to get involved. Babies are not attractive to me, as you well know. I echo the sentiments of the delightful W.C. Fields – 'anyone who hates dogs and little children can't be all bad' – and besides, if I phone I know that there will be the inevitable line about 'When are we going to see you down here?' and I must confess that I have no desire to go. One always ends up listening to that egocentric monologue from Bob which centres round the latest opus. It is all so selfish. And let's face it – he's no Isaiah Berlin. Well now, what to tell you? I continue with the television show[2] on Sundays at the Talk of the Town. What a dump. They tell me that Bernie Delfont is charging the BBC a thousand a night for the hire. I think he should pay them for the plug on the TV every week. The waiters there get treble pay for working on Sundays, and one of them said to me 'You know all that champagne we had for the Sammy Davis show? Well we took it all round the back and had it ourselves, and gave them that perry stuff. They didn't know the difference, the silly bleeders' – and one is supposed to leer one's agreement. I didn't bother to conceal my disgust. 'That is morally dishonest!' I cried 'and you will reap the reward!' and walked away vaguely feeling that I had made no sense whatsoever. I hear from that Windeatt who is doing that landscape garden work on Mount Etna. He says that Bob writes to him regularly, and that he has paid Sarah Miles six months in advance for the house in Hasker Street. Oh and another thing. I was called up to the office of the head of Variety at the Television Centre, and asked if I would like to do a comedy series with – wait for it – Stanley Baxter!! – my old friend of the Army revue days in Singapore, and all my standing on the Anderson Bridge ogling the sailors to no effect. So I said that I had no objection in principle but would like to see the scripts and know the format etc. So they said they would contact Stanley and discuss it. Well he went along and saw them and turned it all down saying that he valued our friendship too much to risk losing it by working

---

[1] The actress Sarah Miles, his wife: married 1967, marriage dissolved 1976, remarried 1988.
[2] 'International Cabaret'.

together. He said that I was very difficult, and that if there was a row we might not be speaking to each other in the middle of the series etc. BUT he told them that he would be quite happy to PRODUCE me in such a series! (he's had no experience in this sphere – Need you ask!!!!) So they came back to me and said that S was willing to produce the series and didn't I think that was an exciting idea? I said I thought it was a bloody awful idea. I really did.

'You mean that you don't want him to produce you?'

'That's right.'

'But why?'

'Because if his argument about our acting together is valid – then it applies just as well to his producing me. In some senses, more so.'

'I think you are being very foolish about this. He has got the know how and has that marvellous revue mind – it could be the greatest thing since Ned Sherrin.'

I know that your mind will be boggling by now, so I won't go on and on with all the rubbish they talked. Of course the next day Stanley was on the blower saying that he had told the BBC he was willing to produce the show. The irony was that we were meeting that night for dinner so the atmosphere was awful. Within five minutes he was on about it again. 'Your career is at the crossroads you know – you can't go on with your International Cabaret series for ever, and it's only realising a fraction of your talent – I am willing to work on this show for you, and then we could take the best of the stuff and present the whole thing on Broadway.' So then I said that I wasn't interested in Broadway unless he meant Hammersmith. Oh it was a dreadful evening . . . Went to see the much heralded Schlesinger film *Far From the Madding Crowd*. It looked entirely like a travelogue, and sounded like an advert for a peasant way of life – a sort of 'under Salazar it ain't so bad' movie. I have not been as bored, for SO long, for quite a time. Not since the appalling *Grand Prix* with Brian Bedford. He has the great accident in it, and you keep seeing him in hospital beds looking bitter with all these bandages round his head. 'He looks like Whistler's mother,' I said to my friend Henry Davies, and we both giggled maliciously. Last night, beneath my windows in Allsop Place, I heard the most terrible shouting, and I looked out, and saw this woman shouting obscenities and raving. There was nobody about at all, and she was urinating copiously against the wall of Madame Tussaud. Of course there wasn't a policeman in sight. It lasted from 10.25 to 10.40 . . . then she pulled up her knickers and disappeared into the night crying 'Fuck you all!' which is a tag line I have often wanted to use myself; especially at the end of some lamentable blackout sketches in revue. But I have the censor to cope with. No one bothered her.

> love,
> [K]

To JOHN WINDEATT

15 November 1967

My dear John,
Thank you for your letter of the eleventh which arrived this morning. Listen ducky – don't be quite so prompt or I won't be able to keep up the pace. Letter writing is something best attempted once a fortnight or onc finds there is little to report and that the missives being exchanged become scrappy, uninformative, and rather a waste of your actual postage. Heard that doleful Marylebone Church clock chiming every hour, right up till four. I got up eventually at 7.30. Found your letter on the amber mat, and one from the Stokers' Mess of HMS Leverton at Malta. Asking for the words of the Rambling Syd Rumpo songs. Well to write all those out again would take ages. I have sent them the address of the producer of the series at the BBC and suggested that they write to him. He has got a secretary and she can type all those things out at a far greater speed than me. Let's face it. I sent them the photograph they requested and a single disc of the Ballad of the Woggler's Moulie . . . Most of the time in your letters to me, you are always making jokes and being funny. You don't have to with me you know. When one earns one's living from humour one gets a little tired of reading it. I would much rather you told me the natural happenings of your days – with the odd bit of conversation you might have had with these lads that clear the vines which are causing soil erosion if you are not very careful I can tell you. I think you are a fool to cut down those vines. Our vines have tender roots[1] as the playwright so aptly puts it in the last train to Brooklyn[2] or whatever. Love,

> [K]

---

[1] *Our Vines Have Tender Grapes*: 1945 film directed by Robert Sisk.
[2] An allusion to Hubert Selby's book *Last Exit to Brooklyn* (1964). (See the letter of 24 November, p. 73).

To NOEL WILLMAN

16 November 1967

My dear Noel,
Yes I'll bet you are missing your lovely house – especially now that
you have got used to having so much space – and the luxury of going
upstairs to bed; the apartment you describe does sound pokey, but
probably that's what most of them are used for. Well I went to this
party at Ned Sherrin's new house. That Anthony Blond the publisher
was there. I told him I knew Patrick Skene Catling whose novel 'The
Experiment' he has just published. He asked me how I knew him and
I said that he was writing the profile on me for the Observer – no –
the Weekend Telegraph. Two thousand words and loads of pictures.
Me on the windowsill, on the settee, at the desk, on the phone, etc.
The photographer actually asked for one in the bath – he said I could
wear a bathing costume if I liked. I said I was up to all kinds of tricks
but that wasn't one of them. Then Bert Sheveloff[1] came in with John
Gielgud and the room went suitably hushed. J G said to me 'How
amazing to actually meet you socially. I was told that you lived a
solitary monk-like existence, and that you hated parties – I haven't
seen you for ages' and I said 'What about that time we met on the
stairs at the Corner House and you said I was droll?' and said O dear
he had forgotten and looked as though he didn't want to be reminded
of it. Then he told a really good story about this woman who had
been a mistress of Gerald du Maurier who collapsed on the great
man's opening night and had to be carried out of the auditorium –
J G said 'They carried her out with the skirt all awry and her knickers
showing and du Maurier said they signified what she thought of his
performance.'
     You don't realise you are coming to the bottom of these forms
until it is almost upon you. Our star at the Talk of the Town on Sunday was this Juliet Prowse who stars in this musical 'Sweet Charity'
which got such raves. She threw herself all over the stage, and was
very wanton. The audience looked quite staggered by it all, and
clapped like mad. I think energy counts for an awful lot nowadays.
My stuff went quite well   I told them I'd done the camping in a
portable tent in Hampstead on a diet of chestnut puree and crab
apples – I said 'OH yes it was the full dolce vita . . .' Well I have gone
on enough for now – half the time I only write to you because I want
you to know that you are never far from my thoughts and that you

---

[1] Burt Shevelove (b.1915), director and playwright, specialising in musicals.

are a very dear person. Goodnight sweet prince and flights of etc. etc.

love,
[K]

To JOHN WINDEATT

20 November 1967

My dear John,
Please begin your letters to me properly – not with this 'Kenneth'
scrawled on the top in that bald, brusque fashion. It is usual to start
'my dear' and so on. And don't start getting piqued just because I tell
you the kind of letter I prefer, and tell you that I don't fancy all the
joke-ettes. Florence Nightingale said that all paper wars were futile,
and she was right. I am in the position of avuncular mentor to you,
and when people are fond and loyal to you, you should allow them
to take a few liberties. I take very little with you, so shut your row,
do you hear? I will not tolerate any kind of bolshy stuff, so don't try
it on with me ducky. I'm your friend remember? – I am not here to
mete out honeyed words and give you the flannel. Friendship means
taking the chaff and grain together, and with a breath of kindness
you must blow the rest away. How lucky you are to be in a nice
climate. Here it is truly wintry and miserable. They are all tearing
about the windy streets with their over coats huddled around them;
the English are not very happy. Not at the best of times, but devaluation this time seems to have brought home to the man in the street
that his country really IS on its knees. We are far from the proud
days of 'We – Victoria, Queen of Great Britain, Empress of India . . .'
etc etc. and it's beginning to dawn on everyone that we are just a
rather small, foggy little island that must either make things and sell
them, or die. Yes – I AM right about Scott. Useless little poof. There
are times when we have to make choices. Having made them you
must stick to them. When a relationship is sundered – forget it. Finish
it. Start afresh. Don't fall into the trap of retrospective sentimentalis-
ing. That is death. Remember the bad things – remember what caused
you pain and anguish and ask yourself 'was it really necessary?' –
suffering may be worth while where a profound love is reciprocated.
There, it wasn't. So don't start kidding yourself. You got the bum's
rush dear . . . I do hope that you are letting this new environment
blow a new wind through you – and that you are not dwelling in the
past. You will return and tackle new things in this country – take on
a nursery, or grow flowers and lovely things, and do something

creative. The WORK is what is important. Get that right, and the rest will fit in like a jigsaw puzzle. But if the work is wrong, the rest will never go right. You are QUITE right of course – it would be much better to end up as St Francis than T.E. White.[1] There you have given me a well deserved rebuke. It is true, I beg your pardon. You chose a particularly vicious parallel. I felt awful when I read it. Glad you were there before me about soil erosion. I believe it has wreaked havoc in Sicily. Did you ever read 'Night of the Vespers'?[2] – it's by Runciman – all about the Sicilian revolution. It is a marvellous book, full of imagery and atmosphere and he really seems to have got under the skins of these proud and tragic people. Let me know if you want me to send you a copy. And of course I suppose you saw the film 'The Leopard' – I loved it. I went with Noel Willman. I tell him about your doings when I write to him, about once a week. He loves getting letters. Tom and Clive are both lousy correspondents I warn you. In that sense, they are a great disappointment and an early promise NOT fulfilled as Dr Johnson so rightly remarked.

I get a lot on these air mail forms don't I? – you must admit I am quite adept at it. I only hope I am allowing room for the tearing open business – do let me know if I am going too close to the corners. I went over to Maggie Smith's for lunch on Saturday last. She is now married to Bob Stephens as you know and I saw their baby son – Christopher. Utterly adorable red headed boy who giggles bashfully at you, and seems to be endlessly amused at everything. Must say I thought it was lovely – what you said about bringing you the fruit and things – even if you do have to throw the stuff away. The generosity is heartwarming I think.

      love to you,
      [K]

---

[1] Terence Hanbury White (1906–64), children's writer, champion of the countryside and English mystic medievalism, best known for his Arthurian sequence *The Once and Future King* (1958).
[2] Actually *The Sicilian Vespers: A History of the Mediterranean World in the Later Thirteenth Century*, by the Hon. James Cochran Stevenson (Steven) Runciman.

To NOEL WILLMAN

20 November 1967

Mon cher Noel,

A cottage in the country? – I just said it as a fantasy.[1] It would never work my dear. Not in terms of our getting on together – on the contrary – I think that might work very well – but in terms of the practical business of commuting to and fro, and the preparations that have to be made when one is going to arrive, or leave etc. Look at Mags and Bev. They got that lovely place in Beaumont, Hertfordshire – they said it would be no problem cos they'd found this lovely woman in the village who would pop in etc. and the second week they were away, it was burgled. All their lovely things gone . . . I was amazed to get the letter from you so quickly. Of course I wasn't expecting to hear anything at all. I got your original one from New York and thought 'that's the cue for me to start writing' but I thought it was only for you to do the reading you see. Not that I wasn't delighted. I was. It was just so totally unexpected. I did the TV show last night, from Talk of the Town. The dressing room was packed afterwards. They all stand around and expect you to entertain them all over again! – even with the overcoat on and me briefcase under the arm, they still don't go. You have to actually open the door and usher them out. And I am always getting these Moroccan lads. I mean you meet them on these beaches and think fab, and you say they must look you up if they ever come over etc. and of course you think they never will, and then of course they do just that. But my french is terrible – apart from je suis grande etoile – and they end up thinking I am talking about some splendid lavatory because of my pronunciation not being all it should be. I had a long letter from that Windeatt on Mount Etna. He is getting lots of work done, and has bulldozed a road through, and got the local lads to cut down all the vines for this landscape garden. I wrote and told him what a fool he was to cut down the vines. You always find on the slopes of a mountain that when you cut down the vines you invite soil erosion but of course he will just laugh me out of court I know that. They all think they know it all these lads – I was the same at that age – headstrong and self opinionated.

I expect by now you will have recovered from the shock of devaluation. Do you remember I warned you of this months and months

---

[1] Over the years KW made vague house-sharing proposals to several friends, though Willman's letter expressing interest in this one is not preserved.

ago? – when I was in your car one night? – wish I had taken my own advice. I only did it with about 500 or so. Should have done the lot.

love,
[K]

To NOEL WILLMAN

24 November 1967

My dear Noel,
I went along to the Old Bailey to hear a bit of this Calder [&] Boyars trial. They are the publishers of this American novel about male prostitution called Last Exit To Brooklyn – and the crown maintain that it is obscene. The defending counsel was competent, and so was the crown really, but one was struck by the total lack of ability to marshal arguments and present them well – to be clear, forceful, and dramatic. They were so boring. I saw three members of the jury dropping off to sleep on more than one occasion. The judge was a great fat drear, and he kept craftily popping boiled sweets into his mouth. When the defence was winding up he said 'Gentlemen of the jury – (they were all male) – do you really believe that this book, with its sad story of this pathetic queen, can really deprave and corrupt anyone? – do you think that the story of Harry – the foreman in the factory with his lonely dreams and oral sex – do you think that is liable to make someone go off AND TRY IT? – I put it to you – this book is THIRTY SHILLINGS – who has got that kind of money to spend on a novel? – and look at the language. These American sexual deviates speak in a private jargon of their own – ordinary people would have great difficulty in understanding it – do you really believe that such a book could deprave and corrupt because I really must RAM THIS POINT HOME . . .' At that point I started giggling and I got quite scared cos the judge gave me a filthy look so soon after that I beat a hasty retreat I can tell you. I read in the paper today that the jury voted it obscene. You should have seen that jury. A more stupid bunch of morons you could not have assembled. Two of them had to be led through the affirmation cos they could not speak the lines properly. Looked like the Mafia to me . . . I went with that Ned Sherrin and Bert Shoveloff or whatever that ridiculous name is. Afterwards Ned said he had to dash away, and Shoveloff to Buffalo was left with me in the drizzling rain on the pavement. I muttered some lies about having a dinner

appointment and jumped on a passing 13 which took me to Baker Street.

>   love,
>   [K]

To SUSAN RAY

30 November 1967

Well Susan you are a disgrace and no mistake. Said you would write and say how you were getting on. I have never even heard if you arrived all right. It is the bum's rush I am getting. Oh! yes ducky – you've thrown me over like an old boot, and if I had the chance I would come out there and shout outside your door and embarrass you in front of the neighbours and everything. I suppose you are having the lovely weather and looking brown. Here it is bleak and damp and cold. Everyone huddled in their overcoats and the morale is very low. Yes. Well. I did the Simon Dee show on television on Saturday. That goes out on Channel One – and as you know Cabaret is Two – so I am not very often seen by a big audience. And it went like a bomb. It's rather like a more groovy Eamonn Andrews show – and at one point he asked me if I had someone in, to do the cleaning and I cried out 'No! – I do all my own work! – I shove the Harpic down the loo and run!' and the audience fell about. It was the biggest laugh! isn't it extraordinary what amuses people? I had loads of letters the next day. They all contained expressions like 'God bless you' and 'Your Obedient Servant' which gives you an idea of the sort of audience I attract. I went over to see Maggie Smith last week. Since she has been married to Robert Stephens she has become quite different and laughingly says that her hair is all falling out, but it looked all right to me. She is going to do the film of 'The Prime of Miss Jean Brodie' which should be a marvellous break for her . . . Lots of love,

>   [K]

To NOEL WILLMAN

2 November 1967 [evidently 2 December 1967]

Mon cher Noel,
 . . . Well of course you are quite right about Baxter. He is a very good person fundamentally – and his friendship matters to me. I go right

off people every now and again and am capable of utter treachery. When he refused to do that series with me I felt rejected and started abusing him roundly and going about saying frightful things. When I was faced with it, by him, I just had to admit it and apologise. It was all very lame and unpleasant I can tell you . . .

    love,
    [K]

To JOHN WINDEATT

8 December 1967

Mon cher John,
Just received this marvellous letter. Really good letters are so rare nowadays and mostly one accepts the usual scrappy effort, so when a really good one comes along like this, one is absolutely delighted. This is the best letter I have had from you. Full of atmosphere and loads of information and funny as well. Yes, Paolo at Biagi's explained the newspaper article very well,[1] and of course I went there with Maggie Smith so she heard it all too, and she insisted on being given the article and doing her own translating cos she learned a lot of Italian when she was in Venice for the Honeypot film.[2] She said 'O he looks very handsome doesn't he?' when she saw your photograph – you were standing with the mayor in the doorway of the caravan. So I said yes you were the great trick etc etc. I must say your account of all the work that has been accomplished astonished me. The TV show last Sunday starred Billy Eckstine. He was very good. I was doing a load of rubbish about being asked up to the TV centre 'Very grand, with your deep leather and your sheraton and your framed photos of Anona Winn – they said to me, just sign here, and I said but what is it for, and they said the usual BBC procedure, it simply says that you have never been an atheist, or a communist or a bigamist, and I said But what if I have been a bigamist? And they said, in that case we lock all the doors and you have to tell us what it's like . . .' And that went quite well I can tell you. I have had interviews this week for features about me – with the Daily Mirror, The Daily Telegraph and the Daily Sketch, and The Weekend Mail, and Reveille

[1] Windeatt had sent a Sicilian newspaper article about himself and his landscaping enterprise.
[2] *The Honey Pot* (1966), with Rex Harrison, Susan Hayward. Written and directed by Joseph L. Mankiewicz.

and goodness knows what. All due, I think, to the appearance on the Simon Dee Show on Channel one. I did it last Saturday and the fan mail was fantastic . . .

Do you know those Beatles gave a private party recently at the new Royal Lancaster Hotel and their manager rang and asked if I would go along and compere their cabaret? – have you ever heard such impudence. Just cos you do it on the Telly don't mean you are available for functions does it? – the nerve of it. The morale in the country is at a very low ebb, everyone hating the government and can you blame them? – you can not dear.

> love,
> [K]

To THE STOKERS' MESS ('BIG JIM, ROBBO, BILL, DAVE and DAVEY'), HMS *LEVERTON*

13 December 1967

Well Hallo me dearos, dearios, heartios or what you will – I had to do this interview programme and this disc jockey said 'now we are going to play an excerpt from your latest EP of Rambling Syd songs' and I was amazed cos I didn't even know that it had been issued. So I rang up EMI or Parlophone or whatever their rotten old name is, and said that I thought common courtesy would have been observed if I had been informed and they said they were sorry but it was an oversight so I said what about a complimentary copy of the record and they said 'we are very sorry but that is another building – we don't have any stocks here – we are purely administrative' so I hung up cos I thought it was overt dishonesty or a load of codswallop and I went to a shop. There I got the record and put it between hard covers to send to you, and bore it to the post office. They said 'is this for Christmas?' and I said 'well it's not for August bleedin Bank Holiday' which I thought was rather witty but I only got a withering look and they said 'where is it going?' and I replied 'to the Stokers of the Leverton' and they said 'don't be silly there aren't any stokers in the modern navy – it is all automatic firing' I said 'don't talk rubbish – they're up to their knees in the coal – shovelling it into these great roaring furnaces, with their shovels red hot to the hilt!' they said 'it's not their shovels that are red hot'. By this time there was quite a crowd of would-be Christmas posters in the queue behind me, all getting irate and crying out 'Hurry on for gawd's sake'. So I said 'just tell me how much the postage is, and keep your comments on the modern navy to yourself' and he said 'We have all got a job to do' and I said 'Tough Bananas' paid the one and three and walked out and was accosted by some fool who said 'have you heard about the woman that took the baby to the doctor and said she was worried because it was so thin – and the doctor grabbed hold of her breasts and said "and no wonder the baby is thin! – these rotten old tits of yours are dry and scraggy – mouldy old tits they are! – no milk in them! that's why the baby is emaciated" – and the woman said "But I'm his Aunt!" and the doctor let go of her breasts and said "Oh! – then why did you come?" and she said "I always do if someone squeezes me tits."' And I said no I hadn't heard it, and I didn't think I had suffered from deprivation as a consequence. These people all think that if they tell you their latest joke, you will use it on the television or the radio within the week. It's all prefaced with 'here's a good one for you . . .' Thank you for your letter of the 1st December – I hope you are wrong about the weather forecast for Xmas. We had this load of snow last Friday but then there was a thaw over the week end and by Monday there was rain to wash all the filthy sludge away. And very glad I was to see the last of it. It may look very nice on the cards and pictures but snow is a bloody nuisance in London. It ruins the uppers of your shoes – gets inside the stitching and you start letting water, or treading water or whatever, and you end up with the chill blains and frostbite and the ends dropping off. I could tell you things [to] make your hair curl, but I see you've had the blow wave. Anyway I hope that you won't envy Fez too much – having his Xmas at home – is he called that cos he wears a fez or what? – and I hope that you have as good a Christmas as is possible in the circumstances. I have given your Christmas card pride of place and when people ask I say 'my friends on the Leverton'.

[K]

To JOHN WINDEATT

6 January 1968

My dear John,
Thank you for your letters of the 25th and the 30th which were waiting for me on my return from Morocco. I went off there on the 31st and woke for the New Year amid the palm trees and the African sun and the lovely omes.[1] I had the cold of course, everyone seems

---

[1] 'Polari' slang for 'men' (homo, homme, etc.).

to have one – there has been quite an epidemic, and the trip helped me enormously to get over it. Back yesterday to start work on the television script. Oh! how I wish I was finished with it all. The very thought of work nowadays fills me with ennui – I just don't want to know. Enthusiasm of any kind is anathema to me. Who told you that I was a member of the Spartan? – and anyway, what business is it of yours? – I became a member years ago. It is a very nice little club and a very useful place for meeting one's sympathetic friends. Writing this letter is like slogging up hill. I feel totally depressed – this bloody fan equipment for the flats has gone wrong, and there is a terrible drumming noise over my head the whole time. It makes concentration impossible – and it is not constant. It diminishes and then grows intermittently. All that crap you talk about money is too ridiculous to reply to. It makes me angry to read such utter rubbish. To pretend that one really doesn't need money in this world is so ludicrous that it's otiose. Only a fool would not agree. Moreover – you are the first person to USE money – buying expensive things like clocks and grand pianos and cribs for the Bolts and sending out for firms of caterers to send the hot dinner to the house. It's all so hypocritical to live like that, and then pretend not to care about money. But I don't intend to raise this subject with you again. I must say your description of Christmas with the Patanes was absolutely fabulous. I laughed over that I can tell you. Especially your comments about your happiness on not being able to repeat the performance next year. The new muscle man sounds fantasy. I cannot believe that you haven't had something. I just can't believe it. I can't write any more – I am too depressed.

> yours,
> [K]

To NOEL WILLMAN

6 February 1968

My dear Noel,
Thank you so much for your letter of the 29th January which I received yesterday. I was sorry to hear that you entertain no hopes for the musical – but it may have transpired by now that you have had a pleasant surprise. I can quite understand you wanting to be back in your own abode – possession may be theft, but it is very comforting to have one's own things about one. Now the radio series, Round the Horne, has started again. We began yesterday at the Paris.

The usual load of camp with me screaming my head off about 'I could have been another Hayley Mills – I'm not being serviced properly on this show – Terence Rattigan now! – he'd service me – he'd know how to handle me . . .' etc. It's all rather outrageous and pointless, but nowadays it seems we're all going up to Heaven in a formless din. On the front page of The Times last week, they had this photograph of a young Vietcong officer being shot through the head by the chief of police in Saigon. The correspondence columns have been full of it ever since. The general tone of all the letters is 'We don't want to see this kind of thing', in fact one writer actually says 'Surely we should keep quiet about these sort of outrages?' Of course some of them admit it is good journalism in so far as the paper is doing its job and reporting what actually happens etc. but I must admit it was a very shocking picture and I was amazed to see it in the Times. A clergyman wrote 'I submit that you should not have published it because it was horrific and because such a picture is inadequate and deceptive and therefore evil. Even in a non-Christian context, here is taking place the profoundest experience of mortal man, the ending of his mortality by the apparent agency of evil. No representation can depict this. All it does is to harden and to make us callous. And what was the photographer doing?' It has caused a great furore . . .

Went to the Old Bailey with my friend the Hon. George Borwick last Thursday. It was the Savundra case.[1] Embezzlement. When we came out of the court one of the secretaries rushed up and said 'O Mister Williams – the Judge would like your autograph, and he asked me to say that he never misses the Television shows' – I murmured something about being honoured and signed for her. I was amazed the Judge even noticed me sitting in the court. He had seemed to be engrossed by the case. Well I don't think there is anything more to tell you. Have you any idea when the 'Love Match' will go on?[2] – or any idea of when you will return?

Love,
[K]

---

[1] Dr Emil Savundra, charged with fraud after the collapse of the Fire, Auto and Marine insurance company. He was sentenced to eight years' imprisonment and fined £50,000 for what the judge called 'a gigantic swindle'.
[2] These projects of Willman's may not have materialised: his work during 1968 is listed by reference books as *Darling of the Day*, at the George Abbott Theater in New York, and the film *The Vengeance of She*. 'Love Match' was certainly not the British farce about football by Glenn Melvyn.

To NOEL WILLMAN

15 February 1968

My dear Noel,

Well the bum has been really dreadful. Screaming and misbehaving till I became quite lunatic with it. Went again to the grand and diplomatic Mr Mulvany in Harley Street, and this time he said that this sort of thing could be brought on by emotional stress, and asked me if I was under any sort of strain. I said (in that loud and common voice) 'Well it's not easy if you're a homosexual and live alone and celibate – O! no! – it's not funny ducky I can tell you! – especially if you fancy a bit and have a few drinks and with me that is always death because I start shouting the odds and all dignity dies and –' he said 'Quite so' and dismissed the whole subject. Obviously didn't want to know about this garrulous queeny figure screaming on about her privations. He said I would have to go into hospital on the 19th February – but it will only be for a couple of nights and nothing to worry about. I said 'I don't like it when they shave your bum' and he looked mildly amused but conceded that he'd arrange to have it done under anaesthaetic or however you spell that ridiculous word. I was delighted to get your letter of the 12th February so quickly! – I am so sorry that it was incorrectly addressed. You see how distraught I am! – I will see it doesn't happen again. I thought of you last Friday, cos Tom and Clive drove me down to Brighton for the day, and it reminded me of our drive to Pevensey that time when I remarked to you about Lot having it off with his own daughters and you said 'I know my dear. It is all very worrying' and it made me laugh out loud. We had a constitutional along the promenade, and a wintry sun tried to get through the cloud once or twice. That long front was deserted apart from a disconsolate kosher queen bundled in one of those beach shelters. We went to the Queen's Hotel for lunch and there was a new woman serving at the bar. Said she was a Czech but the accent was very curious and had that sing-song quality one associates with Scandinavia. She said 'You got ta enchoy yourself in dis life – what choo vant kids for? – O blimey! – dat vood reely brown me off!' and we all chorused agreement and swallowed the gin and tonics. After lunch we went into an empty children's playground and larked on the swings till the rain drove us back to the car and we drove back to London.

Yesterday I felt very buoyant and walked to the agent's office with a light step. I felt quite jocular and made funny faces at a lot of people – they were all the same – first they looked startled and then they do the double take. With all the elderly crabby old women coming out of Debenham's I did the lips pushed out and the wink. By the time they get it, I am past and way off in the distance. I came upon this lovely bit in the Johnson book where Boswell says that it is midnight and very late and the Doctor replies 'What is that to you and I?' and the pair of them get into coats etc and go round to Mrs Williams for tea! This woman seems to have the kettle on all night! And a marvellous bit where this drear keeps on at Johnson about the advantages of drinking – 'Do you not agree that it keeps a man's mind off dreary things?' The Doctor: 'Why yes Sir – if he is sitting next to you!'

You remember I made that LP and it cost me a thousand to set it up? – and we sold the whole thing to Decca? – well I got the first royalty today. On a year's sales. It is for £9.4.6d. I must say I think it is screamingly funny. They all said to me at the time 'You will make a bomb out of this ducky.' Well I can't think of anything else to tell you, so I shall stick this up and post it, and brave this cold and frosty morning.

> love,
> [K]

To STANLEY BAXTER

5 June 1968

My dear Stanley,
Love could I only tell thee. Great and deep joy in the eyebold[1] with your letter. Of course I was delighted to read your remarks apropos the Eamonn Andrews.[2] I got a marvellous write up in the Mirror for it, but was brought sharply to earth by that Watson. He sent a stinging missive 'you were camp and cheap . . . you must not confuse RUDE-NESS with WIT . . . I felt ashamed as I watched you – the audience laughed with EMBARRASSMENT AT YOU . . .' every page was filled with this kind of nastiness. I really do think I'll have to finish with her. The years only make me MORE vulnerable to this kind of attack.

Anyway – to my main news. I'm off to Tangé on Thursday, but I

---

[1] Standard phrase from the repertoire of the nonsense monologuist 'Professor' Stanley Unwin (b.1911), of whose work KW was fond.
[2] KW had appeared on Andrews's TV show on 2 June. His first appearance with Andrews, in June 1966, had marked the beginning of his successful chat-show career.

would like you to send me the odd air mail form 'cos I do love it when I'm away from home. I must get away from the atmosphere of England into sun and calm. The odd sherry and the lie down.

Love,
Kenyeth[1]

To ANDREW RAY

3 August 1968

My dear Andrew,

. . . I saw Noel Willman recently. He is playing one of the 3 Musketeers in a BBC Television serial. He has grown a beard and everything and looks very distinguished. Said that he was hating every minute of it. Gordon Jackson is in this Maggie Smith film at Pinewood – The Prime of Miss Jean Brodie – and his wife Rona is in that Brian Rix production at the Garrick, Let Sleeping Wives Lie. She is enjoying being back in the theatre, but they are finding it difficult to get someone to look after the children. I had to go up and baby sit for them last Wednesday cos she had the matinee and G was away on location. George Borwick put on Night Must Fall with Adam Faith and they had a profitable provincial tour, but then Emily Williams[2] wrote from Geneva (her tax dodge haven) to say that he would not allow them to bring his play into London, so it had to come off. Adam Faith said in the paper that it was heartbreaking and that he wanted to go on with the legitimate theatre and that he would never sing again, and that he wanted to play Hamlet. It is all happening here as you can see. I went to the great shindig at Gerald Thomas's house in Burnham. Very lavish party. Peter Rogers and Betty Box and Ralph Thomas and Joan Sims, all that lot – you know. I got rather sloshed and had to stay the night, and in the morning I was roped in to open a Spastic Children's Charity fete in a field nearby. Do you remember that John Windeatt? – he was a young landscape gardener I met down at the Bolts' once? – well he committed suicide the same week as Tony Hancock! It was all very weird. We have had terrible weather here. love,

[K]

[1] Favourite form of address used by Gordon Jackson in his letters to KW.
[2] Emlyn Williams (1905–87), actor, dramatist, director.

To ANDREW RAY

12 August 1968

My dear Andrew,
What a superb letter! it really sprang off the paper. I have never had
such a good letter from you. I certainly get the picture of the acting
set-up. I know one of them myself! – the Neill creature used to be a
friend of Peter Nichols I think. I remember it well. But a leading man
with your actual halitosis is disgraceful. No – I could not put up with
that. I would have to stop in rehearsals and say 'Phew – your breath
is really shocking you know – I wish you'd take some pastilles or
something out of consideration for those working with you.' All right,
so it may be embarrassing etc. but at least it's a step toward alleviation,
and why be afraid? What the hell can anyone do to you? As I told
you in my last letter, I did the David Frost Show with your Dad.[1] It
was good to see him again after all this time, and he was certainly
very nice about you. The thing for which we had been engaged had
to be cancelled cos they couldn't have the sets etc. so Frost asked us
to ad lib . . . Pickets were outside the building. They shouted as we
went in 'Don't work with them Kenny! You belong to the union same
as us' but I just smiled and said 'It's the money loveys' and went on
in. Ted and I got loads of laughs and at the end Frost asked us if we
would both do it again. We agreed. But they phoned and said that
the strike this week was worse, and that the entire show has been
cancelled.
    Yes I know what you mean about acting being a drag. Brando was
quite right. It is strictly for adolescents. But if it's the only profession
you've got, then stop moaning and belly aching, and do it. That is
what you have to settle for. If I had the money, I would certainly not
do any work that I can think of. I would be delightfully social. Go
around the world on a yacht and call on people for the odd cup of
tea and the cucumber sandwich. O bliss. There must be another world
somewhere. Shades of West side bumholes. Well I have got to get on.
There are loads of jobs to be done. The teeth to be brushed. The laces
to be tied. There is always the laces. It has been a rich life.

    love,
    [K]

[1] Ted Ray (Olden) (1907–77), comedian and actor.

To PETER ROGERS and GERALD THOMAS[1]

12 September 1968

Dear Mr Rogers and Mr Thomas,
I don't think you will regret your decision to offer me this part of Dr Soper.[2] You have taken a step in the right direction, and I admire your perspicacity; more power to your elbows! I am not without some experience in the dramatic field, having served with the Tavistock Players as far back as 1939, and was described by the St Pancras Gazette as: 'Bleached and boisterous Bloomsbury Blonde who reveres the late King Charles and jokes that might have been prevalent during that monarch's lifetime' and went on to serve King and Country with the Royal Engineers in the South East Asia Command. I was a great favourite with the lads and was frequently called upon to render 'He Tickled The Lady's Fancy With The End Of His Long Cigar' which frequently brought the house down, and several pairs of trousers. But I won't bore you with the details. I have also been booked for Methodist socials (When I Was Young And Twenty I Had A Dainty Quim) and the odd seance up at Madame Rawalpindi Smith's. I was actually present when her crystal ball exploded on the fateful night she materialised Fatty Arbuckle, and had to sit on a bit of the broken glass throughout. We were knee-deep in ectoplasm, and the room suddenly went cold, and there was this terrible smell of haddock. I remember thinking 'Hallo! someone's brought their tea!' I was also an initiate of the Septuagesamites, and performed as an acolyte, but was unfairly blamed when the Bishop tripped over his surplice and ruptured himself – by the size of the surplus, I thought he was a Canon. But I am digressing here, and I am sure you worthy gentlemen don't want to be bored with an old Thespian's reminiscences. As to character references, you will find glowing testimonials to my prowess written up all over the City, and at the Scabies Cleansing Station at Paddington. There is a furtive fellow called Edie in Cork Street who can give you the low down on my personal proclivities should you deem it desirable. I am always good for a Barclays[3] (no, I don't mean the card) and am a dab hand at the old abdominal breathing. Very heavy down the phone. By including me in your undertaking, you are setting the seal of success upon your enterprise, and we shall go forward together and it will not affect the pound in your pocket so bugger the

[1] Producer and director, respectively, of the Carry On films. Thomas died in 1993.
[2] *Carry On Again, Doctor.*
[3] Rhyming slang: Barclays Bank = wank.

gnomes of Zurich. Remember always that I do a very good turn (see Chapter 5 of Godfrey Winn's 'Performers I Have Poked') and that, thick or thin, late or tardy, in sickness and in health, I shall be right behind you.

> your devoted servt.,
> Fred Bumhole
> pronounced Bummel.

To NORA STAPLETON[1]

18 September 1968

Well Nora, you know it's a funny thing but when we were discussing the old days and that Michael Harald and the touch up and you said 'O yes and Denis Goacher!' I was suddenly reminded of how much of an influence he had been regarding poetry, and I was looking through the bookshelves and I came on an old copy of the Randall Jarrell book which he gave me, and I thought you might be interested to hear some of these bits from it.

'Art matters not merely because it is the most magnificent ornament and the most nearly unfailing occupation of our lives, but because it is life itself. From Christ to Freud we have believed that, if we know the truth, the truth will set us free; art is indispensable because so much of this truth can be learned through works of art, and through works of art alone. Which of us could have learned for himself what Proust and Chekhov and Hardy and Yeats and Rilke, Shakespeare and Homer learned for us? . . . Art has always been a matter of a few . . .'[2]

And this marvellous quotation from Marcel Proust – 'All that we can say is that everything is arranged in this life as though we entered it carrying the burden of obligations contracted in a former life, there is no reason inherent in the conditions of life here on this earth that can make us consider ourselves obliged to do good, to be fastidious, to be polite even, nor make the talented artist consider himself obliged to begin over again a score of times, a piece of work, the admiration aroused by which will matter little to his body devoured by worms, like the patch of yellow wall painted with so much knowledge and

---

[1] A friend since the mid-fifties. Stage manager (or deputy) on several productions in which K W played.

[2] The quotation is from 'The Obscurity of the Poet', an essay in Jarrell's *Poetry and the Age* (1955). In detaching the final line from a later phase in the argument, however, KW slightly distorts its meaning. Jarrell wrote: 'If, knowing all this, we say: *Art has always been a matter of a few*, we are using a truism to hide a disaster.'

skill by an artist who must remain forever unknown, and is barely identified under the name Vermeer. All these obligations which have not their sanction in our present life seem to belong to a different world, founded upon kindness, scrupulosity, self-sacrifice, a world entirely different from this, which we leave in order to be born into this world, before perhaps returning to the other to live once again beneath the sway of those unknown laws which we have obeyed because we bore their precepts in our hearts, knowing not whose hand had traced them there – those laws to which every profound work of the intellect brings us nearer and which are invisible only, and still! – to fools.'[1]

And this quote from Goethe: 'The only way in which we can come to terms with the great superiority of another person is love. But we can also come to terms with superiority, with True Excellence, by denying such a thing as Excellence can exist; and in doing so, we help to destroy it and ourselves.'[2]

    love,
    [K]

To DAVID HATCH[3]

18 September 1968

Dear David,
Well I certainly meant it – I felt absolutely useless at the run through[4] but Nicholas & Clement were marvellous & you kept telling me it was all right and I actually got thro' it! I'd no *idea* a game could be so difficult. Bless you for writing. If only people knew how tiny the actor's ego actually *IS*! I rang John Simmonds today to ask you about 2 seats on Friday for my mother. See you then.

    Yours,
    Kenneth

[1] This quotation concludes Jarrell's essay.
[2] Also quoted by Jarrell in the same essay.
[3] At this time producer of the new panel game 'Just a Minute'. Progressed from performer ('I'm Sorry I'll Read That Again') to Head of Light Entertainment, to Network Controller and then Managing Director, BBC Radio. Became Special Assistant to the Director-General in the 1993 Birtian shake-up.
[4] Of 'Just a Minute', with Nicholas Parsons and Clement Freud.

To TOM

28 September 1968

Well Tom, that was a lovely letter and that's a fact, but I am sorry if
I misled Clive in the line about 'not getting on with people less intelligent than myself' – cos I assure you it was not aimed at him. You
quote the Tennyson to him: 'Let no man dream, but that I love thee
still . . .'[1] and if any doubt remains about the origins of 'our trouble'
I must tell you here and now that Stanley certainly put the whole
thing in perspective when he said 'it's absurdly petty' and he was
quite right. That is what I was being – petty. It is a side of myself
which you know exists and which I should be able to control far
better than I do. It was absolutely disgraceful to involve Clive in such
an imbroglio. Our interval, pause, or gap taught me that. I still think
it was rather disgraceful going on and on about looseness in morals
on Wednesday, and then having to admit, in the last analysis, that I
was as hedonistic as the next man! – all that stuff I was using to try
and make a case – quoting friendships which I pretended had given
me no pleasure etc. What a load of rubbish. That's another thing you
see – the tendency to get carried away by my own eloquence. O! I
tell you, I shouldn't be allowed out! I have been reading the Ackerley
biography 'My Father and Myself'[2] and it is incredibly illuminating.
Again and again it makes the point that, if you put off the proffered
love or affection – because you are waiting for your Ideal Love – then
you never find love at all. It is frank and sad and poignant, and the
descriptions of trade and rent encounters are really quite marvellously
objective. I would offer it to you, but alas, you never read any books.
Now about the phone. It doesn't apply to you and Clive. It never did.
The reason I had it changed was that I had got to the stage where
FAR too many people knew it, and especially employers. If casting
directors or film people, or the BBC, speak to you direct, it is practically impossible to refuse the work. If it goes through the agent, as it
should, then it is easy to tell Peter to put them off in some diplomatic
fashion. But I shall give it to you, and then I want you to memorise
it, and not write it down anywhere, so no one else can get hold of it,
and if anyone asks you, you can say that you don't know it yourself

---

[1] 'My love thro' flesh hath wrought into my life/So far, that my doom is, I love
thee still./Let no man dream but that I love thee still.' From 'Guinevere' (*Idylls of the
King*).
[2] An account of his father's double life, published 1968. J.R. Ackerley (1896–1967)
had been literary editor of the *Listener* from 1932 to 1959.

and that I am very peculiar about such things and a bit of a crank etc and you can say that you always write, which would certainly contain more truth than most explanations people offer. If you ever have to telephone me, it is best after ten. But as you know, I do have a pathological loathing of the machine – hence all that code crap[1] – so if the letter can substitute, I certainly prefer it. I did the Radio show from the Playhouse last night and it was absolute death. I am no good at these panel games and that's a fact.

> love to you and Clive,
> [K]

Intended for GEORGE MELLY[2]

29 September 1968

Dear Mr Melly,
It's all very well for you to complain about 'critic-knocking'[3] but heavens! we performers have been having it for years – the knocking I mean. I have had notice after notice in which I have been called 'epicene' and 'feminine' and 'camp' and a 'purveyor of homosexuality' and heaven knows what, and this, when I was performing stuff written by professional writers, not myself. When I first read these sort of notices I was appalled and deeply hurt. I thought to myself 'surely I do not come over like that?' but then it happened so often that I began to think it must be true. True that is, for the objective outsider, but NOT for me. If I really believed that I look in life, like the kind of effeminate poof the critics describe, I think I would do away with myself, and goodness knows there are plenty of occasions in life when I feel near to it. Of course this letter is a private one to you and I would be grateful if you would treat it as confidential. I wouldn't write to the papers cos I realise that if you put yourself on show you have got to accept adversity in whatever form it comes. The reason I wanted to write to you was because you drag in the old queer bit again this Sunday in your column when you say of me 'Kenneth

---

[1] KW would answer the phone only if it rang a certain number of times (see letter to Andrew Hathaway of 19 November 1971, pp. 139–40).
[2] Then television critic of the *Observer*. This carbon copy is marked 'Later torn up and never sent. F. Nightingale: "Never start a paper war".'
[3] Melly had opened his *Observer* piece (29 September 1968): ' "Critics are like eunuchs," said lovely little Kenneth Williams to David Frost. "They know how it's done, they watch other people do it every night, but they can't do it themselves." Critic-knocking is a favourite actors' sport on TV . . .'

Williams — whom God preserve, if She really exists . . .' which I suppose means that if there is any God interested in preserving me, you
think this God must be feminine, and not masculine. I don't think
such a line about God, is in very good taste, but I notice you go on
to accuse Laurence Harvey of just this. I was acutely embarrassed by
the way he behaved, and I agree with what you say about him, but
two wrongs don't make a right. I take my God very seriously — for
me, the word embodies indestructible values that are outside of man,
values like Truth and Goodness and Beauty, which I think we can
strive after though alas, most of the time we fail, and I think your
line quoted above is unworthy. It's the sort of thing one might expect
to hear from the smartie queen at the cocktail party. You start the
column by saying that I made the remark about the critics being
eunuchs, but in fact I said on the television that I was quoting a man
'much greater than myself' and it was Brendan Behan. But in fact I
think Randall Jarrell makes a valid point when he says 'there is something fundamentally ridiculous about criticism; what is good, is good
without our saying so . . .' You may think that we're 'show-off's' but
that's what we are employed for, and in a chat spot we are actually
at the moment of creation and we KNOW critics are watching. Ask
yourself how you'd feel if there was someone over your shoulder
analysing each sentence as it got to paper. I realise that I have been
trapped in the facade of the persona I have adopted, but it was forced
on me. If anyone calls you a pervert often enough, you adopt any
shield you can get hold of to protect yourself. It seems to me that
critics should deal directly with the object. If a bloke is supposed to
be comical they should say whether or not he has succeeded in being
comical; not whether he is queer, or psychologically maladjusted or
something. Forgive me going on like this but I think your heart is in
the right place and wanted you to know how I feel.

[KW]

To MR BARBER[1]

Peter Eade Ltd,
9 Cork Street,
London, W1
3 October 1968

Dear Mr Barber,
Obviously it is best to begin any kind of speech with some touch of
humour, and an odd local reference, open with some line about 'It's
very good to see you all here, and my wife and myself are delighted
with your presence – in fact some of the presents have been quite an
eye-opener; we've got enough blankets to start a youth club! – but
of course we are very grateful, and seriously ladies and gentlemen, it
certainly does give me great pleasure – and has done, since I was
fourteen. I don't want anyone here to run away with the idea that I
am some sort of libertine – I am really very naive – you might say
innocent. On the other hand you might not. They told me when I
was very young that whenever I saw a girl, and I wanted a date, I
should cry out to her "Where are you going to, my pretty maid?"
and they said if I did this, everything would work out fine. Well I saw
the girl and I did cry out "Where are you going to, my pretty maid?"
and when she actually turned round, I couldn't have cared less. She
could have kept right on going, for all I cared. But it was different
with my wife. When I asked her where she was going she said "with
you buster" and that was the beginning of a partnership. And marriage
is a partnership, there has got to be the ebb and tide of mutual ideas,
there has got to be intellectual flow. But my wife would not agree
about intellectual flow. In fact every time she saw Flo she threw her
out. Muttered something about two's company – there's no point in
quoting the rest. My wife made it clear to me from the start. She told
me exactly what she wanted. She said "I want a man with guts and
go and lots of money" and I said to her "I've got the guts and I've
got the go, and I am sure we can come to some arrangement." But I
don't want to bore you with the reminiscences of an elderly bride-
groom, so I shall ask you to raise your glasses now, and join me in a
toast to the parents of the bride, without whom, obviously, none of
us would be here today – ladies and gentlemen, I give you . . .' etc
etc.

   If on the other hand you feel that all those would be outrageously

---

[1] Apparently a fan who, admiring KW's way with words on television, had written
to request advice on speech-making.

out of place and that the guests would be expecting something utterly formal I would simply stick to some dull platitudes about 'something old and something new, something borrowed something blue . . .' and say that you've got the lot, that you thank them for coming to celebrate such a happy occasion and ask them to join you in the toast. It is proper for the groom to toast the parents of the bride. They are the ones he is supposed to be particularly beholden to. And in a way, that does make sense.

Thank you very much for inviting me to the wedding. Unfortunately I am like yourself. I hate weddings. Indeed I hate all functions with any sense of formality to them. I realise the need for formal virtues but am an absolute coward about my duty in them.

yours sincerely,
Kenneth C. Williams

To HANS SCHMIDT[1]

11 October 1968

Dear Hans,
When I arrived back from the film studios tonight, I found your letter waiting for me, and I was delighted to see the post-mark and the foreign stamp on the envelope. It is always exciting I think to receive a letter from another country, and I think you are enormously clever to be able to write another language. It is clever enough to speak it, but to write as well, is marvellous. I find it difficult to say anything – even a phrase – in another language. I actually become inhibited about it, and stupidly self-conscious. Of course this doesn't happen when it comes up in the course of a play, but that is quite different.

I was very sorry to learn about the road accident! – but glad to know that you were not hurt. You must always tell these drivers to go at a reasonable speed. I always admonish the chauffeur who takes me to the studios to keep to the speed limit. He races along at seventy miles an hour, and tells me that he is saving time. But I respond by saying that I don't want to 'save time' – you cannot make people understand that 'time' is to be USED, it is not to be SAVED. It is ludicrous to rush about getting from A to B and saving five minutes. What are you going to do with this precious five minutes? Most of the time, it is nothing.

---

[1] KW's German pen-friend, writing (in excellent English) from Munich. KW was disappointed to learn of Schmidt's girlfriend, but pursued the correspondence anyway.

In your letter to me, you quote some French which you saw written on a wall of the Faculty of Medicine, with a caricature of de Gaulle, but I don't speak French, so will you please tell me what it says in English?[1]

Of course I was delighted to read that you will be visiting London in July/August of 69. I do not know how you will like Croydon. I went there once, intending to look round it, and see the new theatre they have built there, but after one look at the main street, I fled in horror and never returned, except to pass through it on my way to the coast. But most certainly when you come, you must tell me in ADVANCE and also tell me what you would like to do – any show you want to see – or restaurant you would like to try, and I will be happy to arrange it. Now please don't forget to TELL me.

Do not worry about replying promptly to my letters. I know very well how much time is demanded of you, with all your studying, and it is very important that all goes well for the degree, and you must work hard to attain that. All good wishes to you –

> yours ever,
> [K]

To the DIRECTOR OF BROADCASTING, South African Broadcasting Corporation

30 December 1968

Dear Sir,
Having just finished filming the sixteenth Carry On – this time 'Carry On Camping' – and at the moment in the process of finishing a sound radio series for the BBC entitled 'Just A Minute' – I have about a month free before starting the next series for the BBC which will be 'Round The Horne' once again.

There is a possibility of my being able to visit your country – end of Jan/beginning Feb. period – and I was wondering if you would be interested in my doing a cabaret type radio show – chatting between

---

[1] Hans Schmidt replied enumerating the following inscribed remains of 'the events' of Paris, 1968: under the caricature of de Gaulle, 'Run, my friend, the old world is behind you'; then, 'It is forbidden to forbid', 'Walls have ears (a proverb!); your ears have walls'; 'I don't like to scribble on walls'; 'I decree the state of eternal happiness'; 'Under the cobblestones is the beach'; 'Forget everything you've learnt, begin to dream'; 'We are all German Jews'; and 'When the finger points at the moon, a stupid man looks at the finger'.

discs, not in the conventional disc jockey fashion, but with a narrative in surrealistic-comedy vein.

I did this with success for three years on BBC Television under the title 'International Cabaret' and I think that the scripts would easily lend themselves to broadcasting.

All this is of course dependent on my being able to take this holiday (which would of course be at my own expense) and being in your country, and the only thing that might interfere is my mother's health, which is causing some anxiety at the moment.

Why I am writing, therefore, is to ask whether you would be interested in compiling such a programme for sound – of say six or so episodes, if and when I was able to visit you?[1]

> yours faithfully,
> Kenneth Williams

To DAVID HATCH

8 January 1969

Dear David,

Thank you for your letter. Yes, I know exactly what you mean.[2] The note of acrimony DOES creep in & I honestly don't think there's anything one can do about it that WON'T result in INHIBITION and that's death to convey. I think the real truth is what I've *always* suspected (for years) that the principal offender has a meanness of spirit which basically resents the laughter caused by others and expressed this resentment by making the sort of niggling remarks which are generally of a personal nature & ill mannered. But if one replies on this level, the whole thing just gets NASTY. One must grin and bear it.

> Sincerely,
> Kenneth

[1] KW seems here to have momentarily overcome his loathing of Apartheid, which, he generally claimed, ruled out the possibility of his paying any sort of visit to South Africa. He never did go.
[2] In the normal course of producer's post-mortem work, Hatch had evidently suggested to KW that the atmosphere on the latest recording of 'Just a Minute' had not been ideally playful – a frequent occurrence on a mentally taxing show that is played with varying degrees of competitiveness by the panellists.

To DAVID HATCH

22 January 1969

My dear David,
You can't imagine how welcome your letter was! – I've been in a
lousy state for some time, due to some old trouble & everything culminated in a dreadful BLACK MONDAY which was all pain & worry.
Landed up on Tuesday with the surgeon who originally operated and
he handled everything superbly so this morning I was feeling tentative
etc. and then your letter came through the box. I honestly think that
praise is like medicine for an actor – and needless to say, your words
acted like a tonic for me. My unspeakable thanks for all you say about
my work in the series and for your kindness and understanding about
the odd psychological difficulties we have encountered. Old Guthrie
always used to say, the first criteri[on] for a Director was – 'one who
could create an atmosphere in which the cast is uninhibited . . .' & I
think this is why I've enjoyed so much working with you – you seem
implicitly to understand this. Look forward to seeing you on Friday.

> Gratefully,
> Kenneth

To GERALD THOMAS

25 June 1969

My dear Gerald,
Thank you for your letter. I tried to telephone you at 3 o'c. today and
a recorded voice said that the lines were engaged, and again at 4 o'c.
when I got the engaged signal. So I am writing a reply instead. I agree
with what you say about Camping.[1] I did not enjoy it at all, and seeing
the trade show suddenly brought it all back to me. I remembered the
awful conditions and everything. I remembered complaining to you
about having to sit in a coach all day at Black Park with all those
extras and not being used even, and being virtually treated like a
crowd artiste, and I began to think about my whole position – all
the years one has worked together one feels there should be some
improvement in one's position. Peter says there can be no improvement in salary, yet the cost of living has risen while I have been

---

[1] Thomas had remarked that after the trade show of *Carry On Camping*, KW had
not seemed very happy. (Thomas added that *Camping* was not his own favourite 'Carry
On' either.)

getting the same money – my car hire bills have trebled since '64. When I complained to you about conditions in Camping you said you could not afford to differentiate between people and that the circumstances of work would not permit it. So one starts to feel that if there is no improvement, either in salary OR working conditions – where is one heading? Taking this into consideration and the fact that you and Peter both told me that you felt I was not sustaining the character in the picture, I have been thinking that perhaps I should not be in the next one. That is why I have been so tardy about contacting you. That is why, when Louie gave me your message, I didn't reply straightway. I have been uneasy in my mind and I realise from your letter that you have perceived this instinctively. Whether it is rational or not, I feel I should be treated differently than other people – I think I should get more attention when it comes to making out a call sheet – because I think I AM different. I do not think that everyone is the same. I think some are more talented than others, and often, more conscientious than others. I knew that if I had lunch with you and Peter, my natural affection for you as people would inhibit my speaking my mind, so perhaps it is as well that I have received your letter today, because it has forced me to clarify my position.

> yours ever,
> [K]

To MICHAEL MILLS (Head of Comedy, BBC Television)

26 June 1969

Dear Michael,
Thank you for your letter. No – I did not write to you saying that I did not think the circumstances apropos the Comedy Playhouse were propitious, simply to hurry anyone along.

I have decided not to do it. I have changed my mind.[1]

When I was first sent the half written script, I thought it was intriguing, and told you, when I met you in the Centre.

When I read the completed version I was greatly disappointed. I

---

[1] KW agonised greatly over pilot shows and half-realised formats, many of which were never performed. This one was a Comedy Playhouse production provisionally titled 'Colonel and the Bat Man', by Myles Rudge. The unavailability of Richard Pearson, a fine actor and a solid family man of the kind KW liked, was the immediate cause of his withdrawal here. They had worked together in Peter Shaffer's *The Private Ear* and *The Public Eye*, with Maggie Smith, in 1962.

felt that the writing did not accelerate, that it did not build to any kind of conclusion, and there was no comedy ending.

The suggestion was made about bringing in the old lady at the end in an attempt to remedy this.

I see now, that this would be something 'stuck on' so to speak and not intrinsic. But over and above all that, I realise that I could not agree to perform this kind of writing – bearing in mind the sexual undertones – without being very sure of myself. And I am not. Perhaps with Richard Pearson I would have been sure, there is an extraordinary reciprocity in our work together.

I could not attempt this script at the moment, let alone work with an actor I don't even know. I am too vulnerable. I have hardly slept during the last week with worry about it and I suppose the whole thing culminated yesterday, when I wrote to you.

In all conscience I am sorry, but I can't do it.

>   yours sincerely,
>   [K]

To TOM and CLIVE

6 July 1969

My dear Tom and Clive,
Quite an eventful few days . . . we went to Hyde Park. There was a vast crowd of people there because the Rolling Stones were playing in the open air, and it all turned into a sort of memorial service for Brian Jones, who as you know was found dead in his swimming pool. Apparently Mick Jagger got up and spoke of him very movingly and quoted the poem 'He is not dead He is not sleeping . . .'[1] and everyone got quite emotional. I don't know what's the matter with this rotten typewriter but the spacing seems to be all over the place. Yes, well then we left the park and had some tea which was nice, and then in the evening we saw this marvellous film 'The Italian Job' with Noël Coward and Michael Caine. The ending is wickedly inconclusive and a bit of a cheat, but the rest of it is magnificently photographed and well cut. The only marred element is the casting of Benny Hill. You are asked to believe that he is Britain's cleverest computer expert, and of course you don't. He looks like a silly fat man, and no more suggests a mathematical intellect than fly in the air. The stunt stuff

[1] Jagger read from Shelley's *Adonais*: 'Peace, peace! He is not dead, he doth not sleep/He hath awakened from the dream of life . . .'.

with the cars is terriffic. I mean terrific. It's this typewriter you see. Yes, well then we came out of there and walked in the heat of the evening to the Steak House for dinner. I had the wine etc., and then the Manager asked if I would have a brandy on the house! Well I thought – in for a penny, in for a pound – and so I had the brandy and then another and you can imajeen how I felt when I came out! Instead of going to the block I kept on walking. Went past the entrance. Would you believe reeled? and tottered along crying out 'Hallo dearie' to all and sundry. The 'all' didn't much bother, and the 'sundry' was in short supply, but eventually I found E. – 'look I'm supposed to be meeting my girl friend, but I'll come up with you just for a chat all right?' so I said yes and in the lift he said 'Just a chat mind! – no actions!' and I was bellying alongside him in the corridors slurring agreement. Indeed we did sit there and chat. You might say it was the story of my life. When I let him out it was quite late, and then, on the corner of the street I got involved with the charming young driver of a GPO van which had broken down and did I know where he could reach a phone? – so he came in and did the phoning and we talked for ages before the rescue van came and by the time I fell into bed it must have been about three! Curiously enough, I look incredibly lovely today, in spite of it all. All love . . .

[K]

To the Hon. GEORGE BORWICK

2 August 1969

Dear George,

. . . I had the phone call from Stanley B. He is going to do this musical which Harold Fielding is presenting.[1] The book is to be by Beverley Cross and he said 'Bev is a sweetie, and has agreed to incorporate any ideas I want into the script, which is nice, and the producer is dear old Wally Douglas who I like, and of course there is my old chum Boo Laye in it!' I said that it all sounded very cosy indeed. Like I always say to Stanley when he has made up his mind about a job. You just have to tell him everything is going to be lovely even if you see the disaster looming. Cos you know that the WARNING is NOT what he wants to hear. When he told me about that ill fated Australian venture[2] – I knew it was death. When he told me about the Orton

---

[1] *Phil the Fluter*, at the Palace Theatre.
[2] Baxter had toured in Australia with *Chase Me Comrade*.

venture[1] – I knew that was disaster, but you have to sit and watch him career down the toboggan track, and think yourself lucky if you can put a few cushions in for him. By way of, at least, bolstering the ego; cos if there isn't a little bit of that, there is no actor at all. The weather here has gone off steadily ever since you left. Today it is really quite cool and overcast and there has been this mist all day. As misty as Niagara where of course Dr Livingstone met the celebrated lady who is forever commemorated in that lovely verse –

> If you can keep your hair, when all around are losing theirs
> And in the midst of baldness – make your mark!
> If you can keep a smiling face despite the falling hairs
> You're a better man than I am Ethel Clark.

Well the bum was a joke this morning I can tell you! and after the bowel motion I thought I should become demented or something. But thank goodness the ointment and the suppository shoved up, has quietened everything down and I was able to venture into the street, looking like most other pedestrians. No one actually screamed out 'Got a touch of the Farmers then?' – I said to the chemist 'there is so much talcum powder up there that I daren't blow off . . . everyone would be covered in the dust' and he just said shortly 'rather you than me' and rang up the till. Money is all they think about nowadays. It's the banks they should all go to on Sundays and all go and kneel outside the Midland, or Lloyd's, and intone 'And deliver us not into Inflation . . .'

> your old chum,
> [K]

To the Hon. GEORGE BORWICK

6 August 1969

My dear George,
I have waited for something to pop through the letter box from my old chum, but lackaday, I have waited in vain. On Saturday, Stanley came to see me. He arrived at 12 o'clock, and we went to lunch at the G[rill] & C[heese]. He said that Nigel Patrick[2] had telephoned him

---

[1] The production of Orton's *What the Butler Saw* which had opened at the Queen's Theatre on 5 March 1969, with Sir Ralph Richardson, Coral Browne etc. 'A notorious production' (John Lahr).
[2] Leading actor (1913–81), for a time ubiquitous in British films.

and adopted the most patronising tone – 'Now look here old son – I've heard from Georgie that you don't want to do these plays because you don't think the parts are very good! – now look here chummy – if you don't want to do the plays, well fair enough, that is your own business, but don't tell me that the parts aren't GOOD old son! – have you read them properly? – they are bloody marvellous acting parts that any actor would give his eye teeth for! – I think you would be foolish to turn down an opportunity like this – I think you would like our company – Michael and Gracie are sweeties and we would simply put on a damned good show and have some fun – so be a good chum and have a proper look at those parts will you old son?' He said he did read them again, and still said no, because he thought they none of them merited revival, and he said 'You can see it all, with Noël turning up and saying "You're not quite getting the point my dear – in the 1926 production there was an enormous laugh on the exit line and you are just missing it" etc . . .' In the evening he took me to dinner at Mick's Diner which is one of those sheesh places. It was boiling hot, and of course the seats were . . . yes – you've guessed it. The bums were soaking at the finish . . . I stopped a taxi and the driver said 'Are you joking? Baker Street is only up the road – you can walk it!' I said 'I should get soaking wet!' and he said 'All right, get in – but it will cost you money!' When I did get in he shouted over his shoulder 'You're that fucking geezer on the telly ain't you? I can't remember your fucking name . . .' I was too exhausted and depressed by then to care, so I just didn't answer. Got into the flat and reflected that I had spent a really disagreeable day, and went ruefully to bed. On Monday and Tuesday I did some massive dubbing sessions for Richard Williams – the animation film man, and the voice was very croaky at the end of it.[1] I saw Nora Stapleton in the evening. She asked to be remembered to you. She is now with the Contemporary Ballet Company, and she says it is a very exciting set up and that the male dancers are all lovely lads. She has just returned from a tour of the South of France with them and she looks very tanned indeed. I said 'Did you have it off out there?' and mimed wanking, but she just said wearily 'O don't be disgusting . . .' love,

[K]

---

[1] 'Loads of voices for *Majestic Fool*, it really was quite exhausting.' (KW's diary, Tuesday 5 August.)

To the Hon. GEORGE BORWICK

11 August 1969

My dear George,
What a day! the heat has been absolutely gruelling. Everyone is complaining. Work is practically impossible; even at 8 o'clock this morning while I was sitting having my coffee, the sweat was rolling off me! It is awful. Went to the Centre and worked with John Law; he sends his regards to you, cos as you know we often refer to the 'George Voice' when we are doing the scripts so you figure in the public and the private life you see. Whenever THAT character comes up, JL always shouts 'Give me the sole meuniere!' We did quite a bit of work, and packed it in about four, and I got the taxi home. When I got home, there was a call from that D.[1] – you remember? – he said that he had got involved with some crooks in a money deal – borrowing three hundred – and added 'They are real villains, and now they've been on the phone & they say if they don't get it by September the first, they will come round and get it – you know – in a nasty way. I am a bit frightened Ken, cos they're the sort that come round in a car of tough guys and give you a going over . . . I was wondering if you could let me have the money?' I said that I hadn't got that kind of money, and I said that if they were threatening he should call the police into it, but he said he could not on any account do that, so I suppose the whole deal is a bit shady, and then I rang off . . . I hope all is going well with you & that you are sipping your eau de vie to the dregs – all love,

   [K]

To SHEILA HANCOCK

22 September 1969

My dear Sheila,
How sweet of you to write. I hope my laboured attempt at humour with the telegram gave you a smile. All my other tries, like falling through your dressing room door at the Duke of York's and pretending to be dead, always failed miserably & you used to say 'O! get up! you silly sod.' Singularly discouraging.[2] It was good to read all your lovely

---

[1] An acquaintance not mentioned elsewhere in this volume.
[2] Sheila Hancock habitually stood up to KW rather in the manner this incident suggests.

notices![1] The Barker one was fabe and the Bryden one is to be preserved.[2] He is one of the few I really think of in terms of scholarship.
Poor old Hobson[3] seems to be in dementia & it's reported that she's
actually dressing up as the pope & delivering her stuff to the paper
ex cathedra. I'm at the Centre every day writing & free only at night
& then *you* are working, so there's no point in talking about meetings
in restaurants but I understand we're meeting on the radio thing
'Just A Minute' so I will talk to you then & we shall revolve many
memories.

> Your old chum,
> Kenneth

To SIMON BRETT[4]

27 September 1969

Dear Simon,
I am sorry about the second show on Friday – I know I was lousy. I
felt v. resentful about the way it was all getting like a slanging match
without being amusing but admit that doesn't excuse going off into
a great sulk which is what I did.[5]

> Apologetically,
> Kenneth

To SIMON BRETT

3 October 1969

Dear Simon,
Your letter does indeed say 'Piccadilly Studio' – I looked it up. I was
utterly wrong, and you were right.[6] Will you *please* accept my humble

---

[1] She was playing in Leonard Webb's *So What About Love?* at the Criterion, with
her future husband John Thaw.
[2] Felix Barker and Ronald Bryden, drama critics for the *Evening News* and the
Observer, respectively.
[3] Harold Hobson, drama critic for the *Sunday Times*.
[4] Novelist and editor, at that time a BBC producer, who had taken over 'Just a
Minute' from David Hatch.
[5] KW's famous tirades on the programme occurred when his desire to entertain
was fuelled by his annoyance. When he was really angry, he fell silent.
[6] Clearly KW had presented himself at the usual studio (the Paris), found nobody
there, and unjustly blamed Brett for the confusion.

apologies? I am truly sorry & now wish that I hadn't shouted the odds so foolishly tonight. I am greatly discountenanced.

Your contrite
Kenneth W.

To PETER EADE[1]

4 October 1969

Dear Peter,
I was rather disturbed by your attack in the office on Thursday when you said you thought I had become bitter, and that other people had spoken to you expressing similar sentiments. Your attitude seemed to be based on the fact that you feel I am not doing enough work and you added that it was good to be occupied (quoting my past work in the theatre) and you said that actors thrive on adulation. I think that you were irritated by my reference to my personal troubles – it was my mentioning the crabs that seemed to set you off. I can't see what your objection here was based on. You have discussed such things before. If it was because of Laurena[2] being present then you should tell her that it's because I am unconventional that I have any talent at all. When I protested that you were the very person I should be able to talk frankly with, you told me that I should 'change the record'. By this, I take it that you feel my conversation is monotonous.

If what you say is true (about actors thriving on adulation) you didn't seem to care much for my prosperity on Thursday. I came out of your office with my confidence round my ankles. I do not spend very much time with you, either socially or in your office, so I find it difficult to understand the charge of monotony. I think I take up a comparatively small amount of your time; you can hardly say you have to tout around finding me work.

You told me once that you really did not like being an agent. I did not reprove you for it. I don't really like being an actor; you should not reprove me either. I am simply in the trap of someone who has chosen a profession which once enchanted him, and now finds it does not. I think Marlon Brando was absolutely right when he said that 'acting is only satisfying for adolescents'. While I may not be totally

---

[1] KW's agent since 1951 (see letter of 20 March 1951, p. 7). He died in April 1979.
[2] Laurena Dewar, of Peter Eade's office, who briefly took over the business after Eade's death in 1979.

mature in many things, I am certainly not intellectually adolescent any more.

That is why I try to steer clear of the theatre. To speak lines of banality is one thing in a film, or on television, or radio; but to have to do it night after night in a theatre is to have the whole thing blown up into embarrassing proportions. It constitutes a torture which I am not prepared to submit to, unless sheer economic necessity forces me. I went through all this in that last debacle at Wyndham's.[1] I think it is unbelievably stupid when I am told to 'forget this'. If such a process were possible the intellect would never store any knowledge at all. All trials are indeed trials for your life. And all sentences are sentences of death.

I am not without a conscience. I try to do what I can do reasonably well, within certain limits. Like Voltaire said – you can only dig in your own bit of garden. I think I have given something to the profession – as opposed to most actors who just take out – even if it is only writing a bit of material in my own style. I have tried to be authentic. I observe values like Truth and Goodness and Beauty, and I try to measure myself by them in my life. A lot of the time I fail. But I try.

After the David Frost Show on the 15 June, you said to me 'you have never been better', well after your admonishment on the 2nd of October I could never have been worse. Our relationship really has its basis in that sympathetic response you once evinced in a railway carriage when we were returning from Guildford together; it is about loyalties. Not about business. If you can read this letter in the light of this, then don't reply and let us not speak of accusations of bitterness again.

> yours,
> [K]

To the EDITOR of the *Spectator*[2]

9 October 1969

Dear Sir,
I was particularly interested to read the article by A.E. Dyson in your 13 September issue, with its reference to our current moral malaise. He says 'The roots go back as far as Rousseau and his romantic

---

[1] *The Platinum Cat* (1965), the occasion of what KW regarded as a nervous breakdown.
[2] This letter appeared in the 18 October issue of the *Spectator*.

disciples, who initiated the replacement of European wisdom by a rag bag of half-baked notions . . .' I thought this article was well written and stimulating. It connected in my mind with a passage which I first read in 1952: 'Willingly or unwillingly Darwin had to give still greater force to that system of unsystematised, inarticulate metaphysical fallacies, which one might term the Creed of the Ontological Invalidity; both in the sense that it dismisses a priori as invalid all ontological assertions about the nature and meaning of Being (as different from the laws governing the processes, connections and interconnections of the phenomenal world, of all that becomes, develops, evolves) as well as in the sense that it has made an incurable invalid of the human intelligence which, grasping their relevance, is capable of responding positively to questions asked about WHAT the world is. To such questions the modern intelligence is prone to respond with that mixture of shame, embarrassment, revulsion and arrogance which is the characteristic reaction of impotence to unfortunately unmanageable demands. This invalid has been left ever since in the nursing care of unhappy poets, dreamers or religious eccentrics, if he was not satisfied with the treatment he received as an outpatient of the Church.' This is from 'The Disinherited Mind' by Erich Heller, and I think it is relevant to the problems postulated in the article you published. For the man of conscience, the modern world is a place where one does indeed walk precariously, and the more individual responsibility diminishes, the more it is taken over by the State, the bureaucracy, & facelessness with which we are increasingly surrounded. I believe Mr Dyson is right when he talks about the values of Christian belief, and what Blake called the 'mental fight' has been going on with me since 1946.

> yours sincerely,
> [KW]

To GEORGE ROSE

20 October 1969

My dear George,
My first thought on receiving your letter was 'about time too!' for I consider you have shamefully neglected me; nevertheless the old surge of affection came back as I read on, and heard the voice of my old chum, and the hilarious account of the Tangier visit! I do wish you had written to me before you arrived in London! We could have revolved many memories – fancy you being in El Piano! that Sid &

Dennis who run it are a scream. Last time I was there the former threw a glass of tonic water over a titled Englishman and cried out 'Piss off out of it dear! You're just another queen to me!' and the milord withdrew discomforted and soaked to the skin. I was out there from August 20th to September 3rd this year. It never lets me down. Always the weather is good and I have the saunter round the beaches and visit the odd bar, and have all the chats. I don't bother with the other, cos I'm only interested in the cuddles and these Arab lads are all intent on something far more penetrating. You ask what I am doing. Well, apart from one of those panel games on radio, I have been trying to compile the material for my own TV series with the BBC. I certainly have no wish to return to the theatre, and only HOPE that economic pressures never force me into it. The telly and the radio or the odd film – yes, but the other, to me, is a sort of prison sentence. As you know, I have always been in these Carry On films, but I have turned down the latest (Jungle Boy) because I couldn't do that AND the TV series, without one suffering at the expense of the other, and anyway, I just fancied a rest from them. If one has any value in a team at all, it is good, now and again, to remind them of it, by NOT being there. I had a curious letter from Charlie Hawtrey saying he was appalled at my absence and that he was 'surrounded myself by enemies and traitors, but soon I shall leave these evil shores for EVER.' I think she means Australia but the sort of telegraphese he uses is becoming almost unintelligible. Joan Sims is in it with him, and she rang up and said 'It's not the same without you love . . .' which was all very gratifying. I must say I do enjoy NOT working. It gives me a chance to catch up on me reading, and listening to me records. Remember you introduced me to Gerard Souzay? – I have quite a few of his recitals now and have lost none of my enthusiasm for lieder. I have ordered a new gramophone which should arrive any minute so I am getting all worked up about that. John Hussey wrote a few months back that he was being dunned. I had to give him 300 nicker. Poor boy seems never to be solvent. Now he is at the Bristol Old Vic, but of course he won't save anything. Apart from Stanley Baxter, who is shortly opening in this new musical 'Phil The Fluter' at the Palace, the only other consistent chum is Gordon Jackson of whom I'm inordinately fond; he is on tour at the moment with a new play.

I was sorry to hear about the death of your Mum; mine is still going strong, and leaves on the 25th for a cruise in the Med. I told her to be careful 'Keep your hand on your ha'penny dear' I said, 'they're all after a bit out there' and she retorted 'Don't worry yourself, I want nourishment, not punishment' so I think she knows what she is doing. Certainly at 69 she ought to . . .

[K]

To the EDITOR of the *Spectator*[1]

21 October 1969

Dear Sir,
Reading Mr Hollis is not at all easy. First, he reminds us that Christ told us not to judge, and then he proceeds to ask IF there is an Omniscient God at all. Later on, he seems to be proffering the doctrine of original sin, but follows this with a bracketed doubt about whether an innocent Adam could have been persuaded to eat the apple. He then tells us to 'invoke the courts as rarely as possible' (a ludicrous statement if you examine the amount of work which burdens the Central Criminal Court in London alone) because in punishing a criminal we actually do MORE HARM to society! If this is true, our concepts of Justice are completely mistaken, and what is happening in our courts every day is very odd indeed. Mr Hollis goes on to tell us that 'we cannot take it upon ourselves to punish others without danger to our own souls' but later on he says we have the RIGHT to defend ourselves against the wrongdoer by 'shutting him up'. The inference here seems to be that punishment & imprisonment are different things. This muddled kind of writing is irritating. All men make judgments – why on earth should they not? – there ARE certain common assumptions in all societies, there have to be. Obviously Hitler was an evil criminal and should have been destroyed. If someone informs me that it would be better to imprison him and submit him to 'remedial treatment' because he really represented the evils of society and was the victim of circumstance etc etc., I should reply that they were talking rubbish and dangerous rubbish at that. As Isaiah Berlin has written: 'To this we can only answer that to accept this doctrine is to do violence to the basic notions of our morality, to misrepresent our sense of the past, and to ignore some among the general concepts and categories of normal thought. Those who are concerned with human affairs are committed to the use of moral

---

[1] This letter was not published by the *Spectator*. Christopher Hollis's 18 October 'Personal Column' ('Swinging Together') had begun: 'One of the most important and one of the most oddly overlooked of the sayings of Christ is that which forbids us to judge.'

categories and concepts which normal language incorporates and expresses.'

Of course all freedom carries the burden of responsibility, and to argue that in punishing the wrongdoer you become as wicked as he is, is as foolish as saying that in recovering your property from the man who purloined it, you become a thief.

> yours faithfully,
> [KW]

To GORDON JACKSON[1]

23 October 1969

My dear Gordon,
I telephoned Rona this evening and said I had obeyed your injunction to do nothing about the play[2] opening – no telegrams or fuss etc. – and I said that I had read that marvellous notice for you in the Times and how very gratifying it was to see your name connected with such praise, and she told me about Sir Bernard[3] rushing round like a whirlwind full of notes & suggested revisions etc. I said I only hoped that nobody acted upon them because you know my feelings about an original vision. It must be adhered to; no matter how many opinions are offered . . .

It was like a bit of the past last week for me, because I flew to Dublin for this late night Television show. Eamonn Andrews type format, only there he's called Gay Byrne. One of the guests he had was an American columnist lady who giggled and said: 'Do you know what your first name would mean in New York?' and he looked extremely po faced & replied 'I know EXACTLY what it would mean but now we're in Dublin where it's the abbreviation for Gabriel so let's proceed on that assumption shall we . . .' I met Siobhan McKenna while I was over there – that's why it was like a bit of the past . . . Mister Pakenham bored the arse off them. I say Mister cos although he is the son of a Lord (and a very distinguished one at that, in my opinion) he stated categorically that he would refuse the title. He said 'I don't mind a few ornaments on my house – I've got

---

[1] Scottish actor (1923–90), married to actress Rona Anderson. Valued friends since KW and Jackson appeared together in Orson Welles's *Moby Dick* (1955).
[2] *The Signalman's Apprentice*, by Brian Phelan, at the Oxford Playhouse. 'Gordon Jackson's superb, rimless spectacled, beautifully timed Alfred would gain ascendancy without benefit of stage' (*The Times*).
[3] This sounds like a visit from Sir Bernard Miles, the actor-producer and founder of the Mermaid Theatre. The credited director was Vivian Matalon.

battlements, actually, all round it – but I don't want any on my name.'
I felt like shouting 'Good for you girl!' but in fact just sat there nodding
and looking sage. There was one moment when they talked of the
endless mismanagement of the Whitehall government, and the historical sufferings of the Irish people, and this Pakenham made some
crack about me having a nerve to show my English face in Dublin. I
did the very slow take and riposted 'Wanna get your facts right dear,
I'm Welsh.' That got the biggest laugh of the programme. The fool
should have left it there, but no! she starts on about Welsh troops
being used against the Irish during the rebellion! I said that the poor
fellows were doing no worse than the Irish troops who helped the
British crush the Indian Mutiny, and that the coal mining despoliation
of the countryside and the disruption of the Welsh economy was
entirely due to mismanagement from Whitehall. I said 'my country
could feel equally aggrieved as yours' and then I rose and pointed the
quivering finger and cried out 'Remember the Pindaric Ode! – the
vision of those Druid priests in sacred robes seeing the defeat of Llewel-
lyn at the hands of the dreaded Edward! Remember their words –
RUIN SEIZE THEE RUTHLESS KING . . .' And then there was
a clap which was just as well cos I didn't know any more of the poem,
and I'm not what you'd call a dab hand at your impromptu pindarics.
Nonetheless, I did not enjoy the evening.

At one point, a bloke in the audience, during the transmission, was
asked what he thought about a play called 'The Barracks' which was
running at the Olympia Theatre. (It had been adapted for the stage
by Hugh Leonard who was on the panel of this chat show.[1]) The
camera was turned on to this fellow in the audience and he said 'Well
like I think it's ironic like that these plays get on in the Dublin festival
– I mean like it's always the same – plays about ordinary country folk
and their sufferings and their troubles – and these plays are being
watched by people like you!' At this point, he seemed to be addressing
the panel, and nobody seemed to be replying, so I said, very loudly
and firmly, 'Are you saying that there is something fundamentally
patronising about cultivated people watching a play depicting very
simple people, and that you resent this?' He seemed to gulp air a bit,
and then said plainly 'Yes.' I said 'You're wrong' and then thankfully
Leonard spoke up for his play. Then a Dublin press critic got up – he
was drama critic for the Irish Press I believe – and attacked this same
piece, saying that it was a vulgarisation of the original novel. Leonard

---

[1] Adapted from the novel of the same name by John McGahern. Hugh Leonard,
b.1926 (as John Keyes Byrne).

replied that the author of the novel had written him a letter congratulating him on the realisation of his characters on the stage, and complimenting him on his faithfulness to the author's intention. I said to this critic 'There you see — the author himself says he is happy with the work, and yet you condemn the piece in your paper and in so doing, you WOUND the writer — Mr Leonard here — you have actually wounded him, do you realise that?' And this man suddenly burst out and said 'Do you people NEVER accept criticism? Do you think you are perfect?' and straightway I said 'Yes. Because if I DON'T think that, I could never get on the stage at all; and my confidence would vanish, and I would be reduced to the same inarticulate stammering that you're exhibiting now.' Well he didn't like me I can tell you. After the show, when we were all in the hospitality room having the gins and tonics I saw him give me a look of utter despite, and I suddenly thought that he was really a very nice fellow, but like a lot of critics, he would never really understand an artist, never understand the vulnerability, or the critic's FUNDAMENTAL USELESS-NESS: which is expressed in the line 'What is good, is good without our saying so' and probably it's all just as well. With some disputes there never will be any bridging. The antipathies run too deep. You can only explain — clarify — and cleanse the water that runs between.

Well apart from the weekly radio show I do no work. I sit here in my drawer in the sky, watching the reconstruction of the Nash Terraces reflecting on the utter stupidity of the Fine Arts Commission, the GLC and the Town and Country Planning Acts which have forced the wretched builders to scoop out the backs, not touch the fronts, and then try to match old foundations with new. Still I suppose we're better off than the Venetians. According to the papers they are simply sinking a bit further into the sea every year. They will eventually be lost without trace, like Atlantis, and the money from the Train Robbery, and the National Theatre on the South Bank.

I haven't seen anything of La Baixter, but then it's into purdah before the openings isn't it? — don't come near me cos I'm doing the lines. I have seen Tom & Clive of course. We all had dinner at the Garden last Monday. I hadn't seen them for a week and they had me out to dinner on the last occasion, and it was all very pleasant, except for that slavish sycophancy that goes on all the time — 'is everything to your liking?', one's praise sought for every single thing you are helped to; becomes a great bore. That Dominic[1] had the effrontery to tell ME a story! — I could hardly believe it! 'This Nun she rushes in

[1] Of the restaurant staff.

to the Mother Superior! and she says "O Mother Superior! there is a
new case of syphilis" and the Mother Superior says "O thank goodness! – I was utterly sick of the Beaujolais."' I did one of those hollow
laughs and he went off eventually . . .

I have written a letter to the Spectator, and they have printed it in
the latest issue (October 18th) so you might look out for it when you
are next in one of those waiting rooms. Today I have written them
another one, but that wouldn't appear till the issue of October 31st
and even then I think it's stretching luck a bit. But it is nice to see
one's name in your actual print, gave me quite a thrill I can tell you.
I wrote another one today. Sent that to the Times.[1]

> love,
> [K]

To MIKE FIELD, Editor of *Rag* Magazine, University of Wales

24 October 1969

Dear Sir,
Considering that your deadline for going to print is so imminent, you
might have thought to put a fivepenny stamp on the envelope
you addressed to me. He said with asperity. Nevertheless I will tell
you one of my favourite stories.

It is about a bejewelled 'grande dame' alighting from a luxurious
Rolls Royce, swathed in sables, while a liveried chauffeur holds the
door for her with one hand, and clutches her poodle in the other. A
wretched old woman – dressed entirely in rags – hobbles up to her
and cries 'Lady! I haven't eaten for three days!' & the reply is: 'Well
my dear, you must simply FORCE yourself.'

> yours faithfully,
> [KW]

To IAN LITTLE[2]

29 October 1969

My dear Ian,
Well you certainly don't make things easy. You seem determined to
reject God because he is not a benevolent superman who has ordered

---

[1] *The Times* did not print this letter, and KW did not keep a copy.
[2] A correspondent in Stockport.

everything in humanity, in a way of which you can approve. You
want the suffering and the stupidity and the horror and the squalor
OUT – and you want the reasoned, just, humane society IN. It sounds
to me as if you are a materialist. I'm afraid, like them, you throw the
baby out with the bath water. You seem to want a sort of Utopian
existence for men in a world where ignorance and stupidity are
banished for ever. You seem to be either leaving out, or deliberately
ignoring, the concept of freedom. You are an individual. I would say
that God had given you Free Will. That means you have the right to
choose. You can choose Good or Evil. It could reasonably be said of
you that you have chosen Good (we have to talk in terms of general-
ity) but having made that decision by virtue of your freedom to
choose, you then wish to deprive others of that freedom by prohibiting
cruelty, misery, privation, squalor, and all the other things you list in
your letter. (It read like some of the complaining chapters of the bible.)
If you really value your freedom to choose Good, you must equally
value another man's freedom to choose BAD. And a lot of men do
choose Bad. Quite apart from the ignorant men who choose it, there
are actually people who deliberately choose to pursue Evil. There are
people who derive pleasure from pain. There are the sadists and there
are the masochists who often appear as something quite other when
they are doing their shopping up the high street. The world is teeming
with myriad entities, millions of individuals – each one, like you, with
a will of his own and a power to choose – it is because of these million
differences that we find humanity so fascinating, marvellous and
unendingly mysterious. If you reduce the whole thing to conformity,
and the Utopian place where everybody is reasonable and good, you
will do violence to the human spirit. Part of that spirit does lie in the
Ideal and the Aspirational, and all that is uplifting and fine in the
world; but another part of that same spirit lies in Promethean arrogance, insatiable curiosity, despair and malevolence.

O don't you see Ian? – there are things and people who are
BETTER than we are? – and we have to acknowledge them? – if we
don't we are denying something in our spiritual selves which will not
be denied without protest. In a sense the troubles of humanity in this
world are like some great sprawling train disaster; if you come along
and do a bit of bandaging, it might not be much, indeed it might be
very small, but if you try to take the whole train on your shoulders
and free the victims pinned underneath, you will kill yourself. We
are human, and we are limited. When we try to become gods we kill
ourselves and other people.

I'll tell you what. Give yourself an intellectual exercise. You reject

God on the grounds of Reason. A great Liberal philosopher once did the same, largely because he could not accept the Dogma. The set of rules devised by the church seemed to him to be intolerably harsh and unjust. He said that rules should be fluid things, flexible, changing with the state of humanity. He said that in order for there to be a profitable dialogue between men, one should be open minded, and WILLING to see the other point of view. He said the cornerstone of an enlightened and liberal philosophy would have to be: It is my Duty To Admit Doubt. And he made the first line of his Dogma. You see the trap?

   Goodness knows why I am talking to you on this subject. I find organised religion frightening. I cannot take it at all. I cannot worship in community. I cannot accept the idea of sex (outside of a good marriage) as being anything but sinful. But there are a hundred things in the human spirit which sustain and comfort me. They may come in the form of poetry – or painting – or music – or in the sights and sounds that England gives me, but I know in my heart that they come from God. Like Emerson said about his friends: 'they came to me unsought, the good God gave them to me . . .'

       love,
       [K]

To the EDITOR, *Jeremy* Magazine

1 November 1969

Dear Sir,
I first read about your magazine in the Times and having taken an interest in Homosexual Law reform for many years, I was looking forward greatly to reading it. After repeated requests, my newsagent eventually produced it today. On the front, it says Volume One, Number Two, but there is no date of issue. I got through it all in a few minutes, and I thought to myself 'what a rotten fraud!' – six shillings for a lot of dreary photographs of two very ordinary looking people with pretentious quotations underneath, padding out a vacuity of material. It is not enough to have leading articles extolling the virtues of sexual liberalism – we're all for that dear, otherwise we wouldn't be buying your journal – one wants some interesting articles as well. Doesn't the gay world possess any writers of wit and original-ity? – can't you find anything better to put in than that banal 'Con-fessions of a Kept Boy' rubbish? – if I have read that kind of thing once, I've read it twice. I hope it's better next time 'cos I rushed

around telling everyone it was to be the most enlightened thing of its kind & if it doesn't improve I'm going to look very foolish indeed. At the moment Gay Guide is the only authentic thing in the book; it's written with a delightful sense of humour & conveys the information neatly & succinctly. I hope the rest catches up with it.

> your[s] faithfully,
> [KW]

To SIMON BRETT

4 November 1969

Dear Simon,
Thank you for your letter. Yes, I did go quite 'numb' on that second show I remember. I'm afraid it ALWAYS occurs when the chair gets weak. Decisions should be made & points awarded without these ENDLESS holdups where the justice of the thing is discussed. It is just boring. On that game, he kept asking the audience to vote for everything & it just SLOWS you down. It destroys the momentum of the game. Its essence is speed. Once you LOSE it, you lose everything. All the playing interest goes for me.

> Yours,
> Ken

To SIMON BRETT

8 November 1969

Dear Simon,
Oh! please help me! try to erase that gaffe of mine about DARWIN (being responsible for the theory of gravity! – instead of Newton) from the tape of the 1st show on Friday 7th at the Playhouse. I mean, if you say it cannot be done, I will have to accept it. But if you could cut the MISTAKE out altogether, I would be eternally grateful. It makes me look a complete fool to *NO* purpose. i.e. – I know the truth of the matter – and it was purely nerves and stress that led me into the Darwin/Newton mix-up. Now IF it was screamingly funny I wouldn't mind, but it *isn't* – it's just stupid and I honestly don't want to appear THAT stupid. *Please* help me in this matter. I know I was terrible as

the Chairman in the No. 2 show. I accept that: but I did have a 'go'. It's just that I'm better in the role of rebel & being demonic, than an adjudicator and responsible.

> Yours ever,
> Kenneth

To NOEL WILLMAN

13 November 1969

My dear Noel,
Heard that radio production on the Third the other night. The satire I told you about, which was a send up of all those eulogistic radio tributes, called 'A Bannister Called Freda' — the life of Dame Fred[a] Bannister in which I play all the men in her life. It was quite good and made me laugh immoderately, though I realised that my acting had grossly deteriorated through doing so much revue type work. Pulled me up shortly I can tell you. Say not the struggle nought availeth. No indeed. I linger on the threshold you see, or rather, the ante room of greatness, cos I'm really afraid. The artist is often on the side of the devil and every time I see him I get the screaming ab dabs. Walk the floor of my brain, up and down, up and down, and eventually end up with a headache, and O so much guilt. Must send Stanley Baxter a telegram tonight. He is opening in this new musical called 'Phil The Fluter' — book by my old chum Beverley Cross, about the composer of 'The Mountains of Mourne'.[1] I do hope he has a success, cos otherwise I fear he will be splintered for ever. I don't think there is any special news to be conveyed to you. They are still bashing away at the modernising of the Nash terraces underneath me, and sometimes the noise is ear splitting. I dream of cottages in the country, but of course the damp always deters me; all those wet leaves drearing about like Henry James. I saw this verse in the Spectator the other week —

> 'There is only one omission
> In the Shape of Things to come:
> We need a Royal Commission
> To redesign the bum'[2]

---

[1] W. Percy French (1854—1920) wrote 'Mountains o' Mourne' with Houston Collison. French also wrote the song 'Phil the Fluter's Ball', which gave the musical its title.
[2] Printed in the *Spectator* of 2 August 1969, signed 'E.M.B.', and prefaced 'Thoughts on sitting too long in a first class railway carriage on the Southern Region'.

It gave me pause for reflection in between shoving up the supposi-
tories I can tell you. The weather has been very good, and this morning
it's all sunshine and light. The trees all turning to gold, and that
autumnal feeling everywhere. I am always a little surprised to find
the light failing in the afternoon. Well I hope your production proceeds apace and that things are brightening for you, and that you will
soon be safely back in London, where you are sorely missed by

> your loving chum,
> [K]

To DAVID[1]

15 November 1969

Dear David,
You did well to give the false promise. You were working against time
and being placed in jeopardy. If release from capture necessitates a
bogus confession I think it is absolutely justified – like an American
in Vietnam or a Kusnetzov in Russia. In any case the provocation you
describe is monstrous. You should have kept all the doodlings: they
sound quite damning. I think it was Havelock Ellis who said that
those who castigate most heavily are sufferers themselves and this one
sounds latent indeed. Now obviously, the company, ideally, should be
avoided. One should never see or hear it again. But from all that you
say it sounds as though this is well nigh impossible; therefore, a different strategy must be planned. Don't think this can be evaded. You
must evolve a policy. A sado-masochistic relationship has been established. He has played the tyrant and made use of your weakness with
taunts verbal and written, ending in the extraction of this promise.
Fear has led you into the passive role of acceptance.
     You must now perform the role of the convert. His company should
be sought by you and he must be thanked for all the happiness his
conversion has brought about. You must appear that dazed and smiling thing that owes it all to him . . . 'all over the week end I have
been thinking of all that you have said and it has acted upon me like
a spiritual catharsis. I actually FEEL better because of you! – thank
goodness I had the good fortune to meet you, and be reminded of
wholesome values again. It has changed my life. It is as though a

[1] An acquaintance whose homosexuality had been exploited by a fellow
office-worker, named John, in an alternating pattern of near-seduction and public
ridicule. David had requested K W's advice.

cloud has been lifted from me! my step and my heart is lighter! I am so happy! – and I owe it all to you. How can I ever repay this debt? – what is there that I can do to show my gratitude . . .' Later on he should be told that, all because of him, you have re-established an old friendship with a wonderful girl you have known for years, and discovered a deep affection that was under your nose all the time without realising it etc. This girl must be given a name and everything – perhaps you would have her call, or pick you up at the office – and be mentioned to him so often that eventually he is sick of hearing about her (or jealous of your new-found mentor) and the whole conversion BIT.

In this fashion you will shift the emphasis in the relationship – subtly. The entire process can be concentrated, or watered down, according to your inclinations, and your acting abilities. But your behaviour must have a policy; a purpose. You must be POSITIVE. Only then can you render him NEGATIVE. And that is the whole point of the exercise. He forced a promise from you; he should be awarded with its enactment. He should be thanked to the point of embarrassment.

The TV series which I rehearse in December is called 'The Kenneth Williams Show' which you must admit shows the kind of originality that [can] only be produced by conceit or mental confusion. Heigh ho.

> yours ever,
> [K]

To DAVID

6 December 1969

Dear David,

Amazed to hear of the developments in the John Saga. One feels it is bound to end in disaster for him; the entire episode spells out that kind of foredoomed quality. It is very good of you to adopt this forgiving attitude, but please take my advice and keep away from it. Right away from it. It doesn't matter how many times he tries to see or talk to you. Simply don't cooperate. Don't talk at all. Your forgiving attitude will not avail you in this case. You are dealing with maladjustment. He may seem to be letting it rest, at the moment; he did last time. But he will start again. These mental predators need victims like ophidians need live mice.

We flew from Gatwick on Thursday at 5.45 and landed at Gibraltar at 8. The evening air was warm and balmy and I thought everything was going to be nice. Then the trouble started. The small plane that does the trip over to Morocco was fully booked for the entire week! – that left only one alternative. The Boat. Tried to book on that and we were told she is in Dry Dock! Ludicrous, and strangely typical of the Rock. So we went off to the hotel in dire spirits. About 9.30 we started a stroll round the town – well there is no town – rather down Main Street, which is all there is of Gibraltar, and ended up in the Sugar Bowl. The pub is run by this queen they call Sugar. She is a disgrace and rushes round doing daft dances with castanets and kissing the sailors. Gets away with murder. When I walked in she flung her arms round me and cried out 'Ah Kenny! – you haven't forgotten your old sweetheart!' and kissed me passionately and all the matelots started cheering. I told her to piss off and stop making an exhibition of herself and give me the gin and tonic but of course I had created the desired effect and thereafter the entire place revolved around my presence.

The sailors kept asking my friend Tom 'Are you his bouncer?' cos he does look quite tough, but he indignantly denied it and kept repeating 'No! – just a friend' and I was being bought loads of drinks when this rather appealing young man said 'Come away to my place – you will never have any peace in here!' and I thought that was really rather charming so I gave Tom the wink and we shot out the back way with this young fellow. Well 'his place' turned out to be miles! – we walked and walked, and eventually ended up in the Naval Married Quarters and walked up the stairs of a particularly sordid sort of tenement block and by this time it was about 12.30. He opened the door, and we found – HANG ON! – we found Mum and Dad, sitting in domestic bliss, watching the telly. Peyton Place actually. I was furious. His invitation had been couched in totally dissimilar terms if you see what I mean.

We shot back to the Sugar Bowl – cos everything goes on there till about three or four in the morning, and this time we got in with a crowd of boys from the ship HMS Blake – they were all very charming and insisted on buying us drinks till they were coming out of our ears and we all sang dreadful songs and lurched back to the hotel at about 5 in the morning. I had to get the page to put the key in the lock. Eventually woke at 7 with an awful headache!

Later on that morning, we were sitting disconsolate in the lounge of the hotel, watching the rain pouring down outside the windows in the Mediterranean haze, and I noticed these two young fellows sitting nearby and I said to Tom 'Shall I chat them up?' and he said

'No. They look too aloof' and then the waiter came up with two
drinks and said they were sent with the compliments of these fellows!
I said to Tom 'Well you were QUITE wrong, ducky' and called these
two over, and asked them to join us. They were dressed in elegant
lounge suits with those rather opulent looking cuff links and I said
'Are you waiting to cross over to Morocco?' and they said no, they
were ON LEAVE in Gibraltar, from the aircraft carrier HMS Hermes.
I cried out 'OH! have you got any messages?' and they said what did
I mean and I said that Hermes was the Messenger of the Gods and
they muttered 'Oh yeah?' and looked perplexed so I thought 'you'd
better cut out your Greek mythology bit, dearie!' and we were just
starting another round of drinks when I was called to the telephone.
It was Johnny Koon – he owns the Lotus House and the China Garden
in London – and he said he was opening a new restaurant in Gibraltar
that night and would I be the guest of honour. I said 'That is very
nice of you dear, but I am with a few friends actually – my young
secretary and two boys we picked up – I mean two cousins of mine
on my mother's side – whom we have bumped into at the hotel here!
– quite extraordinary how these things happen isn't it?' and he said
yes it was and why didn't I bring them all along? so I did. We all
bowled into this not very ritzy establishment and had the champagne
and one of the guests was – HOLD IT! – the Captain of the Hermes!
Of course it was a riot when I introduced my two cousins! He asked
what they were doing in Gibraltar and they both stammered and said
'Well – we are on your ship sir' and explained they were Naval ratings.
I said gaily 'I should have thought you'd have recognised them captain!' and he retorted 'I've got two thousand men under my command
on that ship!' and I said 'But then, as Doctor Johnson properly
observed, "In naval matters sir, no man is under oath"' (which is
completely untrue) and he said 'Oh yes – of course' and we all sat
down to dinner. It all went very well, and I told them some amusing
anecdotes – Orson Welles on the opening night of Moby Dick, leaning
across and whispering to me in the middle of the Carpenter Scene
'Piss Off!' and I did, saying 'God bless you my darling' – that went
down quite well with the Captain, and eventually they drove us to
the airport where we got the midnight plane to London. Got in at
about 3.30 in the morning. The Customs said 'Have you anything to
declare?' and I said 'A complete waste of a fifty pounds air fare.'

yours,
[K]

To the Hon. GEORGE BORWICK

24 December 1969

My dear George,
Well I never thought I would be writing to you at Christmas! – but
here I am doing so! – as you know I never send cards, but I wanted
you to know that you are in my thoughts; indeed you are never far
from them. When I was at Noel Willman's house, he had a Hester
Chapman to dinner. She is a writer. Mainly biography. She said to
me 'I went out to Tangier in August 68 as the guest of Margaret
Huntingdon, and it was one endless round of parties parties all the
time and Margaret said we could all have a good laugh at these queers.
There are hundreds of these queers out there – they all go there
because they cannot behave properly in this country you see – and
out there they can behave disgracefully and go around openly with
their men-friends you know! – One party I went to, there was this
fellow David and his friend had hardly anything on! and in this alcove
in his house we found loads of these filthy paper-backs my dear! –
not a decent book in the house! – and I met these two young fellows
who were on holiday there and they said they thought it was all a
bit too much and they gave me a lift home and Margaret just left me
– went off with some French woman and said I could make my own
way home – so these fellows gave me a lift back, and I sat on my
own and had this bread and cheese, and that was my visit to Tangier!'
I was saying 'How Dreadful' and etc. at odd intervals, but it was really
an endless monologue. I received a very funny Christmas card from
Stefan and Arnee, and it showed a bloke swimming from Gibraltar to
Tangier! – on the Tangier side there was a huge cock. I can't think
what it is supposed to mean. Louie's birthday was the 20 December
so we went up to the Jacksons and they gave us drinks, and then we
all went to the Carrier restaurant for supper. Giovanni was absolutely
marvellous and gave Louie a Birthday Cake and everything! Made a
great fuss of her. She kept admiring the candles on the table and
eventually asked if she could take one home with her and said to him
'It'll come in handy 'cos I live alone, you see!' And everyone laughed
though I thought it was rather outrageous. Spare a thought for a
lonely old man in Baker Street,

love,
[K]

To SUSANNE FERGUSON[1]

c/o Peter Eade Esq,
9 Cork Street,
London W1
31 January 1970

Dear Susanne,
Yes, I find myself in agreement with most of the things that you say.
In many ways, letters are like Strachey's view of History – the idea
of little buckets being lowered into the ocean which are pulled up,
made to disgorge their contents, and tell us something about the area
we cannot see. The reason I have been low in spirits lately is because
the flat I occupy has become noisy and I cannot concentrate under
such conditions . . . It is all very complicated because I hold a 90 year
lease on the apartment, and in every other sense, it suits me very
well. It took me ages to find a place where I did not hear noise through
the walls, or radios playing etc. I thought of going out of London, but
that would mean endless travelling on trains because I don't drive,
and most of my work is in the centre. Nevertheless I will probably be
reduced to that in the long run.

Oh I know what you mean about the Sunderland experience! – in
1963 I went off with a chum, and we did the Greek Islands and on
Skiathos I could hardly believe the silence. It was languorously warm
and the air was heavy with myrtle. Eventually we came to some
straggling little houses and an old lady gave us some grilled mullet
and a bottle of retsina and it was to die. The scrubbed cleanliness of
everything, the simplicity and the quiet and the beauty. We met some
fishermen later on who told us that there was no work, and unless
you were lucky enough to own a boat and be able to fish, there was
no alternative but to go to the mainland and get employment. Even
so he added 'sixty per cent men have no work . . .'

This next door neighbour of mine is a heart specialist. He & his wife
asked me in for a sherry. Their flat is adjoining mine. I couldn't believe
it! – it was as quiet as the grave. I said how pleasant it was, and told
them of my predicament, and this fellow said 'You want to try and
find a buyer for it – advertise for a deaf sailor who is used to the
sound of a ship's engine' and he fell about laughing at his joke. I said
that I didn't find any of it funny. They both got contrite and said that

---

[1] A correspondent from Edinburgh who had detected signs of melancholy in K W
and wrote to offer comfort and thanks. Her healing experience of nature (see K W's
second paragraph) occurred not in Sunderland, however, but in Sutherland.

if ever I wanted to study I could go in and use their spare room. Of course it is impossible to tell such people that these kind of offers are useless. What one needs is privacy in every sense of the word. I have always lived alone. I cannot work if there is anyone about. Even in the next room. O I don't know what the answer to it all is! I suppose really that there is no answer. We are all orphans in this vast orphanage where no one knows his origin and no one comes to claim us. I used to like acting because I used to like showing off. I don't any more. But at 44[1] you can't start all over again. And I don't know any other way of making money. And there is me mother and the dependants. It is a Gordian knot all right. I remember talking to Robert Bolt once – when I was in his play at the Queen's[2] – and I said how dreary it all was (we'd had a great flop) and he said 'Yes – it's a Vale of tears for three score years and ten. My only consolation is that I am half way through . . .'

yours,
[KW]

To HANS SCHMIDT

12 February 1970

Dear Hans,
It is extraordinary that you should write about the Warhol film:[3] I have seen it. Ordinarily I would not have done so, but on January 17 I went to dinner with Michael Codron (who presented both the revues I did in London) and after the meal, he casually let it drop that he had got tickets for this film, and took me along to see it. Afterwards, I wrote in my diary: 'Technically, it was appalling, but there were moments of great truthfulness and beauty. The dialogue naturalistic and liberally sprinkled with filthy epithets; all very lively. It achieves with ease all that Midnight Cowboy failed to do.' And now you write saying practically the same thing! – isn't it amazing? The police have since confiscated the film and have now handed it to the Director of Public Prosecutions I don't think he will act upon it though, because this venture has the blessing of Trevelyan – our eminently respectable film censor. But several people have commented on what seems to be a reaction against the permissiveness of

---

[1] He was actually still forty-three, until 22 February.
[2] *Gentle Jack* (1963).
[3] *Flesh.*

the latest liberal measures; they feel the pendulum is swinging faintly in the direction of puritanism again. They may be wrong, but I have heard it evinced on more than one occasion.

On Saturday I have got to do this programme at the Playhouse Theatre for the BBC. It is a mammoth reading of prose and poetry for 50 minutes – the choices being entirely personal, and marking stages in one's life – intellectual development etc. It has been a murderous task to actually compile the script. I wish you had been around, I can tell you! I am including most of 'Lady of Shalott' – from Part II. It has always held a special place in my affections. How marvellous that you have published a piece on D.H. Lawrence! What a pity it is not in English. I would have been very proud to have a copy. Alas, I will never be able to read German. A leopard doesn't change his spots, and obviously I will not start, at this late stage, to learn another language. So many people have to learn English now. Because of the Americans, I suppose; they have the Empire now. Same thing, different clothes.

My television series 'The Kenneth Williams Show' is now going out every Monday night on BBC1 at 9.10 at night. Very good spot – just after the news. It had a very good review in the Daily Mail, which called it 'intellectually stimulating' and the Telegraph dismissed it as 'rubbish'. I don't know if I told you, but I wrote it with John Law and he was ill at the opening of rehearsals, and during the second episode, he died. It was very sad. He was only 40 and we had been friends since 1960. Pity that you are not over here to see them. You will never have a second chance. I doubt if I could ever be persuaded to take on a series again. It is a daunting task indeed, to prepare all those scripts in advance. When this Saturday is finished, providing nothing important turns up, I think I shall go away. Probably Tangier – cos I know a few people there, and it isn't fun to go somewhere where you are going to be alone. I shall have to find out what their weather is like, only a few weeks ago, they were having awful floods.

> your friend as ever,
> [K]

To N.

7 April 1970

N:
I have re-read your letter of March 31st and I have decided after much thought that I was wrong to reply as I did, defending the character

of Tom. I have nothing to be defensive about. In fact, I see now that it was insulting and rude of you to speak of someone dear to me in such derisory terms. I think it best for both of us that we do not meet or correspond in any way in future.

> Sincerely,
> Kenneth

To ANNETTE KERR

80 Queen Alexandra Mansions,[1]
  Hastings Street,
London WC1H 9DP
1 May 1970

My dear Annette,
Oh! darling I was so pleased and touched to have your letter. It is wonderful to receive praise from someone perceptive but doubly appreciated when it's accompanied by professional awareness. You have been a good and steadfast friend . . . I am filming at Pinewood at the moment[2] – up at 6 o'c every morning – charming & I must admit I *do* enjoy it. They're a lovely crowd down there & all so nice to me – the camera crew & the stage staff – oh! it's all marvellous. All my life would have been wonderful if I'd stayed off the milk. It was the milk that did it.

> All my love,
> Kenneth

To B.

10 August 1970

My dear B.,
Last Thursday we went to Provan's for dinner. That Stuart Grimshaw was very pleasant and we were enjoying the sweet when the waiter said we had to vacate the table and we were shoved downstairs on that bonkette for the coffee. There were three gentlemen already on it and they had to squeeze up to make room, so they introduced

---

[1]   KW was actually living at number 92, while building work was being carried out, but his mail was delivered to his new flat, number 80, into which he moved on 20 June.
[2]   *Carry On Loving.*

themselves – 'I am Jack, and this is Eric. We run a hotel in Euston Street. And this is our friend Bernt from Bangkok . . .' Well we all said 'fancy that!' and so on, but this Jack said 'my dears if you want a really good holiday, go to Bangkok – we have just come back and honestly it is a BALL! – outside the barracks, the sergeant came up to us 'cos we were admiring the sentries and he said "you want one boy? or two boy? or three boy? – I get for you" Oh he was charming! and they come running out of the gates, the boots going bang bang bang and they salute you with those flashing eyes and smile at you and ask if you like them . . . Oh my dears, I am never going anywhere else for a holiday.' Their friend Bernt actually lives there and said 'yes it is ideal if you are gay, because everyone in Thailand is gay if they are under thirty – you must take my card . . .' V. took it without hesitation and was writing down various details like she was fixing a travel itinerary, and kept murmuring 'Hm yes – I've always wanted to visit Bangkok . . . lovely name . . .' Then into the restaurant came a great party of men, mostly Americans, with that lawyer Tony, and so it was 'my dears what are you all doing on this bonkette?' and then the waiter said that their table wasn't ready and so we all had to squeeze up even more so that they could all sit on the damn thing too! The sweat was running off all of us, and the Bangkok Saga was repeated all over again with lots more detail and several had the half hard. When I was walking back to V's I said 'Of course you could make Morocco sound just like all that stuff they were describing' and he said 'Oh yes, my dear, take it all with a pinch of salt – I know these Thai boys and believe me, they are very possessive . . .' That Barry was in the restaurant too! – the hair has practically covered the face now! Tom has had an extraordinary adventure with a DOCKER!! – ending up in an apartment in Lisle Street and the cock was actually bitten. When the doctor examined it after he said 'Oh it's merely broken the skin very slightly . . . I must say, it IS rather a large penis . . . hm . . . yes . . . I expect that is quite a size when it's up . . . very large indeed . . .' and Tom anxiously asking 'Is it serious – this cut?' and the doctor still holding it, and peering intently 'Oh nothing to worry about at all . . . but I must say this is really quite a size – you must have made a lot of people very happy.' 'Well yes, but what about the treatment?' 'None – it will clear up in a day – just don't let them get their teeth into it again that's all . . . it certainly IS a very large one – try not to get an erection for a day or so . . . my word . . . it is a beauty.' The more one hears about these clinics the more accommodating the National Health Service appears to be. I am going to see Louie tonight and she says that the arthritis is better. I hope you are enjoying your FULLY BOOKED holiday in Tangier. Glad to hear that your bum has turned such an attractive shade. Pity you can't exhibit it in town. I should think that 'Oh Calcutta' would jump at it. And no need to make up either.

lots of love
[K]

To BEVERLEY CROSS

5 October 1970

My dear Beverley,
Got your air letter of 30 September this morning. Quite a treat to see it lying on the floor under the letter box, and it is so comforting to get letters in the morning. I had to laugh about your adventures with the mule, and your tottering into the Monastery of the Miraculous Ikon! – those animals can only be mounted safely with their masters holding the bridle all the time. That is the way I ascended the formidable height of the Acropolis at Lindos and it worked very well. As we rounded a craggy turn of the path going up, with some apprehension as the mule dislodged stones which went cascading down into the sea below, I was chatting away to Tom over my shoulder when we encountered some riders coming down. At that point I was saying 'Of course, you know I am a superb rider . . . oh yes my dear . . . it was me that taught John Wayne . . . he always says he owes his style in the saddle to me . . .' etc. Well of course they were English and they heard the whole thing. When they passed us it was the full raised eyebrows and 'get the Madam' look. Like the time with you in Crete when I said about those two approaching blond young men 'Here come a couple of Krauts' and they stop'd and said 'No – we are Swedish – and you should not speak so rudely' and I was terribly embarrassed and said it was amazing that they had heard me from that distance and you said it was the voice projection. The Carry On Henry script bears no relation to any kind of historical accuracy. Wolsey and Tom Cromwell are plotters with Guy Fakes I mean Fawkes to blow up the King who has only one prospective wife in the film and she is called Marie and eats so much garlic that he cannot bear to go near the bedchamber, and there, his place is usurped by a character called Sir Roger de Lodgerly who obliges her considerably, and is played, surprisingly, by Charlie Hawtrey. There is a lot of by-play with the King going off hunting, getting thrown from his horse, and landing up in the hay with rude country girls and so on and so forth, but it

would be pointless to pretend that they have based it on any incident from the past. I really do not see any point in doing it, except that Peter Rogers has got this thing about Carry On films 'always look good in costume' and as the final arbiter is always the box office as far as these films are concerned then there is no reason to bother about scripts which are irrelevant to the subject. The joke is that they have bought the costumes from 'Anne of the Thousand Days' because they are so concerned about it looking authentic, and I am assured that this film totally lacked authenticity in that sense. Willman said 'the costumes were all wrong my dear' with an air of such weary finality that one felt it MUST be so. I expect you know about our strikes over here. Refuse has not been collected for over a week now and the stuff is piling up everywhere, and the sewage is an appalling problem. The country seems never to have rallied since the fall of Macmillan. Do you realise that? – ever since that period there has been a sort of malaise which has pervaded the national atmosphere with a kind of despair & hopelessness. The total result, in terms of 'fuck you Jack' & permissive society, drugs, rising illiteracy, contempt for morality etc. makes it all terribly depressing. Some days you throw it off, but it keeps coming back, as Roy Fuller says somewhere, 'like the all pervasive odour of a fart . . .' Give my love to Gayden.

[K]

To NOEL WILLMAN

5 October 1970

My dear Noel,
I was probably not expressing myself very well last time I talked to you when I was trying to oppose your argument that Good can, in the light of history, be shown to come from immorality and sometimes from Evil. I really do think it is a dangerous kind of thinking and further, I think it is fallacious. It must of necessity put into jeopardy any kind of contemporary judgment. I had to go back to my books for support, and I found it in this passage by Isaiah Berlin:
'It needs more than infatuation with a programme to overthrow some of the most deeply rooted moral and intellectual habits of human beings, whether they be plumbers or historians. We are told that it is foolish to judge Charlemagne or Napoleon or Genghis Khan or Hitler or Stalin for their massacres, that it is at most a comment upon ourselves and not upon "the facts". Likewise we are told that we should

not so describe those benefactors of humanity whom the followers of Comte so faithfully celebrated; or at least that to do so is not our business as historians: because as historians our categories are "neutral" and differ from our categories as ordinary human beings as those of chemists undeniably do. We are also told that as historians it is our task to describe, let us say, the great revolutions of our own time without so much as hinting that certain individuals involved in them not merely caused, but were responsible for, great misery and destruction — using such words according to the standards not merely of the twentieth century which is soon over, or of our declining capitalist society, but of the human race at all times and in all places in which we have known it; and told that we should practise such austerities out of respect for some imaginary scientific canon which distinguishes between facts and values very sharply, so sharply that it enables us to regard the former as being objective, "inexorable" and therefore self-justifying, and the latter merely as a subjective gloss upon events — due to the moment, the *milieu*, the individual temperament — and consequently unworthy of serious scholarship. To this we can only answer that to accept this doctrine is to do violence to the basic notions of our morality, to misrepresent our sense of the past, and to ignore some amongst the most general concepts and categories of normal thought. Those who are concerned with human affairs are committed to the use of moral categories and concepts which normal language incorporates and expresses.'[1]

There is also a relevant passage in Burckhardt's 'Reflections on World History'[2] where he says 'From the fact, however, that Good may come from Evil, and from disaster relative happiness, it does not follow that Evil and disaster are not what they are.' Values for him, are as real and more so, than facts and happenings. In this, he is with Schopenhauer a Platonic Idealist, despising what he calls the 'frivolous pretence of objectivity' which instead of achieving what it aims at, merely loses itself in a welter of relativities. In the same book he dismisses the comfort of the Hegelian 'master plan' for the world; he

---

[1] From Isaiah Berlin's 'On Historical Inevitability', in *Four Essays on Liberty*.
[2] The whole passage that follows consists of closely paraphrased extracts from the 'Burckhardt and Nietzsche' chapter of Erich Heller's *The Disinherited Mind*. The Burckhardt quotations appear on pp.75 and 77 of the 1961 Penguin edition, and the Schopenhauer passage about Plato on p.67. At the end of the same chapter appears the quotation from Burckhardt: 'At every moment, I would be prepared to exchange my life for a never-having-been' (from a letter to Riggenbach, 12 December 1838), which in his diaries K W misattributes to Schopenhauer.

says 'Every successful wickedness is, to say the least of it, a scandal. The only lesson to be derived from the successful misdeeds of the strong, is to hold life here and now in no higher esteem than it deserves . . .'

In Schopenhauer himself, we read: 'Those who regard the philosophy of history as the aim of all philosophy, ought to read some Plato, who indefatigably repeats that the object of philosophy lies in the unchangeable and in what lasts, and not in the things which are now like this, and now again like that. All those who postulate such constructions about the world in motion, or, as they call it, history, have not grasped the fundamental truth of philosophy: that, philosophically speaking, what REALLY is, is the same at all times . . . a real philosophy of history ought to bear in mind that what forever IS and never DEVELOPS . . . that what we have before us [is?] the ONE creature, essentially identical and unchangeable, busying itself with the very same things today and yesterday, and forever . . . This identity preserved through all changes is founded on the fundamental qualities of human hearts and brains, many bad, few good . . .'

You know I can't live without the Idea of Morality. Whenever I feel that these fundamental values are being put at hazard I tend to become the very thing I ought not to become – emotional. I should resort to quiet reason. Perhaps because I lack this facility, I so admire the writing of someone like Berlin – or indeed Erich Heller. It was Erich who first showed me the devastating effect that Darwin had on the Ontological creed, and that sad story is still being told, and is giving rise to all these terrible invalidities. I suppose the modern poet is in the worst dilemma of all, and for the most part he seems to take refuge either in the esoteric or the 'difficult' – or resorts to rhetoric. Certainly he no longer addresses himself, or is listened to, by all. Perhaps he never was, though one feels that in Chaucer's and Shakespeare's age he did. I have gone on and on haven't I! – you see what comes of being alone and in the house all day. I suppose it is cowardly but the staring and the nudging and the whispering really does set my nerves SCREAMING on those days when I am not very buoyant[1] and I'm now beginning to think that I can't type either. I saw Tea and Sympathy [Tom and Clive] on Sunday when they had me up to lunch at Highgate. Somehow the conversation came round to Tax

---

[1]   KW had written in his diary the previous day: 'I cannot walk anywhere without the STARING, without the idiot who stops me with some rubbishy remark (either banal compliment, or insult), and I LONG to be unknown. Because I'm not a star and have never earned those astronomical sums I am not rich and cannot afford the seclusion of the country retreat.'

and T said that he thought I deserved to keep more money than I did and that I should form a company etc etc. I said in reply 'Oh dear – I couldn't LIVE like that, and anyway the real truth is that I think I DESERVE nothing . . .' He retorted, 'I think you deserve more than two rooms in a tenement block.'

That did it. I kept talking all right. But inside I was finished. The fact that anyone can formulate and label like that. All right, perhaps we all do it . . . but to say it flatly 'that's the sum total of your life, that's how you have ended up.' It was the same in the Corner House last year with Peter Eade when he said 'Let's face it, you are synonymous with CAMP as far as casting is concerned.' I felt any sense of achievement that I might have possessed draining slowly away. Look forward to seeing you on Thursday.

      love,
      [K]

To PETER MARTIN (*Nova* magazine)

c/o Peter Eade Ltd,
9 Cork Street,
London W1X 1PD
15 October 1970

Dear Mr Martin,
I would have replied to your letter earlier, but you sent the missive to Peter Eade, and addressed it to St James Place – wherever that might be – and he has never had an office there; by the time your envelope got to me it was covered in various re-addressings and was, of course, very late. You say that you have heard I do not take holidays. You have been totally misinformed. I take them whenever I can. Herodotus is supposed to have said 'Everything changes except the law of change' and a change of environment is something I heartily recommend. I often find the atmosphere of London stultifying and it is a delight to get away. Last thing I did was a cruise to the Greek Islands and Turkey which entailed a charter flight, to join the ship, from Gatwick to Venice. We were told to report at 13.00 hours and did so. The take off was at 23.00 hours. By the time we arrived in the small hours of the following day at Venice and [were] taken to the docks and put on board the ship, we were an unshaven, hungry and disgruntled crowd indeed. The following day we were in Corfu and sitting in the sunshine having coffee, writing postcards full of lies

to everyone saying it was fabulous. In Kusadasi the sun was like a burning bowl, and the ride to Ephesus was airless and sticky. I stood in the auditorium where Paul was faced by that chanting mob raving about 'Diana of the Ephesians' and thought 'With seating for twenty four thousand, it must have been the longest barracking in history!' and outside the gates found a shop with more postcards. Most of them depicted the god BES – who was some sort of fertility symbol I imagine, cos he is shown with the most enormous penis which is out of all proportion to the rest of his body. I posted one off to my agent, and wrote on the back 'These foolish things remind me of you' and he assured me later that his secretary was eyeing him with renewed interest. Of course none of this will be of any interest to you since your article for Nova is concerned with people who do not take holidays, but I thought I would send you a few lines to make it clear that when I receive letters I am generally diligent about my replies.

yours sincerely,
Kenneth Williams

To the Hon. GEORGE BORWICK

15 October 1970

Mon cher George,
I got your long letter this morning and was of course delighted. Thought I had better type the reply because of your complaints about the spider hand writing. I was sorry not to see you before your departure, but you know very well that you can always get me through Peter Eade at his office number, so there is really no excuse. Much of the time was taken up with script conferences and costume fittings for the film 'Carry On Henry' and Peter Rogers gave a great reception at the Dorchester and we all had to go and meet the press and drink champagne to celebrate the launching of the 21st Carry On film. They asked Charlie Hawtrey to put his arm round Barbara Windsor and kiss her for a photograph and he cried 'No thank you – find me a gentleman instead!' and reeled off to another part of the room. The photographer looked utterly bewildered and asked me 'Is he for real?' but of course I took refuge in the usual rubbish about the eccentricities of actors etc. Barbara and I went off together in a taxi, and picked up her husband Ronnie[1] at a club which he runs. It was quite full, and

---

[1] Ronnie Knight, from whom she later parted. Pursued by the British police, he took refuge in Spain.

the atmosphere smoke laden. One drunk reeled up to me and said 'I remember you when you lived with Danny La Rue at those awful flats in Victoria' and I smiled, looked nostalgic and said 'Ah! those were the days!' because as you well know I am unacquainted with the drag, or the district. Then a young lady rushed up and put her arms round me, and kissed me — then holding me at arm's length said 'Is it true that you are a queer?' and I replied 'I'm afraid so my dear' and she said 'Oh! but it's such a WASTE — I think you are the most attractive man in this room' and I said 'that is true, but neverthe- less I take it up the arse' at which point Ronnie came round from behind the bar and said 'Come on — we are going out to eat.' When we got into the street he asked 'What did you say all that for?' and I told him there was no point in doing anything else; people who ask ludicrous questions deserve to be told ludicrous lies; and he said 'I think it is wrong for your image' but I answered 'It's my conscience I have to live with — not my image' cos as you know I simply cannot take that kind of language seriously. I started the film on Monday, and my first scenes were with Kenneth Connor and Bill Maynard. Everyone at Pinewood raving about the film that Ken Russell is making there.[1] One of the electricians said to me 'You wanna get over to their set and see what's going on! — he's got all these lesbians kissing each other and there is this girl being had by the biggest Alsatian you have ever seen!' I said 'You mean a man from Alsace?' and he said 'No I fucking don't! I mean a bleeding dog!' I said 'O dear — I thought all that sort of thing went out in the thirties' and he said it was coming back in the seventies. I am glad you are enjoying yourself and keeping yourself occupied. Cultivate the good people and give only cursory interest to the others. Lots of love from your old chum —

[K]

To MARJORIE ROULSTONE[2]

Peter Eade Ltd,
9 Cork Street,
London W1
30 December 1970

Dear Miss Roulstone,
My answer to your letter HAS to be 'I do not know' since what you ask — i.e. Have I influenced the language habits of adolescents? — is

---

[1] *The Devils.* 'A pointless pantomime for misogynists' (*Halliwell's Film Guide*).
[2] A teacher of English in Birmingham.

impossible to ascertain. The burden of your letter would seem to be a condemnation of the use of double entendre in comedy written for broadcasting. I would therefore point out that you should correspond on such a subject with the scriptwriters or the producers of such series, and, if you think it warrants it, to Controllers of networks. The actor is the last person to discuss it with. The actor is given a script and has to speak the lines which are set down for him. That is what I have done in the radio shows which you have specified in your letter. I have never written anything for a radio comedy in my life. When I had to address a hundred pupils at a Secondary school recently, I was warned by a teacher to avoid a particular line in a poem I was quoting; it was the line

> 'Out flew the web and floated wide
> The mirror cracked from side to side
> The Curse is come upon me cried
> The Lady of Shalott.'

I ignored his advice, and I went ahead and used the poem. There was no sniggering; they listened and they were interested throughout. When I have played 'Twelfth Night' to children I have always noticed that they GET the double entendre in Malvolio's letter speech – the one running 'Her Cs, her U's . . .' etc. whereas when you play it to adults, they either don't, or they pretend they don't get it. I find it odd that you should single out the radio shows I have been in. All comedy material on radio & television leans heavily on double entendre, but I think it will need a lot more than sniggering at it to debilitate the English language.

> yours faithfully,
> [KW]

To the EDITOR, *Daily Mail*

Cambridge Theatre,
London W.C.
n.d. [probably 21 July 1971]

Dear Sir,
I must compliment you on Tuesday's edition of the Daily Mail.

The article 'Reputation Wreckers', by Walter Terry, was good journalism at its most perceptive; the Monica Dickens piece a delight; and Virginia Ironside, always a lively critic, proved that style and integrity can go hand in hand to entertain her readers. Another thing: Your financial section is excellent because it clarifies the gain figures. Congratulations to you all! Long may your paper flourish.[1]

Kenneth Williams

To the Hon. GEORGE BORWICK

24 August 1971

My dear George,
. . . I posted 59 letters off at midday today. I was at the desk from 8 till 11.30. I started again at 4 and now it is 8 o'clock by the Borwick desk clock which is ticking away here on the desk. Needless to say, this is the ONLY proper letter. The others were all notes . . . I hope you are keeping well. DO NOT feel you have got to sit down & reply, I'll simply keep you posted – your old chum,

[K]

To MICHAEL[2]

21 September 1971

Dear Michael,
Thank you for your letter of the 18th, which I received today. It was interesting about the soldier electing a court martial. I suppose he must have felt very strongly about his case; probably feels that, in the end, justice will be on his side. All this business about the military and their relations with the local population is complicated and difficult. It must be appalling to have to serve as a soldier in Ulster at the moment, and I feel sympathy with the military in a situation like that. I suppose the real fault lies in the political expediency. It seems that the only reason we are there is because of this religious schism, and we are told that the Catholics hate the Protestants and vice versa. We are also told that the unemployment in the North is exacerbating the situation and that the province is subsidised by Whitehall. I think we should get out of that country. I think it is as simple as that. Just

---

[1] The Deputy Editor of the *Daily Mail*, Louis Kirby, replied to KW on 22 July, remarking 'You sound like the ideal *Daily Mail* reader.' The letter was printed some days later under the heading 'Well done!'
[2] A serviceman lately stationed in Northern Ireland, who had moved on to Sharjah. He had mentioned a soldier who, charged with failing to pay a small taxi fare, preferred court martial to the local judicial system.

get out. No matter what they say about the likelihood of dreadful consequences, the fact is that nothing could be worse than the mess that has been left ever since the ludicrous and artificial partitioning of Ireland took place. It is the same with the Americans in Vietnam. They should simply go. I think public opinion in the United States will eventually ensure that they do go. If you really examine it, you will find again and again that it is simply a question of PRIDE. A question of governments – or countries – not wanting to lose face. Of course, in the end they lose not only their faces but a lot of lives as well. The television and the sound radio here is daily transmitting interviews with Irish ladies saying 'Oh! I'm just terrified I tell you! – terrified! – you never know when a bomb is going to come through the window and I haven't slept for over a week . . .' etc etc. It's like some endless black-out sketch with women repeating their fears until you want to scream at them 'well MOVE out dear! – go somewhere else! – don't keep sitting there telling us you are terrified! shut your stupid great mouth!' but of course one can say nothing of the kind. One thing is certain: no one – no one in England is interested. It may be on the television and it may be on the radio (we've got no papers at the moment cos of the strike) but it is not a topic of conversation with anybody I meet. Since I returned from Morocco I have had quite a job catching up with all the letters, but at last the back-log is clearing. Haven't had much work to do – only the 'Just A Minute' broadcasts from the Playhouse Theatre, and they are really quite fun. I mean they are not hard work. I start the film in October and it is called 'Carry On Matron' so I suppose they have found a lot more old jokes about life in hospitals! London is very pleasant at the moment – the days are sunny and warm, but already the evenings are chill with the reminder that winter is on the way and we have got all that drear to look forward to!

> your old chum,
> [K]

To the EDITOR, *Radio Times*[1]

Peter Eade Ltd,
9 Cork Street,
London W1X 1PD
25 September 1971

Dear Sir,
I hope that Mr Garnham will think again about his reply to Mrs D'Arch Smith which appeared in the Radio Times issue of 18 September on page 62. If he re-reads his sentence 'You clearly both desired and expected yet another programme that would allow you to wallow in largely escapist aesthetic values' he will realise that it is not only bad English but palpable nonsense. He goes on with a malignant thrust at the 'Civilisation' series by comparing it to a drug – more bad English (coupled now with denigration of Kenneth Clark) and more nonsense.

There was nothing escapist about the 'Civilisation' series, and its illuminating outline of European economic conditions was honest and sometimes brutally so – quote 'for seven hundred years capitalism has continued to grow to its present monstrous proportions.' – in fact Clark's description of the industrial and banking conditions in thirteenth century Florence has the clarity and precision of a J.S. Mill.

Mr Garnham asks about 'the reasons why an artist or a craftsman creates his objects' and says they are relevant to our finding the objects beautiful. They are not.

Mr Garnham is rash to infer that Mrs D'Arch Smith needs any sociological correction, and impertinent to sneer at the scholarship and care manifest in the 'Civilisation' series. He ends with the Freudian quotation about all civilisation being the result of repression and asks 'is the price worth paying?' He says he does not know the answer. Of course he doesn't. He doesn't know the price either.

     yours faithfully,
     Kenneth Williams

---

[1] Published by the *Radio Times* as the first of four letters attacking Garnham, under the heading 'Was Nicholas Garnham rude and wrong?' A Mrs D'Arch Smith had written to criticise Garnham's programme 'Has the Past Got a Future?'. The wording of KW's letter, as published, was adjusted to make this clear.

To JOHN HUSSEY

2 October 1971

My dear John,
Well hang on to your safety belts cos this is going to rock you baby!
– I went to this do at the Dorchester on Wed last and who should be
whooshing around the dance floor doing a very creditable Charleston?
– Oliver Ford! I was amazed to see him after all these years! he came
over to my table and we talked and talked. He is the Design Consultant
at the Dorchester and he is doing Clarence House at the moment for
the Queen Mother. He said 'we can't talk properly here, why don't
you come down to my country house?' So, two days later I got the
train from Paddington and he met me at the station and drove me to
this lovely Queen Anne House in Sutton Courtenay in Berkshire.
Really lovely place with a magnificent garden and swimming pool
and all. I said 'Well you have got it made haven't you?' and looked
round it all with envy. We talked about you, and I reminded him of
how he'd made you sit in that tiny sofa and you'd said 'If two people
sit here they can't help touching' and he replied 'That's the idea!' and
how we laughed at the time. It was when you were in Bournemouth
and he was then designing for Harvey Nichols – do you remember?
Oh! we sat drinking cups of tea and revolving many memories. Isn't
it incredible how the whirligig of time brings in his revenges? He
hasn't changed all that much except that the hair is almost gone. He
said to me 'Your father told me in 1948 that I would be bald by the
time I was thirty; and he turned out to be quite right.' I told him all
about my flat problem and how I couldn't find anywhere that was
quiet and he said I could go and live down there and share his house
& showed me the guest suite which is completely independent and
he said 'You would have complete privacy and you could do what
you liked – don't worry! I wouldn't be chasing you round the bed or
anything!' I smiled wryly – 'you'd have a job I can tell you, cos I have
had two operations on me bum since we last met and the surgeon
said that my arse is like a patchwork quilt.' Oliver winced with distaste
and said 'Yes well there's no need to go on and on about it . . .' He
obviously thought me appallingly vulgar cos later on he said 'You
talk about things that I would just NEVER discuss!' He has got a
housekeeper who seems very nice (he calls her Wally) and a chauffeur
who didn't appear to be called anything, but also helps out with the
garden. I must say I fell about at your line 'Age shall not wither her
nor iron bars a cage.' I thought 'How true that is even today.' Baxter
came back from Greece yesterday and looked very fit. He has gone

for all this Carnaby Street gear and looks very smart with the flowered shirts and ties to match. All very trendy and mod. You obviously received my letters out of sequence and by now I expect you will have got my last one which railed against you for not writing to me. It is no good you getting irritated because you know very well that I am right and that you should reply to me regularly. Every relationship in this world needs sustenance, and plants that aren't fed tend to die. Letters are the only way to keep things alive. You know how I NEED this reciprocation cos of my deep depressions and inferiority complex. Louie comes back from her holiday today, and I have to go out to Luton Airport to meet her so I just hope that the plane comes in on time. It is awful having to wait around at those places and get stared at all the time. I have washed me hair and everything. Tell me about the parties and the drink-ettes and the bars out there. Write to me. Love,

[K]

To JOHN HUSSEY

4 October 1971

My dear John,
I was saddened to get this air letter form from you, postmarked 30 September, and saying that I had only succeeded in depressing you. I certainly had no such intention. I sit here and compose letters to you because I want very much for you to feel that you have a regular correspondent – someone who wants to tell you all the news and generally keeps you in touch. I have never done it in order to lower your spirits. I have fancied once or twice I may have been able to provide the odd giggle. Alas – I am wrong. I have put my foot in it. But please do not make mountains out of molehills, and don't start paper wars because it is all quite without foundation. It is daft to write & say 'your acquaintances look on me with enmity and bitterness' and if you read my letter again you will see that it is not true. I wrote 'You have no idea of the number of people who I talk to and when the subject of your success comes up, they speak with disguised envy . . .' I was telling you about the reaction to SUCCESS. The reaction of people I happen to be talking to. I talk to an awful lot of people in the course of the work. But the reaction to success is NOT a reaction to YOU. It is the reaction to SUCCESS. Sharing other people's success is not a notable feature with actors. They generally resent it. That is all I was commenting upon. Thought you would be

interested to hear about it. Again I was wrong. Put me foot in it. But to construe this as 'Enmity and bitterness' is just D A F T. Obviously I incurred your wrath because I wrote asking for a letter and saying I was livid cos you didn't write. Well what the hell is wrong with that? What the hell is wrong with a friend saying he wants to hear from his friend? Even if he says it rudely – or without tact – or whatever! No matter how he words it it is still the same thing, A N A P P E A L for reciprocation. Yes I know you are busy. So have I been busy. I have been doing stage, television on Sundays, filming during the days, broadcasting in two series, and writing my own material. It does not stop me writing to you. Because I consider that letters to you are important. I think they are a life line when one is thousands of miles away.

I suddenly realise – this has all happened before. It was the same last time you were in Africa. I wrote & wrote asking for replies. I have still got the letter. I have still got the replies saying you were up to your eyes in it and that there was no time for writing.

I would have thought by now that you know me better than anybody. Certainly you know all about my psychological lack of security and the inferiority which led to the breakdown in 65[1] and which has been a torment ever since. Nonetheless you choose to send me this N A S T Y little letter – simply because I asked for a reply. There are records of suicides who were waiting for replies.

I went to Camden Rates Department and checked for you. You are paid up until September 30. The demands are only just being sent out for the next lot of payments. I couldn't get any information re your cheque for £55 because they don't disclose your method [of] payment to people without proper authority.

> yours,
> [K]

To FRED HILL[2]

9 November 1971

Dear Fred,
It was a pleasure to get your letter this morning but I don't think the Post Office is doing a very good job, since your envelope is marked 4

---

[1] In December 1965, after the failure of *The Platinum Cat*, K W escaped to Beirut for a not very restorative Christmas.
[2] A New York acquaintance who had recently visited London.

Above The much-travelled Hon. George Borwick in tropical kit on board the *Windsor Castle*. Lady Ellerman, his later wife, came from the well-known shipping family.

Left Susan and Andrew Ray in August 1959, shortly before their marriage.

Below left Joe Orton, photographed amid their collages in the flat he shared with Kenneth Halliwell at 25 Noel Road, Islington, 1 October 1966. The following day KW wrote in his diary: 'all the reviews for Joe Orton's *Loot* at the Jeannetta Cochrane Theatre are marvellous . . . What irony.' He had suffered a terrible flop in the original production of the play.

Below right Noel Willman in a characteristically hard-hearted character pose, from the 'Paul Temple' TV series (episode entitled 'Antique Death') in May 1970.

In performance at the BBC: KW, Peter France and Arthur Marshall record a programme of playlets called *Seventy Glorious Years* for radio at the Bristol studios, 12/13 December 1976. Marshall, in his radio-revue guise as 'Nurse Dugdale', had figured among KW's repertoire of impersonations in the post-war CSE troupe. 'He is a diverting, considerate, kind and delicious companion' (KW on AM, Diary, 13 December).

Sheila Hancock and an ashtray-seeking KW, probably 1973.

... with the children at the Police Presentation at Hornsey Town Hall.' The ceremony took ... ace on 25 April 1975; KW refers to it in his letter of 7 May (p.212). His flat had been burgled ... ree days before the event.

Above left Newly arrived in Tenerife: KW, Louie and resident in the Harp Bar, 21 December 1977. 'We got v. sloshed.'

Above KW and Michael Whittaker on a day-trip to Lichfield, 3 March 1978. They visited Samuel Johnson's birthplace, in which KW had a special interest, and the cathedral, where Whittaker had sung in the choir.

Left Michael Codron, KW's most patient West End producer, 1978.

November, and we are now five days later than that. I am just coming
to the end of the filming – most of my sequences have nearly finished
– it is mainly the post-synch dialogue that I have to do. There isn't
much going on at the studio. Bette Davis has finished on 'Madame
Sin' and she looked rather quaint shouldering around in a mini skirt.
She made a speech on the last day of the shooting, and said 'I'd just
like to say that if the artists on this movie had been HALF as good
as the technicians, we might have made a better picture!' Apparently
it just stunned everybody. [Robert] Wagner is the co-star, and he
always wears dark glasses in the studio restaurant but the other day
he took them off and I saw the reason. Looks as though he never gets
to bed. For sleep I mean. The other film being made is 'Lamb' which
is Robert Bolt's screen play and he is directing it himself. It's about
Byron and Lady Caroline Lamb. Robert keeps touching the wood of
the table top and saying 'I just hope I can pull it off Kenneth! I must
pull it off! I have got to pull it off! . . .' and it all begins to sound like
a case of delayed circumcision to me. But then I am not sufficiently
serious am I? I have received some curiously lively letters from a boy
who wants to be a 'pen friend' or something of that nature. He is
called Andrew Hathaway and lives at Beachwood, New Jersey. He
actually wrote 'Send me a photo of you, and your car, so I can see
you standing beside your trusty steed.' I couldn't believe it! TRUSTY
STEED! I think he will be bitterly disillusioned if he ever saw this
tenement block I live in, not to mention the fact that there is no car
to be photographed against! His writing sounds like a cross between
Andy Hardy and Sir Walter Scott. He sent me a photo of himself. I
wrote back 'there doesn't seem to be anything wrong that a good diet
wouldn't cure. You are obviously overweight, and I should check your
oil while you are about it.' So far, I haven't heard any more . . . Write
when you get time – your old chum –

    [K]

To ANDREW HATHAWAY

19 November 1971

Dear Andrew,
No I don't give my telephone number, & I am not listed in the direc-
tories, and the identification has been removed by an engineer from
the instrument, so it will be apparent to you that I do not approve of
the invention. Most of the time, a letter is just as effective, and if
something is urgent, there is the telegraph service. I don't answer the

telephone even if it does ring. Not unless it rings a certain number of times. The number is a code which I have with my agent and about three other people. I did not write about 'the merits or demerits of the States', as you put it. You asked me if I was going to visit the country, and I said that I wasn't because it sounded awfully violent. The statistics for the number of murders you have DAILY is horrifying. Then you started on about the IRA and those idiots in Eire. And what do you mean about the need 'to suspend this discussion' because 'it isn't getting us anywhere'!!! I wasn't aware that we were going anywhere. I wasn't even aware that we were travelling. And what is this enigmatic reference to certain dates supposed to mean? I am not a historian so I don't know the significance of 1776–1783 but I notice you call the British behaviour 'filthy' so I assume this is the colonial rebellion you are referring to. It is very big of you to say that you are willing to overlook this filthy behaviour, but really Andrew, since it took place in 1776 you haven't really got much choice in the matter. The trouble with all colonial histories is that they are all full of guilt about their lawlessness. You can dress it up in all sorts of fancy names like 'life, liberty and the pursuit of happiness' but the fact of rebellion against the rightful sovereign is something that no amount of mendacity or sophistry can wipe away. It is a fundamental wrong. It is no use talking about OTHER WRONGS as a justification of this. Either you have a monarch and believe that the installation and the Holy Anointing SYMBOLISES the nation in terms both of family unity and constitutional government, or you have rebels and republics. And that is what you've got. And a sorry business it is, but you are stuck with it, so you might as well acknowledge it, stop all this waffling about impediments on a fictional journey (which neither of us is making) and admit to being the guilty party. I remember Peter Nichols telling me about these relatives he had come over from America and they stayed at the Ritz Hotel and they confided to Peter 'it is very old you know' and Peter said that it was nothing of the sort since it was built in the late nineteenth century. He said 'it is only about a hundred years old' and his American Aunt cried out 'brother that's old enough for me!' and obviously meant it. You see Andrew, the real truth is that the average European THINKS in a different way from the North American. The European doesn't really like the idea of Americans. This is often confused (by Americans) as disliking Americans. When my friend Gordon came back from Hollywood and said how awful it all was, he added ruefully 'it would not be so bad if we didn't speak the same language; that is what makes it so much worse' and he meant that the immediacy of difference was emphasised. Again and again, in London you hear in conversation 'we have these Americans coming over – and we will have to cope you know – would you care to come over on Tuesday evening? – God knows what we'll talk about . . .' Most of the time Americans leave they are laughed at on departure. A lot of Americans know this and are secretly hurt by it, though they SAY things like 'to hell with them' and affect not to care. But there you are, the Americans are the Imperialists now. They are the people with the Empire (albeit an economic/socio one) and the world influence. When a part of that territory steps out of line, like Cuba or Chile, or anywhere else really that American interests are involved, then America gets very angry indeed. I suppose you could say that Washington is to North Vietnam what the Court of St James's was to Massachusetts. No you are wrong about the actor I spoke about in the Carry On picture. Her name is HATTIE JACQUES and she is in the Eric Sykes show on Television. I don't think that series has ever been shown in the States. I should think it would be far too esoteric. I have not got television as you know, but I do see it in other people's houses and I generally find it unfunny. That Rowan & Martin Laugh-In thing I thought was perfectly terrible. I think Jack Benny is brilliant. I can't think of anyone that can touch that man. The long suffering and the self deprecation are wonderful to see. Last time he came over I was raving to someone the next day & they said 'Well yes, but he's showing his age, his timing now is much slower' and I said 'it's still TWICE as good as most of the other stuff around.' Yes, well I will have to stop now, but for goodness sake don't 'get up tight' about your wicked country & its history! who knows you might even get a Sioux Indian to 'overlook' some filthy behaviour. If you're lucky. I've finished the shooting on the picture. Now it is post-synch on the dialogue which I HATE. So goodbye for now my old Captain, and think no evil of us,

   [K]

To Dr J.B. BATCHELOR[1]

27 November 1971

Dear Mr Batchelor,
Your letter about the play 'The Wit To Woo' sent me to my files of old letters where I thought I might find some comments that I might have made at the time, and which would refresh my memory about

[1]   J.B. Batchelor (Ph.D. Cantab), Lecturer in English at Birmingham University.

the production, and I was amazed to find a complete blank from 1957 to 1963 so there was no help there.

I read the play in February 1957 and I was struck by the nature of the dialogue. It is always the words that interest me, and I hardly ever find myself thinking in critical terms of construction or plot or technical details of stage mechanics. Mervyn Peake's dialogue for the play was full of verbal conceits, wonderful imagery, natural fluency, and above all, theatrically effective. I had no hesitation in accepting the part of Pike; I thought it glittered with malevolence and vituperative wit & knew that I could encompass it vocally. I was a bit perturbed about the physical side of the role but I know that I managed to get a lot of slithering into it.

The play needed wholehearted theatrical bravura acting and vocal relish. In the event it was played in a modern high comedy manner with considerable 'throw away' technique.

Essentially, the actor playing Percy must be capable of a very real duality on the stage. It is so vital that his characterisation as Percy is completely different to October. This is the 'acting within acting' thing, which is peculiarly difficult to accomplish.

You will understand it would be impolitic of me to discuss what I regard as shortcomings in performers or in the director. You say in your letter 'it did not have a very successful run' and this is somewhat misleading, because it was put on at the Arts Theatre for a limited period only. It did not go into a commercial west-end theatre where it could be judged as having 'a run'. With the right cast and management (a rare combination I admit, but not an impossibility) I think 'The Wit To Woo' could be an entertaining Gothic comedy and a profitable venture.

      yours sincerely,
      [KW]

P.S. I always remember talking to Mervyn in the stalls one day at rehearsal & saying to him: You love the word PLUM don't you?' & being shocked and delighted when he replied 'Yes, and BUM and COME . . . lovely sounds . . .'

To DAVID

29 November 1971

Dear David,
Thank you for your letter and the news of yourself but please remember my post-code next time; the Post Office have gone to a great deal

of trouble about this, with the sole purpose of ensuring good delivery, and the least we can do is to cooperate with them. All the people I know who are most voiceiforous [sic] in their complaints about the public services are generally the ones who reject the post-code and mouth a lot of rubbish about 'they are turning us all into numbers'. I was somewhat surprised that you should be in such earnestness about this business of the occult and what lies beyond the grave. What you heard me say on the radio is true. I do not believe in ghosts, or the power of the dead to return. But this should not disturb you. Because I say that I don't believe in such things, it need not affect your belief in them. I do believe in God – not in terms of an old man in the sky, but of TRUTH GOODNESS & BEAUTY – and I hear denunciation of Him every day! – but it doesn't shake my belief in Him. I suppose it is because I believe in God that I cannot believe in ANY superstitions. Walking under ladders only involves the risk of something falling on your head, and as for getting in touch with the dead, well, I don't really think there are any corpses I fancy chatting with. You say that 'there has got to be a continuation' and in saying that, you are saying that you cannot accept mortality. I can. I think 'three score years and ten' is quite long enough. Of course the spirit of a man who has ever infected another human being with some kind of affection will go on living as long as these kind of men exist, but they will not (these spirits) manifest themselves in any mortal terms or forms, but only by their precepts which we carry in our hearts.

    yours,
    [K]

To the Hon. GEORGE BORWICK

9 December 1971

My dear George,
On Tuesday, I did the Pete Murray radio show. It was live. They have the listeners phone in, and you have to answer their questions. One woman said 'Can you give me any housekeeping hints?' and I said 'Oh yes dearie! Don't fart about between the slats of your venetian blinds. Take them down and shove them straight into a bathful of soapy water, and avoid all the loo cleaners that don't have a screw top. You must have a good screw and then it doesn't give off that pungent stink that goes right up your hooter and half suffocates you, and let's face it, nothing is worse than a brown loo! when your friends go away saying to each other DID YOU SEE THE BROWN then

it is socially catastrophic, and keep the room simply ordered. Shove all the furniture up one end and do all your low dusting. Keep a wary eye on your rear. Then shove all the furniture back, and do the other bit. Does that answer your enquiry?' and there was a pause and a rather weak 'er, yes. Thank you' and the line went dead. I rushed from that studio to another one, and did a story for children. It had been written by a child too, and needed considerable cutting and editing, and it was all left till the last minute which did not endear me to the producer. On Monday, I had to go to Doctor Clarke cos I had this boil come up on me nose. It looked like an electric light bulb. Peter Eade gave me lunch at the Pastoria, and the manager told us that the opera singer who fell to her death on Tuesday night had eaten at his restaurant that night![1] He said that she seemed all right and had said she would see him for lunch the next day. Then he said he closed the restaurant, and was walking to the bus stop and she landed at his feet. Fallen from the fourth floor of those flats, over what used to be the Vega restaurant. He said he helped to get her into the ambulance, but she was dead on arrival at Charing Cross. I hope you are keeping well and enjoying your fully booked holiday in the sun. All good wishes and love from your old chum —

    [K]

To CHRISTOPHER

10 December 1971

My dear Christopher,
How kind of you to remember an old man furtively picking his way around King's Cross! Goodness knows there are few enough pleasures left in this prohibitive world of ours, so it was a pleasant surprise to be invited out I can tell you! It is a shame that they banned the drunken driving.[2] That was nice because it did ensure that the odd innocent pedestrian got knocked down and thereafter forced to totter about on crutches. The manufacture of crutches has gone down considerably and one old totterer told me that he had been on the waiting

---

[1] 'Opera singer Maria Collier fell to her death today from the window of her second-floor flat in London's Leicester Square. She leaned over a radiator to open the window, overbalanced, and fell. Forty-four-year-old Maria was famous for her performances in Puccini's opera *Tosca* — who falls to her death in the last act' (*Evening Standard* report).
[2] The Bill introducing the breathalyser test had been published in January 1966. Its provisions had recently been tightened.

list for over a month. He said you couldn't get a crutch for love or money, not for money nor love. Now they are starting on the fags. It will soon be against the law to do it, except in the gents. They will be crowded out in all the loos and the air will be so thick with tobacco fumes that no one will be able to single out his neighbour. They will have to feel their way in and out, so to speak. It will be dreadful for all those who are legitimately in search of proper urination, but it will doubtless delight that band of deviates who go to such places in search of titillation. This practice is extremely embarrassing to the urinators. Only the other day I was in John Lewis and I was bursting for a pee so I ventured into the door marked 'Gentlemen' on their basement floor. There were no gentlemen in there I can assure you! but there was a lot of heavy breathing. Three of them standing at the stalls were quite shameless and seemed oblivious of the fact that it was eleven and time for coffee, not for wanking. I had to go to the cubicle cos the effect was distinctly pornographic & gave me the half hard (as dear old Edward Everett Horton used to term it). That wasn't a good idea, as it turned out, because the adjoining cubicle was occupied by someone who was emptying the bowels copiously and noisily. The smell was atrocious and certainly put paid to the half hard. Edward Everett Horton or no Edward Everett Horton. I staggered out of there with the handkerchief clasped to the nostrils and shot off to the perfume counter for some cheap four-seven-eleven. In the event, I had to make do with something called 'Water of Florence' and judging from the odour (and the price) I would say Florence is a very smart cookie and doing very well out of it, thank you. Anyway, I eventually met that T. who is in charge of stationery and I said 'Do you know what is going on in your loo in the basement? – it is a disgrace down there!' He seemed far from appalled and said 'How opportune! It's time for my coffee break anyway!' and rushed off in the direction of the basement like there was no tomorrow. 'So different,' as Lady Castlereagh reflected, 'from the home life of our own dear Queen.'

Love,
[K]

To ANDREW HATHAWAY

14 December 1971

Dear Andrew,
. . . I was interested to hear that you had seen Terry-Thomas. He hasn't appeared here for so long the public won't remember what he

looks like. I appeared in a film of his once. It was called 'His And
Hers' and I had a part as a policeman who found him in the street in
his pyjamas. I had one of those 'What is this all about' lines to say.
It was all on location somewhere, I remember I sat and chatted with
him in a caravan. He seemed very pleasant. I met him years later in
Great Portland Street & he said 'Hello old dear!' and told me he was
making a film with his own money abroad. 'It's the only way, old
thing!' he kept saying. I felt like a Chelsea Pensioner. I have heard
what is happening to George Rose. He is in the Simon Gray play 'Wise
Child' in America. The other actor in it is Donald Pleasence. In London
it was played by Alec Guinness. I went to see it because my friend
Gordon Jackson played the role which is to be done in America by
George. It will be interesting to see whether the play will be a success
over there. It wasn't a very long run in London. It is about a couple
of crooks on the run – one is dressed up as a woman. Alec Guinness
was very funny in the part. On the night I went, when Alec Guinness
came on in drag, a man in the front row of the stalls got up and
shouted 'Disgusting! You ought to be ashamed of yourself Sir Alec!'
and it held the play up, because he was shouting & raving all the way
out of the auditorium. Apparently he thought it shocking that a Knight
should dress up as a lady. I think that was his beef. When I went
round after, Alec said 'Quite a little fracas, wasn't it?' but I made light
of it, and left quickly because Michael Redgrave was in his dressing
room and I couldn't take two Knights in the one day. Can't stand
Redgrave anyway. Fancy your Indians being called Leni Lenape! Are
you kidding? It sounds more like some sort of emigre gangster. Glad
you liked Eric Sykes. He is an acquired taste, I think, like Avocado
pears. He is doing a show in London with Jimmy Edwards at the
moment. Your letters have been taking longer, because of the fact
that they are being forwarded from my agent's office. So I will put
my own address on this one. I live in the central area in a block that
would be charitably described as a slum, but it is a cheap rent and
prices are rocketing in property. To paraphrase Blunden –

> 'I hope one day to leave this rotten room
> Some bell-like evening when the May's in bloom . . .'

Actually we really do have a May tree in this area;[1] I used to pass it
every night on the way to the theatre, it was lovely with the blossom.
Happy Christmas to you,

    [K]

[1]   In Torrington Place.

To ANDREW HATHAWAY

31 December 1971

Dear Andrew,

Now before we go any further – please do not send me anything – do not send tapes or books or records or presents of any kind. A correspondence is one thing. It can be a very valuable thing but let it stay that way. Now to a more gracious note. Thank you for your good wishes for the New Year, and your delightful letter which arrived this morning. It was undated, but postmarked 27 December – no wait a minute, it is dated, but I was misled by the fact that you have written the date in words at the top of the paper, and of course I was looking for numerals. It is interesting that you should have commended the animated film version of 'A Christmas Carol' with the Alastair Sim 'Scrooge' – because it was produced by my friend Richard Williams. I was in his studio in October and he ran some rough-cuts of the film for me, and I thought it was enchanting. I don't care for Redgrave, but I must admit, I thought the narration was very good. What bits I heard of it. After all, I was seeing an unfinished film. Richard is probably the best animation film maker in Europe today. I have done quite a lot of work for him. We made a version of Gogol's 'Diary of a Madman' together[1] & it was very exciting to work with him because he is one of the very few professional directors about who really does know what he wants. And he keeps on till he gets it. He is of Canadian origin and has all that energy and zest of the North American. It is very attractive and infectious when one first meets with it, but after a while, I begin to long for the cynical lassitude of the European. It is more restful. I have seen the film 'Nicholas & Alexandra' and I enjoyed every bit of it. It has received terrible notices here, and nobody had a good word to say for it, but everyone I have talked to who has seen it has said they loved it. The last scene is quite harrowing. As the shots rang out, one man in the theatre was so moved, he actually shouted out 'You barstards!!' and I noticed that when everyone filed out of the theatre, they were all quite silent. It is not the sort of film to see if you are feeling low. One wonders how any regime established on that kind of unspeakable filth can ever come to good.

I got for Christmas a copy of the Hibbert book of personal minutiae

---

[1] In 1963. The soundtrack of the project was later stitched back together by John Whitehall of the BBC and broadcast as a solo performance by KW on Radio 4 (3 February 1991). It was acclaimed by several critics as his finest acting performance, even though much of it had been timed specifically to match the animations.

on Samuel Johnson[1] and I was actually laughing out loud at some of it. He must have been outrageous. I love the man. There is no one in English literature I so admire as Sam Johnson. Taylor says that, when asked what was the most important thing in life, Johnson replied 'Fucking sir, and after fucking, drinking' with such finality that the entire company was stunned. But he also said 'Any man abed before midnight is a scoundrel' & one cannot help feeling that it's a rather unjust sort of generalisation. Well I must get ready to go to my new year party which brings me to my final sentiments – to wish you a very happy 1972, may you rejoice and flourish.

     sincerely,
     [K]

To the Hon. GEORGE BORWICK

2 January 1972

My dear George,
It is proper that my first letter of the New Year should be addressed to you . . . Of course my dear friend, I know what you mean, but there is the dilemma of my kind of loneliness.[2] Sometimes I can take it. Sometimes I can go for days without bothering about any kind of company and be well content with my books and with music, but then (especially when this flat gets intolerable with noise & distraction) I suddenly need to get away from here, and be offered the hospitality of a home. Restaurants can only be sat in for so long. Did I tell you I had finished with Willman? He was furious because I wouldn't do his play – so that's another relationship up the spout. It is a pity that Stanley is in Scotland. I almost conceived a plan for taking a train & going up to see him in the pantomime in Glasgow! It would be good for me to talk to him. But then I saw the engagement pad and realised that it was not practical. I saw Wendy Toye at the Jacksons. She is having to rehearse understudies galore cos so many of the cast have got flu & she looked tired and strained. She is directing 'She Stoops' for the Young Vic and has got Richard Pearson and Kathleen Harrison!! She is clever with the casting, you must admit! I have twice seen John Hussey by accident in the street, and he just says 'Hello'

[1] *The Personal History of Samuel Johnson* (1971).
[2] Borwick had suggested that certain friends of KW were unworthy of him.

brightly and goes off 'to get a paper' so it sounds like the betting is
ON again!

    your old chum,
    [K]

To GORDON JACKSON

18 January 1972

My dear Gordon,
It was good of you to send the Strachey article.[1] It is a fascinating
piece, and I was most interested to learn about Asquith getting the
half hard with the lady on the sofa. It certainly don't accord with
your actual popular image does it? I was up half the night reading
the Macready journal.[2] O! it is fascinating stuff! – he was born in
what is now Stanhope Street, off the Euston Road, and spent most of
his life living in this area. Some of the accounts of his acting are
hilarious. On one occasion he played a marvellous death scene, and
fell exhausted on the stage, and another actor, coming forward, accidentally trod on his hand! whereupon Macready cried out 'Beast!
Beast of hell!' and then died all over again. The curtain descended on
peals of hysterical laughter from the auditorium. What really staggered
me was his treatment in America. It was really shocking what they
did to him there! They threw everything at him, including the carcass
of a dead sheep! and at the Astor there was pandemonium when they
wrecked the theatre, smashed the windows, tore the guttering from
the walls, threw all the wreckage of the seating on to the stage, and
troops were sent to quell the mob! Macready writes 'the play pro-
ceeded in dumb show, and I remained aloof from such uncivilised
barbarism' but eventually the troops had to fire on the crowd and

---

[1] 'Strachey on Asquith', Lytton Strachey's previously unpublished informal essay
(meant for posthumous publication), was published by the *Times Saturday Review* on
15 January 1972. The most controversial passage concerning H.H. Asquith, the
early-century Prime Minister (d.1928), ran: 'Who would guess from this book of his
which has just come out (*Occasional Addresses*) with its high-minded orotundities and
cultivated respectabilities, that the author of it would take a lady's hand, as she sat
beside him on the sofa, and make her feel his erected instrument under his trousers?
(This I had very directly from Dorothy [Brett], to whose sister it happened at
Garsington . . .)'
[2] William Charles Macready (1793–1873), English tragedian.

over seventy were injured and twenty were killed. It certainly sounds
more dramatic than any of your Master Betty's[1] don't it?

I hope things are going more to your liking in the rehearsals of
your play at the Court. One comes up against these situations again
and again, and we protest and protest, and yet we NEVER become
forearmed, and always allow ourselves to be persuaded by a reputation instead of a character. Before I started at the Cambridge,[2] I
never dreamed it would be the kind of bland stupidity which actually
destroys all the fun, and all the desire to act. Lackaday. Rue. Please
commend me to your good lady.

> your old chum,
> [K]

To TOM

[26 January 1972]

Tom, your letter conceals nothing. You and I both know what the rift
is about. The snub to me was born of a desire for revenge & I don't
want to put myself in that kind of jeopardy ever again, so let's just
leave it alone.

> Ken

To the Hon. GEORGE BORWICK

26 January 1972

My dear George,
I had this letter from Robert Stephens asking me to address the students at RADA and I have to go along there on Thursday – tomorrow
– and take part in some sort of discussion with others on a panel. It
includes John Schlesinger so it will be nice to see him again. Ned
Sherrin rang me up and asked me to have dinner with him, but I
couldn't accept cos I don't know how long the whole thing will take
at RADA do I? Had to go along to Aeolian Hall to talk to some BBC
people about a series and they showed me a pilot script which I
thought was very promising. Now it has to go before the planners
and win their approval. That's the trouble with the BBC, it's all

---

[1] William Henry West Betty (1791–1874), child prodigy of the London theatre,
especially in the 1804/5 season. In later life, success eluded him.
[2] In *Captain Brassbound's Conversion*, with Ingrid Bergman (1971).

hierarchy. Oh! more of the T[om] & C[live] saga. This morning a letter came! The whole thing was one of those chatty 'well how are you?' type letters. He obviously intends to pretend that nothing is amiss. He ends with a suggestion that I telephone and arrange an evening when I could go and have dinner with them! I wrote back a short note, and I started it off with just 'Tom', not 'Dear Tom' because I feel to do otherwise would be blatant hypocrisy. So that is the latest on that score. It is sad in a way, because there is always some good in a relationship (why else does it start?) but they don't seem to comprehend that I am not any ordinary person whom they can treat in a cavalier fashion. They forget that, whatever my faults, I am an actor, and as such very sensitive where ego is concerned, and not to be treated as you would treat the run of the mill personality. I am special. Anyway you look at it. If they want a relationship with me, it is a special relationship. If they put it at risk, then it's their own fault if they lose it, in the process. I am off to meet Geraldine Fitzgerald's son[1] tonight. I have met him once before and I was fascinated. I adored him on sight. He has the sort of good looks and utter charm which floor me. And he is witty. He underplays everything . . . 'we hadn't eaten anything, except a bottle of claret' . . . and most of his jokes are so casual that they are past before you KNOW it. Also he uses Interdens,[2] and as you know, I do too. So as soon as I saw that he was using them, I felt sort of allied to him – you know? Well I hope it hasn't confused you too much with me beginning on the wrong side of the form, but considering I've had the flu and all, it's amazing I've even written!

> your old chum,
> [K]

To ANDREW HATHAWAY

31 January 1972

Dear Andrew,
It will probably be miraculous if this ever reaches you at all. We seem to be sinking into a miasma of inertia over here & now have a Miners' Strike on our hands which is threatening to paralyse everything. Any

---

[1] Michael Lindsay-Hogg (b.1940), film director, son of Geraldine Fitzgerald (b.1912), Irish-born Hollywood actress.
[2] Toothpicks, or, according to the packet, 'Mouth-Freshening Medicated Flavour Dental Sticks'.

moment now, my desk lamp may go out. I think of T.S. Eliot – 'My self possession gutters . . . now we're really in the dark . . .' I got your letter of January 26 (postmarked 27th) this morning. I was still in dressing gown and pyjamas cos I've had the 'flu, and I read it with my coffee and the cigarette. There were other letters. Yours was the only one with style. I was stumping around afterwards muttering to myself 'he writes a damn good letter' and it's a fact that you do. Of course you can't make rules about it but I generally find that the best letter is the one that actually S O U N D S like the person talking. Very interesting what you say about [Clement] Freud on the Cavett show. A second time? – isn't he in danger of over exposure? and anyway, what H A S he got to offer? – I mean, it is not what you would call an exciting mind, is it? – it's not what you would call an intellectual is it? He came to the fore in England by virtue of the fact that he ran a restaurant which became famous for some (O D D) reason, and then he kept going on television talking about food, and cooking etc., and then started to develop a persona of bland rudeness. Host: nice to have you here. Freud: Wish I could say the same. You know the sort of thing. Well like everything else, it was quite funny for a bit, but everyone got tired of it. It was all done before with Alexander Woollcott and Kaufman's 'The Man Who Came To Dinner' only in these cases, they were originals. Thank you for the W.C. Fields quotes. They are marvellous. I was particularly pleased that you chose to end your missive with a Johnsonian line! It was delightfully apt. When you say you are reading Johnson and add that you are now on the Hebrides book, I think you really mean that you are reading Boswell (on Johnson) don't you? Yes, I think that's what you mean. Well, it's a very good way of being introduced to the Doctor, but don't forget he wrote books himself. You couldn't do better than to get his 'Lives of the Poets' – he is great on the narrative stuff. Ignore the judgments on the iambics – just look for his understanding and delineation of character. It is superb. The best essay in the collection is his life of Richard Savage. It is a melancholy tale, but Johnson informs it with such love and such humour, that one is fascinated right to the end. I have got the Boswell of course, but the book I was talking about to you was the minutiae of Johnson, called 'A Personal History of Samuel Johnson' by Christopher Hibbert. He has culled much from many sources, and it is a stream of facets of the old boy. I got the book because I was interested to see that it was by Hibbert. This is the man who wrote 'The Tragedy of Lord Raglan' which is a wonderful account of the C-in-C of the Crimean Campaign. This subject has always interested me, ever since I read Tennyson's 'Charge of the Light Brigade'

& the Hibbert book is as good as 'The Reason Why' by Cecil Woodham Smith which is magnificent. I couldn't put the latter book D O W N – I was up half the night reading it. It is like a thriller. Moves with incredible, almost inexorable speed. Oh yes! I love the stuff that deals with C H A R A C T E R. That is all I am interested in. The character of Johnson is what makes you warm to him, and love him. His uptight nature, his transparent honesty and his sense of honour. Great man. Great time the eighteenth century. Produced a lot of fascinating people – Goldsmith, Steele, Addison, Pope, Swift, one could go on and on. The Victorians were interesting for throwing up a lot of great characters too. If you get the chance, do read Lytton Strachey's book 'Eminent Victorians'. It is a wicked sort of piss take, but incredibly accurate as an I M P R E S S I O N . . . Apropos your question regarding the sound of Bow Bells. I was born in North London – in a street called Bingfield Street, off the Caledonian Road. Its postal area would be N 1 and Bow Bells would be E C so I think there would have to be a lot of favourable wind and ear-strain involved in calling me a Cockney, but really the term is now used for anyone who lives in the London area and speaks without the cultivation of the governing classes. In the 'Spying' film, they asked me to use that type of Cockney speech which is specifically nasal, because I had used it with great success in the radio shows, and it had become known as the S N I D E voice for some reason or another, and it is very popular. On interviews and things, one is invariably asked 'go on – do your S N I D E voice – stay S T O P M E S S - I N G A B O U T' this latter was one of the catch phrases from the radio series. Thank you for the comforting things you say about my choice of career. I am not insensible of the compliment you pay me, and I was very pleased to read such sentiments. Well I seem to have got through my letter without a power cut – my lamp is still on – the radiators are still hot. We have had snow for the last three days. Filthy muck. O! to be rich and fly to Miami! Can you imagine! all that warmth! yours ever,

[K]

To ANDREW HATHAWAY

2 February 1972

Dear Andrew,

I got your letter with the enclosed press reviews[1] this morning, and I must say, I was delighted to be able to see them so quickly. As a matter of fact, I read them over the telephone to my agent, he was interested to hear about the American reaction to the play. It doesn't sound to me as though it will have a very successful run. Those notices are not good, and I should not think you can survive on Broadway without good reviews. From what I hear, the economics are heavily against it. New York costs are fantastically high. I know that Americans who go to the theatre in London are always commenting on the fantastic cheapness of our prices, as compared with theirs. You can have good seats in the theatre here for about one or two pounds. The cinema is reasonably cheap too I think – for instance I got two seats for this Ken Russell film 'The Boy Friend' for a pound each. They are good seats, and are for the second night in the West End. Of course prices are much cheaper than that if one waits to see it at the local cinema. I am interested to see what Russell has done with this Sandy Wilson pastiche musical. I was once in a Sandy Wilson musical on the stage – I played the boy-editor in his 'The Buccaneer'[2] and it was an enormous success at the out of town theatre, which was the Lyric at Hammersmith, but when they transferred it to the West End it went to the Apollo Theatre and folded after about three weeks. Gustav of Sweden came to the first night and I said at the time 'he will put the kiss of death on us' and he did. I had to sing a couple of numbers and I had laryngitis. When we made the LP I was really croaking through the stuff and it sounded terrible. I can't sing anyway. Maggie Smith told me, a long time afterwards, that she had the record sent out to her when she was doing 'New Faces' in New York. She said she played it one night, in her apartment, to some several guests, among whom was Lena Horne. Maggie Smith said that Miss Horne listened in wonder, as my moaning came up, and then she cried out 'Is it a man or a woman or WHAT?' and everyone fell about. Interesting what you say about disliking the city so much because of the bad air and the closeness of the people. I suppose all cities are pretty

[1] For *Wise Child*, the Simon Gray play which in London (1967–8) had starred Alec Guinness and Gordon Jackson. In New York, the parts were now being taken by Donald Pleasence and George Rose.
[2] In 1955 and 1956.

claustrophobic in that sense; well at least all capital cities. The only beautiful city I ever found was Venice . . .

yours,
[K]

To ANDREW HATHAWAY

12 February 1972

Dear Andrew,
Your long letter of February 7 should have got to me on the 10th. But it was insufficiently stamped and it had 6½ pence TO PAY written on the envelope and every time the postman came, I was out, and he wouldn't deliver the letter till he got the money. It was all very difficult. Relations with Albert are rather strained at the best of times. I think he regards actors as lazy parasites and he is probably not far wrong. Don't think I wasn't glad to hear from you. I was. I read your letter avidly. But next time, do check the stamps Andrew. I am terrible at doing it, which is why I always take the easy way out and buy these terrible forms. They are awful things and one does feel rather as if one is rationed in some sort of war time situation, but they never get surcharged. O! you did make me laugh in your letter! O I laughed so much apropos your line regarding Savage's mother 'Boy! she was a BITCH!' Of course you are quite right, but it read so funnily! I can't tell you. Of course it is ages since I read it, but she had farmed him out to some washer-woman hadn't she? – and then married into the aristocracy. Of course she didn't want to know the poor fellow when he turned up at the family mansion! O it is like a Dickensian story. It is truly Dickensian. We tend to forget just how authentically he captured the spirit of his times. Good grief, nothing changes ever. Not as far as human nature is concerned. It is the same endless pattern of haves and have-nots, with some societies in a state of continual compromise/flux (like England) and others dominated by greed and fear (like South Africa) and everyone pretending they don't know each other's business. Well you certainly have disillusioned me about Miami!! I have no desire to go there, after reading what you say about the gnats. I can't stand gnats. One night in Hongkong we were all on this balcony having a drink when a great plague of them descended. You could hardly see. They were everywhere – in your hair and in your drink and up your – well they were everywhere I can tell you. Everyone went on chatting and drinking as though nothing was happening – I saw them picking these things out of their drinks

surreptitiously – and the host said something about 'this is always happening here, no need to worry, they're not in the least harmful' and it
wasn't till one got home and actually saw the BUMPS that you realised
what a liar HE was. Yes, you are right about the unrest etc. being
fomented. It is. With this Miners' strike over here, it is the Communists
. . . The road back to a proper morality and honourable behaviour is
going to be long and arduous, but men are going to be shown it eventually, in blood and fire and anguish. You are so right about 'Carry On
Cabby'. I haven't seen it, but I have heard it was lousy. They made it
originally with a script called 'Call Me A Cab'. That's why I wasn't in it.
I read it and thought that it wouldn't work UNLESS it were done as a
Carry On and that it needed script alterations. They offered me the part
which they eventually gave to Charlie Hawtrey. Anyway, they made it,
and it went out on release and did very bad business indeed. So they
withdrew it, and re-issued it, under the new title 'Carry On Cabbie' and
it cleaned up! They made a lot of money out of it.

    your friend,
    [K]

To RICHARD BURTON and ELIZABETH TAYLOR

18 February 1972

My dear Richard and Elizabeth,
I was absolutely stunned by your telegram.[1] Quite apart from the fact
that it was three pages long, it was totally unexpected! I was delighted
honoured and quite swept away! then I suddenly thought 'What if it
is all a hoax? what if you are not really invited at all?' so I got on to
my agent and they told me to ring the Dorchester Press. They said it
was all quite genuine and that I really had been asked to go to Budapest. I told them I couldn't make it because of these prior arrange-
ments I had to go to France and they said that they would convey
my regrets and so on. Then I thought I would write and tell you how
much I appreciated your gesture. Actually, I would have adored to
come to your birthday party. It sounds like a lovely idea and I laughed
out loud at the sally in the telegram WEAR SOMETHING GAY
FOR SUNDAY AND BRING DARK GLASSES FOR HANG-
OVERS IN BETWEEN! Anyway, to tell you the rest: my last
engagement was on the 17th, when I had the last broadcast in the

[1] An invitation to attend the joint birthday celebrations for Elizabeth Taylor (who
was forty) and her son, in Budapest.

series to do for the BBC and I was dying to go off somewhere cos all these strikes and power cuts have made life a misery I can tell you. (If I'd known about your birthday party THEN I should have taken an aeroplane to Budapest straightway!) Then I had this letter from Beverley Cross, an old chum of mine who wrote HALF A SIX-PENCE telling me that he & his wife had taken this place in Seillans[1] for a year and why didn't I go out there and stay with them? I replied and said I would be delighted because I don't start filming till April so I am quite free. I got this ticket and hope to fly out to Nice on Monday and then join them in Seillans. So that is all about why I can't get to Budapest. But, my unspeakable thanks to you both for asking me. I was dancing about the room I was so thrilled and kept thinking of those lines of Clemence Dane's –

'Sweet as a letter from home on a winter day . . .'

It certainly seems light years away from those halcyon days in Swansea, and that production of 'The Seagull'. I always remember, after the scene with Lydia Sherwood (Arcadina), Richard (Konstantin) used to fling himself into the wings and cry out to anyone who happened to be standing nearby – 'If you're ever in a jam I'm your man!'[2] to the consternation of the stage management who said these asides could be heard on stage, quite apart from the fact that they didn't sound very Chekhovian. You are often in my thoughts, and I wish Elizabeth and Chris a wonderfully happy birthday,

lots of love,
[K]

To BEVERLEY and GAYDEN CROSS

9 March 1972

My dear Bev and Gay,
Well having heard so much about the misery of being in this play[3] at the Court from Gordon, I went to one of the previews last week, to see for myself. You cannot imagine how boring it all is. Gordon does as well as he can, under the circumstances, but O dear! what a yawn it all is! Ostensibly it is about two actors who are on location in Turkey, making this film. Gielgud brays and brays until you long to cry out

---

[1] In Haute Provence, southern France.
[2] 'If you're ever in a jam, here I am/If you ever need a pal, I'm your gal.' Opening lines of the 1939 Cole Porter song 'Friendship'.
[3] *Veterans*, by Charles Wood.

'O shut your mouth and give your arse a chance!' for the monotony of his particular kind of delivery is dolorous indeed . . . I saw Stanley the other day. He looked very red and when I asked why, he said that he lit the oven during the power cuts (to keep warm) and the whole thing blew up in his face and sent him reeling across the room. It has burned all the front of the hair, but he is combing it forward to compensate, and painting in the eyebrows. This, plus the fact that he is growing one of those Zapata moustaches, has combined to give a macabre effect. 'You look AWFUL' I cried and he said 'You are a hell of a morale booster you are!' and I retorted 'Oh!! I could never lie!' (which is about the most ludicrous statement ever made) and went on and on about the best thing to be was frank etc etc. He said that he went to the Whittington Hospital for treatment but they gave him scant attention, calling it 'superficial burns' and obviously not wanting to know. He asked them for some hot sweet tea to allay the feeling of shock, but that this huge Negro nurse had said 'You just go right on home sonny, and have yourself a large gin and tonic!' and Stanley said he didn't think that hospitals should ever sound like that. I admit it certainly don't reflect much credit on the National Health system. I walked all the way to Fleet Street yesterday cos there was this bargain offer of Luvisca pyjamas for only £2 a pair. I rushed in with the money in my hot little hands and the assistant said 'We have only got the 40 size I'm afraid' and I was furious. 'I am 36,' I said, and he said 'Quite so' and I left in disgust. Louie said there were some cheap ones at Lewis's but it turned out they were 20% polyester. I'm not going round in a load of cotton wool.

>   lots of love from your old chum,
>   [K]

To FRED HILL

12 March 1972

My dear Fred,
I got your delightful letter of the 8th March today. Since I last wrote to you, I went off for a week to Seillans in the Haute Provence. Had one or two trips to the coast because it was only an hour from St Tropez and Cannes and Antibes. The resorts seemed to be full of elderly English derelicts, all tottering about on legs like pea sticks and ordering expensive drinks whilst anxiously searching the Times ordinary share index for news of their ill gotten gains. It was not an elevating sight. Still, it got me away from dreary England and the

endless power cuts and strikes and Ulster murders and child rapists. There has been an awful lot of that going on. They tried it on with me once, at Baker Street, when I was coming out of the park during the black-out. Grabbed hold of me and pulled my trousers down and started doing all sorts of unmentionable things until they realised I was a willing party & gave up in disgust. At the police identification parade afterwards, this constable kept saying 'Don't you recognise any of them?' and I said 'It was too dark to see the faces, I would have to feel all the cocks. Then I might recall which one it was' but he said they couldn't extend those sort of facilities and so, like my trousers, the matter was dropped. There were probably many other impressionable young lads like myself who were treated in this derisory fashion, this contributing to what Anna Freud has accurately described as 'a dread of romantic attachment' but we can't delve into the case histories of all the male neurotics in England or we'll be bored to tears . . . So glad you found relief in the old Fernet Branca.[1] I was introduced to it years ago by Maggie Smith. Once when I felt really ghastly at Naples airport I had five in a row. I didn't know you were only supposed to have the one. I didn't know they made you intoxicated! I reeled on to the aeroplane and was chatting to everyone, leaning over the seats and blocking the aisle and generally behaving very badly indeed. When I read your line 'the soft & silent comfort of your flat', I laughed with bitter irony. You should be here. This idiot woman below has a regular crowd in now. There are two negroes with guitars, and four spectre-like girls in cloaks, and they bawl out these madrigals below. It comes up through the floor in such a cacophony it is unbelievable. I have tried playing the Verdi Requiem at the top volume but it doesn't deter them in the least. They bawl out even more lustily. I looked out of the window when they were departing yesterday, and suddenly one of them looked up and saw me! She sneered defiantly, and I withdrew my head so quickly that I banged it on the wall cupboard. I was furious. I shut the window & cried out 'Shit on you ALL! May you rot and perish!' but I don't know that these imprecations are really very effective. I think you have got to go the whole hog and do it round a cauldron and eye of newt and toe of snail and all that paraphernalia . . .

    your old chum,
    [K]

[1] Fernet: highly aromatic herbal bitters, drunk in southern Europe as an aperitif, but more commonly in the north as a hangover 'cure'. The Italian Fernet-Branca, available in miniatures, is the best-known brand.

To ALEC GUINNESS

14 March 1972

My dear Alec,
I am afraid Gordon misled you dreadfully on Saturday apropos the
Michael Codron quote. What really happened was that Rona asked
me to arrange seats for the play at the Court because she was worried
about Gordon being unhappy in the piece and thought that we might
be able to reassure him, but she specifically asked that the arrange-
ments be clandestine because she feared that if our presence was
known by Gordon, that it would inhibit him. Consequently I rang
Michael and explained all this, and Michael entered into the conspiracy immediately and said 'Yes, of course I understand. I will
arrange the seats for you and you'd better go in the Dress.' By this,
he meant that in the Dress Circle we should not be seen, whereas in
the stalls it would all be obvious.

I told Rona about this conversation, and said that it underlined the
safety factor and that it illustrated Michael's tact and kindness. I
thought it a bit odd when she giggled, but put it down to her nervous-
ness over the whole venture. There had been hypertension in the
house because of this play and Gordon had told me that he had never
been so unhappy during a production.

I met Rona on the night arranged, and I thought it was a bit spikey
when she said 'I knew as soon as you walked into the foyer that you
were doing an act. It was "Kenneth Williams goes to the theatre" wasn't
it? – why can't you be yourself?' I thought 'Hallo! she's starting on me!
It's going to be a bumpy night!' Then the play started and I saw Gordon
do his bit and I was enormously relieved to see that the worries were all
totally unfounded; he gave – as he always does – a thoroughly authentic
performance. When I saw him afterwards I told him so, and said he
should stop questioning himself and just enjoy it.

Then I had this letter from Gordon today, saying 'peed with laughter
about Codron telling you to "go in the dress" on the night you came
to the theatre' so I kept re-reading it trying to make sense of it, and
couldn't. So I rang Rona and asked what the line meant & she said
'Oh! Gordon thought that Michael meant you should wear the dress
– you know – a frock! – it is rather funny you see, because the
implication is that you only have ONE dress to wear!' I said 'I see'
rather humourlessly, and I thought I should write to disabuse you of
the idea that Michael ever envisaged me going to the theatre in drag.

> yours ever,
> [K]

To ANDREW HATHAWAY

24 March 1972

Dear Andrew,
I seem to have neglected the correspondence for an awful long time,
but I've been having to do some writing for an undergraduate magazine,[1] and for the Radio Times, and I have been out to luncheons and
then dinners in the evenings, so it's all been busy in a rather trivial
sense. Thank you for your letter of the 20 March which I got yesterday: no, the Kenneth Horne with whom I worked on radio was not
the same Kenneth Horne who was a playwright. Curiously enough,
they were both in the RAF during the war, and both had the same
rank, and a letter intended for the playwright went instead to the
Kenneth Horne I knew; he answered it, and struck up a correspondence with a girl whom he later married. Fancy you seeing 'Carry On
Sergeant' – it was the first one they made in the series. It cost about
75,000 pounds and made a fortune for them. Yes, I remember the
opening scene. I was lying on the bed, and the Sergeant came in and
there was to be an inspection or something, and I had this very rude
speech about 'hanging my left leg on a chandelier' or something to
that effect. Your account of the drunken escapade and the ensuing
wrestling match was quite horrifying! phew! no wonder you're on
the wagon. I must say I do enjoy a drink and the odd olive, specially
the stuffed olive. I am very partial to a stuffed olive I must say. I don't
know who does the actual stuffing and I don't much care, but they
do give an added piquancy, there's no doubt of that. I have this friend
who always says 'Everything looks so much better after a couple of
gins' and I know what he means. Life is difficult ENOUGH to get
through. The Austrian novelist Robert Musil used to say 'Life is so
terrible, the only thing to do is smoke' and that strikes a responsive
chord with me. All this stuff about 'it is bad for your health' is so
much hogwash as far as I can see, for every hour brings us nearer to
death, and it is the one journey we take where the destination is
certain. Burckhardt once said 'I would always have willingly exchanged my life for a never having been' and the moment I read it,
I thought 'Oh yes, I agree with that'.[2] I remember discussing suicide

[1] KW gained confidence for what became a profitable writing career by contributing
to such magazines, viz: 'This is the piece I wrote for the Durham University Rag
Magazine last year. It's the longest piece of mine that has ever appeared in print so
I think it is worth preserving' (Diary, 25 January 1970). This particular addition to
his rag-mag archive was not preserved.
[2] See letter to Noel Willman, 5 October 1970 (p. 127). The correct quotation is
given in the footnote.

once with Robert Bolt and he said 'They do make things very difficult for all the rest of us, because we are all on the same bus really, and if people keep getting up and jumping off, it makes us wonder if the journey is really worth while . . .' This is basically why, on hearing of a suicide, people say 'If only I'd known how unhappy they were, I would have tried to do something to help.' They don't really mean that. They mean, they would have tried to keep them on the bus. I have got to take the journey so you bloody-well-will too! – roughly that sort of thing. There is an unpublished fragment of Rupert Brooke which runs –

> 'You who wake in the morning empty hearted
> Would God, would God you could be comforted . . .'

One feels that this kind of writing is born of empathy. Went to Kenneth More's party last week, and met Rachel Roberts whom I haven't seen since we worked together in 'Crime Passionel' – she cried out 'You don't look any different since you played Hugo!' but I said 'Lackaday dearie! my grey hairs are showing! I think I'll have to have a transplant from the pubics' and we fell to discussing old times. Since her divorce from Rex Harrison, she has been with this Mexican boy who seemed very silent, but charming. Rachel makes up for both with volubility.

>   yours ever,
>   [K]

To LOUISA WILLIAMS

29 March 1972

My darling Louie,
Thought I had better type a letter to you in case you cannot understand my writing. I had expected a post card by now, saying that you had arrived safely,[1] but nothing has come, so I suppose you have been too busy rushing around the night clubs and enjoying yourself. A terrible storm has broken here, and there is thunder and lightning and the rain is pouring down. That cow below has got a load of negroes in the flat, and they are all bawling out songs with piano and drum accompaniment. It is appalling. She should be shot. Or led away into a field and given a bag of hay, and left to graze. Stupid old cow. Rona Anderson has been offered a ten weeks' tour of 'The Secretary

---

[1] In Tenerife.

Bird' with Hubert Gregg, and she has accepted it. She is delighted. I think she welcomes the chance to get away from the children and the housework etc. Gordon is still hating the play at the Royal Court and can't wait for it to finish. He is going to do the TV series 'Upstairs and Downstairs' again, when he returns from the holiday. You remember Jack Hedley? – the one we met in Aquascutum that day? Well, he was at the Billie More dinner party. Phew! he has become terribly fat! you would hardly recognise him! He has got real jowls on the face now. He has moved from the little mews flat he had in Wigmore Street, and taken a big apartment in Eaton Square. Goodness knows where the money comes from. He hasn't worked for about nine months. All right for a pregnancy, but no good for a bank balance. His wife, Jean, is going to have a baby, and all the conversation was about 'What name shall we give it?' I said 'You can't beat Delilah' and Jean said 'You must be mad!' so that fell on stony ground. I got some slippers at Saxone's in Oxford Street and I told them their last pair were a disgrace and the linings all came out and they said 'You should bring them back' and I said I had got something better to do than walk round the streets holding unlined slippers. The new ones seem all right, but they are felt inside, and the brown comes off on the feet. There is always something. There is no getting away from it I tell you. There is no getting away at all. Not at all. At all. No getting away. Rachel Roberts has had rave notices for her play[1] at the Apollo. She wrote me a very nice letter and said that she was pleased to be acting again, and that she'd got this very nice flat in Egerton Gardens, with this Mexican boy friend of hers. She said she had asked Peter Eade to represent her, and invited him to the Connaught and gave him a splendid meal with claret and brandy and cigars and gawd knows what, and when she said 'Will you be my agent?' he just said 'No' and went on drinking. She was livid. Peter told me, on the quiet, that he could never go through with all her tantrums ever again. She was too hot to handle he said. I suppose Rex Harrison felt the same. Poor sod. Yes, well the rain has stopped now, so I can go to the post box with this. I am seeing Nora Stapleton and we might go to the pictures.

> your devoted,
> [K]

---

[1] *Alpha Beta*, by E.A. (Ted) Whitehouse. Rachel Roberts and Albert Finney as Mr and Mrs Eliot.

To BEVERLEY CROSS

8 April 1972

Mon cher Beverley,
You know Hilary Minster (Jack's son) was in the Bergman play with
me – well he rang up the other day and said we could go to the
pictures or something and I said yes, and when he turned up at my
flat, he had a great script under his arm & said he had written it for
me. I was furious. 'How dare you turn a social occasion into a professional one!' I cried. 'If you wish to submit scripts to actors, do it
through their agents or something, but don't USE your friends.' He
stuttered on about 'I didn't think it was usage' and I said 'Don't try
splitting hairs or dressing it up with me. I will not have it. D'you hear?
Either you come here, and we go to the pictures as you suggested on
the phone, and all that, or you can take your script away and stick it
up your arse.' He said 'That is very hurtful' and I said 'I wouldn't
know about that, I've never tried it' and he said 'No, I mean it is
hurtful when you try to write something for somebody and you get
treated like this' and I realised he hadn't taken in anything that I had
said. We went to see this film 'Buck and the Preacher' which was a
western and rather good, but the background music was the worst I
have ever heard . . . My love to Gayden. What has happened to the
lovely snapshots of my hols?

> your old chum,
> [K]

To ANDREW HATHAWAY

14 April 1972

Dear Andrew,
Fancy the Post Office putting the Tutankhamun Exhibition on the
franking stamp of my air letter! Well I don't need to see it on a letter,
I have to pass the British Museum every day, and I am sick to death
of the crowds who queue endlessly to see it. They leave their litter
all over Bloomsbury. I thought it only went on during the day, but
no! – when I came by it last night there were hordes of them floating
out! most of the men in evening dress and the women with furs and
jewels! the evening air was heavy with the aroma of expensive perfume and the odd cigar. I think it was all because of the Dutch royal
family being here on a state visit. As I watched, there was a steady
stream of gleaming Rolls Royce cars gliding into the forecourt to pick

up their distinguished passengers. I thought 'gawd 'elp us! they must want a job! behaving in such a provocative way with a rail strike just around the corner and the possibility of the economy grinding to a halt!' There is something doom ridden about the very rich. From the Bourbons to the Romanovs you see it again and again. Van Dyke captures it brilliantly in all his portraits of Charles, Henrietta Maria and the Stuart Family. I saw them when they were on view at the gallery of Buckingham Palace (the Queen occasionally opens it up and lets a few commoners in) and I was astonished by their haunting and haunted faces. At the dentist's today, he bent over me wearing a face mask! I asked what was the matter and learned that he too had got a cold. Outside, his receptionist was sniffling unhappily. I was glad to get away. I shot over to my doctor for a tonic and a prophylactic. He has just returned from visiting his home in Barbados and I said involuntarily 'O you do look brown' – forgetting that of course, he IS brown anyway. Well as from the 17th I shall be very busy with learning lines and all that so don't be surprised if my replies are sluggish.

> your old friend,
> [K]

To ANDREW HATHAWAY

28 April 1972

Dear Andrew,
We started shooting the picture on the 17th and I suppose we must be about a third of the way through it now. It really is extraordinary that we have been making these films ever since 1958. The cameraman is the same one that we had on the first. There is the usual amount of ad-libbing going on. Kenny Connor has always amused me, ever since I first worked with him in the ill-fated film of 'The Beggar's Opera' starring Laurence Olivier. He used to sing these outrageous parodies like

> 'All at once am I
> Seven inches high.
> I'm a dwarf on the street
> Where you live . . .'

I am a sucker for parodies; they always make me laugh. Tony Curtis came on to our set the other day because he is a friend of someone in the cast. He looked absolutely marvellous. It is a very good face, and he could charm the birds off the trees. The only other person of note I have seen in the restaurant is Michael Caine. He is all right I suppose, but he lacks the aura of Curtis. American stars generally seem to be bigger personalities than English ones, or perhaps it is that they have a tremendous novelty value for us ... I don't know. I remember when I saw Brando in the studios and I was astonished at the sheer magnetism of the man. The eyes were as blue as the Mediterranean. No, I don't much care for Ustinov. I know that he is very clever and civilised and cultivated and heaven knows what else, but I don't warm to him. It is like that Walter Matthau creature; everyone tells you what a clever actor he is, and when you see the work, you have to agree but the fact is, I wouldn't cross the road to see him. Whereas Brando, or Warren Beatty, or Bette Davis ... Interesting about the George Sanders suicide note wasn't it? 'I am getting very bored ...' Apparently he said recently that he found old age ridiculous and that he didn't want to be ridiculous. All a little sad and belated recognition of the truth to say the least. We are ridiculous from the time we come out of the womb. Not to mention the ridiculousness of the sexual gyrations that precede it. Of course you are right about Jane Fonda. Politically she is about as effective as a fart in a wet blancmange. We've got one over here called Vanessa Redgrave. Another pain in the arse.

> your old friend,
> [K]

To STANLEY BAXTER

23 June 1972

My dear Stanley,
Thank you so much for your delightful letter which I received in Tangier. It was sweet of you to write. I had a very good three weeks and got back on the 22nd to find a pile of letters to be dealt with and masses of people to be phoned, etc. etc. I hear the weather here has been lousy. Morocco was fabulous. At dinner with the Hon. David Herbert I sat next to Lady Tweeddale and she is one of your greatest fans – 'Oh! he is superb in those shows of his. There is no one to touch him for their brilliance in characterisation.' She added that I was very fortunate to have you as a friend & looked quite taken aback when I said 'Oh yes – I taught him everything you know ...'

> Love,
> Kenneth

To ANDREW HATHAWAY

26 July 1972

Dear Andrew,

I wrote to you yesterday telling you about my impending move to 8, Marlborough House, Osnaburgh Street, London NW1 3LY, as from August 3rd. And then today I got your airletter of July 23rd. I am not on your side regarding the Chess business. I think Bobby Fischer is superb. All the publicity about his being temperamental & his continual vacillation twixt one decision and another is all marvellous. In an age of mechanics and automatons here is an individual! I like everything about him. Of course he is the spoiled boy genius and all the rest of it, and why not? If I got near him I should certainly want to spoil him. That is one of the effects that highly talented people always have on others. As for Spassky and indeed all the Russians I hear of – O! they are a dull lot. The only one that seemed to brighten up the world was Khrushchev. The shoe banging episode in the UN building with Harold Macmillan asking 'Could I have a translation please?' was really hilarious. But the Russians didn't allow Khrushchev to be a personality for long, and his later years were spent in ignominious anonymity. Don't talk to me about the Russians – no thank you – give me Bobby Fischer any day.

Yes, Camel was a very workmanlike picture. I thought that Angela Douglas was charming in it. She is now married to the actor Kenneth More. Phil Silvers was very boring. Every scene had to be rehearsed and rehearsed until Phil Silvers knew it. By that time everyone else had forgotten it. He said he'd made a lot of money from the song he wrote – Nancy With The Laughing Face – the words for. He said 'Nancy was one of my daughters. I got three lovely daughters and my wife has left me. My wife was lovely! She used to love riding horses – she was a wonderful sight when she was riding! – her hair used to stream in the wind . . .' Jim Dale simpered 'Hm. Mine does that too' and everyone laughed but Phil stumped off furiously.

I expect you have read in your papers about our industrial troubles over here. The government is making loud noises about 'the rule of law must not give way to the law of the jungle' and a lot more in that fashion, but everyone knows when it comes to the crunch that they cannot face up to these nation wide cripplings in a democracy. They could in a fascist state. Franco would shoot the lot.

      your old friend,
      [K]

To ERIC PEEL[1]

31 July 1972

My dear Eric,
I went down to the country on Sunday to see Jean Marsh and she told me the most extraordinary true story about the unsuccessful husband of a very successful actress who was always taken along to the great parties and dinners with her, but warned never to try to outshine the wife who was a great star. At one dinner party he was sitting there unobtrusively while she held forth about her latest success, and the husband was astonished to hear the maid servant (who was serving him with vegetables) whisper in his ear 'Have some carrots you cunt' and he was so shocked that he dropped the dish and the serving spoons and took all the attention of the room and his wife was furious and swore that it was all due to his drinking too much and flatly refused to believe his story about the servant and refused to return to their apartment that night & threatened divorce. The following week, their host rang up and said he'd had a most peculiar experience with his maid servant who had arrived with the morning coffee in his bedroom, and he sipped some while she drew the curtains, and when he commented on its delightful flavour she suddenly turned & cried out that she had peed in it. Of course, in fiction there would be some marvellous denouement but this is a true story so it just peters out at that point. One supposes that the husband was vindicated and everyone lived happily ever after but they probably didn't . . . love,

   [K]

To CARLETON CARPENTER

8 Marlborough House,
Osnaburgh Street,
London NW1[2] ·
18 September 1972

Dear Carleton,
As I know no one called John Gray, or indeed any actor cum writer who would frequent the particular Island you mention,[3] I can only

---

[1]   An acquaintance from Tangier.
[2]   His new address since 3 August 1972.
[3]   Fire Island National Seashore, off Long Island, N.Y., a summer resort area favoured by artists, bohemians and the gay community.

assume that most of the information contained in your letter is a
tissue of lies. You purport to be an author but your missives contain
little of any literary interest. Memory is not the warder of your brain,
and the receipt of reason seems to be a limbeck only. You begin by
accusing me of self-flagellation which is ludicrous since anyone with
my kind of self-regard would never render himself physical harm,
and you continue with what seems to be a paean of complaint about
your waning physical prowess, and your dislike of the work that you
have to do. Get up on the old comic cone and peep at yourself in
passing. That is all you should be allowed – a peep. All vanity leads
to folly, as Doctor Johnson properly remarked, and it would seem
from the last paragraph of your letter (with its disgusting four-letter
epithet) that one should add 'corruption' as well. You take it for
granted, obviously, that I should know something of the American
theatrical scene because you mention – almost cursorily – the end of
the run of something called 'Dylan' and as I sat drinking my coffee
and perusing the mail, I thought to myself 'What on earth is he talking
about?' and the mind began to boggle. Then I came to this description
of yourself as a nun climbing an endless number of mountains & I
realised we were indeed in cloud-cuckoo land where identification
with Julie Andrews completes the syndrome. You ask for my help –
indeed, I would like to give it because your need is manifestly great
– but from this distance diagnosis is not easy. If you cannot change
the environment & go on some completely different kind of holiday,
I suggest you change your reading. Good writing is concerned with
conveying the truth. Its value will be determined by posterity by the
personal vision of the author. It has less to do with saying something
cleverly, than saying something. What you actually say in your latest
effort of the 13th is precious little. I have been occupied with a children's series on television[1] which was written by a Swedish gentleman
who used his country's place names copiously. As their pronunciation
invariably involves the umlaut it was like performing an acrobatic feat
with your mouth. In conversation this should always be avoided since
any kind of verbal superiority embarrasses your collocutor, but
in performance the BBC insist on correct usage because they're so
frightened of scholarly complaints apropos the education of children.
It was exhausting. In the evenings I had to go to the Playhouse to do
this radio programme with Clement Freud who seems to be donning
the mantle of his grandfather more and more as the solemnity and
acerbity are asseverated. He took me to task for using the abbreviated

---

[1] *Agaton Sax and the Max Brothers* in the 'Jackanory' series.

form of his name, and in spite of my abject apologies, he sulked for the rest of the show. I received a telephone call from Nora Stapleton & she said incredulously 'You are not moving again are you?' as if I were some sort of nomad. My move here was complicated & full of tribulation, but I kept my countenance & remained self-possessed.

> your old friend,
> [K]

To DAVID HATCH

19 October 1972

My dear David,
I am now in the first week of rehearsal (in a 3 week schedule) for this play 'Fat Friend'[1] which Michael Codron is presenting. It is being directed disastrously by a gentleman who just loves the sound of his own voice & we are all treated to little homilies on acting and lectures on theory of the 'background of the characters' and the actors are reduced to the status of onlookers. It is unbelievable egocentricity. I came away from the rehearsals today so cast down & exhausted & frustrated and – found your letter awaiting me. Just sat down and practically wept with gratification. There is only ONE thing that makes any real actor tick and that is reassurance from the outside of his own worth. That is what you give to a cast – that reassurance – and that will make an actor work twice as hard for you because he *wants* to please you. [Tyrone] Guthrie described directing as 'the ability to create an atmosphere in which actors become uninhibited' and I wish to God you were directing me in this play right now! In the meantime I can only say thank you for your greatly valued letter. We must meet as soon as this tour is over & I'm back in town . . . I shall need comforting! It has always been a joy working for you –

> Your old chum,
> Kenneth

---

[1] *My Fat Friend*, by Charles Laurence.

To NORA STAPLETON

28 October 1972

My darling Nora,
I was pleased to receive your letter with its exciting postmark and to
know that you are safely arrived in the land of the free, home of the
Red Socks, home of the bean, and home of course of the Boston
beguine. Well dearie it has been utter torment here. I should never
have gone back to the theatre. I have been rehearsing this play for
two weeks, and the director – Eric Thompson – knows about as much
about comedy as my arse. No, on second thoughts I realise that isn't
true. Of course my arse is very funny. In spite of the kicks it has
received at the hands or feet of outrageous fortune and the thousand
natural shocks that flesh is heir to. Lately the farting has had an almost
singeing effect. There is to be a run thro with the management on
Monday at the Queen's. There will have to be some sort of confron-
tation about it there. We have only one week before the opening in
Brighton and I do not know, at this stage, just how much one can
salvage from the wreck. Why does it have to happen to me? Why
can't I find a nice little play, directed by someone who is competent,
which results in a little bit of happiness for spectators and audience
alike? Oh lackaday rue. And Bumholes to you. As the strolling pisspots
were wont to remark. It is awful for me, for I adore the author and
would dearly love him to have a success . . . Gordon and Rona got
burgled! and have had to fit alarms everywhere and they keep going
off at the wrong moment. It is all happening.

      all my love to you dear girl,
      [K]

To PAUL F.[1]

10 December 1972

My dear Paul,
The play in which I am starring, 'My Fat Friend', opened at the Globe
Theatre in London on the 6th of this month. You will remember this
was the theatre in which I had such a success with the 'Private Ear
& Public Eye'[2] when you were in London. It has been very successful
for me this time too! and the audiences are wonderful. Actually they

---

[1] A young Australian friend.
[2] In 1962.

were good all through the tour as well but I thought that one couldn't go by a provincial reaction and was being cautious and rather pessimistic about the London audience. The critics have been lavish in praise for me – apart from one or two shits – and so we are hoping that it will run for some time. It is presented by Michael Codron (who produced both the revues I did in 1960) so it is nice to be working under his banner again. I wished and wished that you could have been there on the opening night. When I was sitting in the dressing room just before the curtain went up, I went back over the years mentally, and thought of the people that really matter at times of real importance in your life – and I remembered our last first night – the Queen's Theatre with the Robert Bolt play.[1] What a shame you cannot be in London to see me do this! – there are some scenes that are really very funny and would appeal to you. I had a telephone call at midnight from Aberdeen and it was Stanley Baxter to ask how it had all gone. He sent me a very funny telegram on the opening night! George Borwick couldn't come, but he sent me a splendid cable & so did Beverley from France. Ingrid Bergman came round and enthused wonderfully, Maggie Smith sent presents and I got so many presents and bottles of champagne it was ridiculous! My dressing room looks like Christmas! The latest Carry On film 'Carry On Abroad' opened the week before the play and that got good notices too! so that made it all doubly satisfying. The producer of my radio show 'Just A Minute' came along to my opening night and we all went to a private room at the Hostaria Romana afterwards, and he said quite confidently to me 'it is a triumph for you – you will be a big success in this – wait till you see the papers tomorrow' but I was saying 'Oh, let's wait and see' and not daring to predict. When our party broke up at about 1 o'clock in the morning, Tom and Clive drove me down to Fleet Street and we swept into the office of the Times and they showed me a proof of the drama column. I read what Irving Wardle had written about me . . . Oh! – I was practically in tears I can tell you! The joy! the utter vindication of all the suffering and the dreary days, when you see one rewarding notice which treats you seriously and talks not only about your comic persona, but about your ability to create pathos as well. I waved it over my head and went out into the loading bays where all the lorries were waiting to take the newly printed papers to the railway stations and I sang 'Bang the drum, light the lights!' from Gypsy, to an astonished horde of drivers and they all applauded me! I don't know how I got to sleep that night! Lay on the

---

[1] *Gentle Jack* in 1963–64.

pillow for hours going back over it all. This is the first letter I have written about these events to ANYONE. I wouldn't do it except with you. The others would think it big headed. Had to write to you though. Now, it is practically dark at three o'clock in the afternoon and the winter is really with us, the trees bare, and the air chill. There is a lot of flu about – remember your cold when you came on that visit? Do write to me if you have a moment. Love from your

      old chum,
      [K]

To MICHAEL CODRON

7 January 1973

My dear Michael,
I never thought I should be writing to you about the deterioration of the performance of the play at THIS juncture . . . if I'd had to hazard a guess about that, I should have said it might have been possible after a couple of months, but not before. Well it has happened: last night . . .

The entire evening upset me greatly. It represents an appalling betrayal. This kind of frivolousness in the approach to the work will simply erode the serious moments in this play and then we will be left in Gagsville and you might as well be in Brian Rix Land. I was ashamed of the performance which the company gave on Saturday.

I know it is difficult to sustain a good interpretation. I know it is easy to slip into something automatic and superficial. This kind of comedy is so delicate that it needs intense concentration in order to achieve apparent effortlessness and style. I have written a letter to Thomas withdrawing from the film[1] in March because I know that the energy for this play MUST be conserved. This morning I went up to see Eric at his house. I told him about the entire episode. He agreed that these kind of cracks in the ship COULD turn into great holes that would sink us completely. He said he would come in but that it would have to look uncontrived, and we both agreed too that the backstage atmosphere in a comedy was all important. I recall saying to you what a lovely company it was to work with. Why, oh

---

[1] *Carry On Girls.*

why do people have to spoil everything? What irony it is that you
are away!

>love,
>[K]

To MICHAEL CODRON

11 January 1973

My dear Michael,
After a long talk with Eric on Sunday last, I went in to the theatre
on Monday the 8th and had a long session in the dressing room.
There was a lot of weeping and gawd knows what went on, but
at last, when we started the show, the seriousness was back in the
performance.

Eric came in last night to see the show, and we all met – the
company and him – in my dressing room in the interval, and he
seemed happy with it, but has called a meeting for today at 7.15 to
give notes. The long and short of it seems to be that the rot has been
stopped, but what alarmed me was the rapidity of its arrival!

Now I have got the Carry On people on my back about the forth-
coming film. I told them I wanted to conserve my energy for the play
and now they are making all sorts of tempting overtures about cutting
the part down and making the hours less and so on. Trouble is, when
I get these people at the stage door who have only come because of
the films – and often admit they have never been to the theatre before
in their lives – I begin to think that perhaps there is a point in keeping
a foot in both camps. No pun intended.

O it is all so bloody difficult and you are not here when I most need
to talk to you. Gordon rang me this morning raving about 'Crown
Matrimonial' which he went to see on Tuesday. He said it was Harry
Packers.

It was Charles Laurence's birthday last night, and he brought his
mother along to see the show and we all had dinner afterwards. He
said he thought the performance was splendid all round, so that was
comforting.

>love,
>[K]

To STANLEY BAXTER

16 January 1973

My dear Stanley,
It is taking me ages to get used to writing this new year in the date!
I have made loads of mistakes on the cheques already. Suppose it
must be a sign of old age, after all, I am within three years of fifty. I
shall be 43 next week. We are having lovely weather I must say −
blue skies and bright sunshine − though it is cold, it is not freezing
and miserable. I went to Marks and Sparks and got these brushed
cotton briefs and they are very comfortable . . . I have just realised
what a mistake I have made in the sentence above! − it should read
− I shall be 47 next week. I was born in the year of the General Strike
which took place in 1926 you see . . . Wasn't it odd that I sent you
a telegram on the very day that your letter arrived, about an hour
later? I had been thinking of you a lot, I always do of course, but our
designer (of the play set) had been chuntering on about you and
saying how clever you were and how he had done your sets for 'On
The Bright Side' and I suddenly thought 'I must have a word with
him' with you, I mean. So I sent this wire you see. Had dinner with
Maggie and Robert on Saturday. Since we are next door to each other
in the theatres, we are always in touch now. She looked tired and
there was an atmosphere twixt her and Robert cos he had stayed out
all night and not been home and she said it made her worry. She said
marriage was a mad institution and that no artist should be subjected
to it. I hope all is going well with you up there?

> love from your old chum,
> [K]

To ERICH HELLER

30 January 1973

My dear Erich,
How kind of you to write to me! as soon as I saw the familiar handwriting on the envelope, pleasure pervaded the morning. I thought to
myself 'I won't open it till I have made the coffee, and then I shall
read it and have a cigarette as well' and I felt greatly indulged. How
extraordinary that you should have attended the Schumann recital

only a few days before you read the article![1] Oh yes, I love the 'Dichter-
liebe' – there were two poets who brought out the best in Schumann:
Eichendorff and Heine. The melancholy and the irony in the latter
poet is wonderfully enhanced by Schumann's music. I am moved as
soon as I hear the opening bars of 'Im wunderschönen Monat Mai'
and I always want to cry over 'Ich grolle nicht, und wenn das Herz
sich bricht' and I would have discovered none of this if it had not
been for you. Have you ever heard Hermann Prey? I have a superb
recording of him singing the Brahms 'Vier Ernste Gesänge' and the
soaring glory of the music and the voice in the phrase: 'aber die Liebe
ist die grösseste unter ihnen' is one of the most beautiful things I
know. I very nearly sent you the Times article myself, but then I
reflected 'No – it will smack too much of sycophancy' and did not do
so. I always talk about you in interviews. It is inevitable when they
ask questions like 'What sort of people have influenced your life?'
etc. When I spoke to Robert Bolt about the preface he wrote to the
play 'Man For All Seasons' I said 'much of what you said about the
private vision and the artist's dream echoes what I have read Erich
Heller saying in another context . . .' and Robert's eyes widened
considerably and he said 'I am very flattered that you put me in the
company of Heller!'

This play at the Globe Theatre is proving more of a strain than I
dreamed it would. I am on stage for most of the evening and never
seem to stop talking. It is a light comedy demanding a deftness of
touch and tremendous panache and drive. The twice nightly houses
on Friday and Saturday leave me exhausted. Sunday is largely spent
in recuperation.

I still go, sometimes, to the Cosmo Restaurant at Swiss Cottage –
the place where you used to give me dinner. You are always there. I
see your face, think of the gestures you might make. You never cease
to occupy my life. I round some corner of my senses and there, as
though the air had carved you out of a sudden thought, I discover
you.

Your letter was somewhat delayed because of an incorrect postal
code – please note that I am NW1 3LY. I hope that, if you visit
London, there will be a chance to meet and talk with you once again,

love,
[K]

---

[1] *The Times Saturday Review* (sent to Heller in Illinois by a Cambridge friend) had
published an interview with KW during which he had mentioned Heller flatteringly,
'and in the neighbourhood of [Dietrich] Fischer-Dieskau at that; just a few days ago
I wept my way through a Chicago Schumann recital of his' (Heller's letter).

To BEVERLEY CROSS

27 March 1973

My dear Beverley,
What a month this is being! first Binkie, and then within four days,
the death of Noël.[1] Both the events made me sad, but I didn't realise
the extent of my sorrow about Coward until about two hours after
I'd heard the news. It all happened on the Monday. I was cleaning
the windows. When I got to the kitchen one, I banged my head on
a jutting ledge. The pain was intense and my first thought was 'please
God! not a bruise on the forehead' cos that would have been awful
for the performance at night, and I rushed to the mirror and saw the
lump was just going to be covered by the hair. Then I thought 'I must
play some music to distract me from the pain of my head' and I put
on a recording of 'Bitter Sweet' and sat listening with rueful affection
to the number 'If Love Were All' – that was about 4 o'clock. It was
about two hours later, when I was on the telephone to Rona, that I
heard about his death. She said 'Isn't it awful about Coward?' and
then told me that it had been announced on the radio. Only then did
it click in my mind – I had been listening to him when he was dying
. . . The things that stay in my head are the things that stay in my
heart, and that man went straight to it from the time I first came
upon his work. I walked to the theatre, and started crying on the
way, and then as I turned into Winnett Street, to go to the Stage door,
I saw Maggie. She was crying too. She said miserably 'How am I going
to go on and say those lines tonight? – first Binkie, then HIM, what
the hell is happening? it's like the end of something real and the
beginning of a nightmare . . . who is there left to turn to?' I went
with her into the dressing room and chatted for a bit, and then I went
into the Globe. Sat in the room and stared into nothingness and every
bloody line became more and more invested with meaning –

> 'Time has paid its debt to me
> And though I know that we
> Must say goodbye
> Oh! my dear,
> If only you'll remember me
> I shall be grateful till I die'[2]

---

[1] Hugh 'Binkie' Beaumont (1908–73), managing director of the H.M. Tennent
theatrical company. Sir Noël Coward (1899–1973), dramatist, actor, songwriter,
cabaret performer etc.
[2] 'All My Life Ago', from *After the Ball*.

He certainly left a lot of himself in me I can tell you – I shouldn't think there is a day of my life when something a propos Coward doesn't occur. Sorry to go on so much, but I feel grief about it and I keep crying. Of course there is the other voice that says 'he would play it all down, and simply want you to go on' and I do that in public. But what do you do in private? where is the misery consolable? I sit down and write to you. One of his lyrics runs 'The thrill has gone/to linger on/would spoil it anyhow/let's creep away from the day/cos the party's over now . . .'[1] That's what I want to do. Creep away from the day. Thank you for your telegram of thanks about the two girls in Sussex Gardens.[2] Glad to be of service,

> love to Gayden –
> [K]

To PAUL F.

29 March 1973

Paul,

When you telephoned me yesterday, you said you were sorry about your behaviour on Tuesday evening, and that you would like to see me and have a talk. I made some quick calculations and decided that this could be arranged if you came along to see me at 11.30. I asked you if that time was convenient and you said it was. I repeated the time, you agreed, and I wrote it down in my engagement book.

In the meantime, I had the BBC on the telephone about all the May, June, July dates for the radio series, and the Codron Management about the understudy rehearsals at the theatre, and the request that I attend there at 12 o'clock. I said yes, because I thought that you would be coming to see me at 11.30 and that we could go there together and talk on the way, and then have lunch afterwards.

You never arrived at 11.30. I waited till 11.40 when I was forced to leave or be late for the theatre.

On arrival at the Globe, I left a message for you – I had already left a note on my door telling you where I'd had to go – and I waited there, thinking that you would come there to meet me. You didn't come. When the time came for me to leave the theatre, I had to go with the agent to a conference at Aeolian, and so I left another message, and this too was not acknowledged.

---

[1] 'The Party's Over Now', from *Words and Music*.
[2] The telegram explaining this favour is not preserved.

This morning I telephoned the St George Hotel at 10 o'clock but the operator said you were not in the building. Now, I have to leave for Broadcasting House in Langham Place, so I will drop this in, on the way.

You say many things that are virtuous, but your actions are not virtuous, and your diligence is lamentable. The real values of a civilised man lie mainly in the extent to which he C A R E S about his friends, and this care manifests itself in consideration. I don't seem to be getting any consideration whatsoever.

I went to a lot of trouble to arrange a meeting for you (which you had requested) and when the time came, you were too drunk to be presented at that meeting, or indeed any other.[1] I spent most of last night explaining that away. Rather lamely as it transpired. I shall do no more explaining in the future.

yours,
[K]

To BEVERLEY CROSS

14 April 1973

My dear Beverley,
Saturday afternoon, and a chance to write you a letter before going off to do the two performances at the theatre later on . . . I had to sell flowers for the Blind on Tuesday last, and I was rattling my box and saying 'something for the blind please!' and one old drear went by and refused to pay anything and I shouted 'it's all right for you, but some people can't SEE' and he turned on me and cried out 'I am eighty four! so fuck them' which didn't seem to be at all logical to me and I was frowning bemusedly at his departure when a charming turbanned Indian gently slipped a folded pound note into the collecting box and said softly 'It is a very good cause' and smiled and went straight on without even taking a rosette. Funny old world all right. That John Perry[2] was driving off in a huge Rolls Royce so I rushed to the car window with the box but he shrugged his shoulders helplessly, wound down the window and said 'I've no change at all dear . . .'

The business is very good at the theatre and we play to nice houses.

---

[1] K W's diary suggests that he was going to introduce his friend to Maggie Smith, who was performing at the adjacent theatre.
[2] Director of the H.M. Tennent organisation.

It has changed very much since the old days – it used to be the end
of the week that was best for laughs but now it's the other way round.
Monday to Wednesday is good for intelligent reaction, and from
Thursday you go into the geriatric territory and the four weeks to live
club, and then the Saturday two houses are all football and pop stuff.

The weather is staying marvellous. It has been an unbelievable year.
Today is languorous and warm. Don't really want to go and do two
shows at all. Would rather be sauntering round St Tropez with you
and Gayden, sipping the odd Pernod and having a giggle . . . O wasn't
that a lovely day we had there on my birthday?[1] – and that warm
warm sunshine, in February!

> your old chum,
> [K]

To ERIC THOMPSON

26 April 1973

My dear Eric,
Further to your telephone conversation this morning: I am sorry but
I think, as a matter of principle, I must protest against the idea of
your rehearsing everybody else, as though the reasons for your calling
the company together are manifold, when we really know that this
is not the case. I appreciate that your reasons are psychological and
that you believe that it is in the best interests of the company morale
and performance at night, to pretend that this is so, but the fact is
that it is not so. Michael saw the play on April 18 and was very
perturbed indeed. You saw it on April 21. You are both aware of what
is basically at fault. I have been writing letters about the kind of rot
that has set in at various points in the production, since January. I
have written an awful lot of letters Eric. Not because I want to (I
know that my endless complaining has irritated Michael more than
once) but because I see damage being done to the fabric of this delicate
little piece EVERY night, I know that it has drifted on to the rocks,
and several parts have just broken up entirely. The morale in the
company has steadily worsened, the playing loses rhythm and sometimes judders to a halt, and we have lost the word of mouth commendation which the WHOLE used to get. Now, the comment again and
again is 'well you are obviously trying to keep it up in the air, but it
is beginning to look like a one man band' etc etc. I really do feel that

[1] In 1972.

the time has come to stop lying and say to this person – 'You are not doing the job the way I want it done. You will either return to first principles and give the sort of faithful interpretation which I require or I shall instruct the management that my authority is not being observed and that the production is deteriorating so badly that something radical must be done if my name remains on the bills.' Every time there is a crisis (like the time I shouted in the theatre) there is a temporary improvement and then BANG! it all slips into such a travesty of vulgarity, face pulling and word-mangling that it was described by one spectator recently as 'incoherent'. I have been with this play since November, and have had months and months of it. I have got enough on my plate trying to play to audiences without actually having to combat the kind of stupid incompetence that I am getting night after night. Once before, in the theatre, it drove me to a nervous breakdown,[1] and I left the boards for seven years. I was off for a week, and then, so was the show. Afterwards, everyone said 'we never realised how much it was affecting you' etc etc., but by then it was too late. I think the time has come to stop telling lies, and that to penalise other members of the cast who have been TRYING to do their best for the piece, is immoral – and totally unjust. If you had seen the blazing anger and the shouting that went on last night when the rehearsal was announced, you would have realised conclusively that all the excuses about lack of energy to perform diligently every night are a pack of lies.

> yours,
> [K]

To BEVERLEY CROSS

30 May 1973

My dear Beverley,
I was delighted to hear from you – always a pleasure to see your hand writing on the envelope . . . Yes, the likeness to Barrault[2] was commented upon by Peter Brook when he directed me in that dreadful film called 'The Beggar's Opera' – we were on the set at Shepperton and he said something about Jean Louis & me to Laurence Olivier and they both agreed there was a resemblance. I had never seen Barrault at the time so it meant very little to me. Then I went to the

---

[1] In 1965, with *The Platinum Cat*.
[2] Jean-Louis Barrault (1910–94), French actor, manager and director.

Academy and saw 'Les Enfants du Paradis' and I thought it was perfectly awful and that he looked like a moon faced twit. I got furious thereafter if anyone commented on this likeness. But they continued to do so – Alec Guinness said it – and I have now become reconciled to it . . .

   You ask in your letter 'Do you remember sitting in St Mark's Square in Venice and reading the French accounts of the Profumo business . . . and Clifford Evans appearing . . . ?' As if I could ever forget! I had said to you, out of the corner of my mouth, 'Don't look obvious, but there is a dreadful queen over on the left in a blue shirt who keeps smiling and beckoning to me' and without hesitation, you looked up, focused on the object, and said shortly 'Take your sunglasses off. It is Clifford Evans.' I was appalled. Eventually, he came over and practically forced us to have lunch with him and Hermione Hannen the next day. They took us to this trattoria. She kept calling you 'John' and then 'Colin' and then 'Benjamin'. I was giggling to myself cos I knew about her being a bit funny. And you told me about Clifford crying out 'Summon my long ships!' and the director 'Cliff, they're not that long.' O I am laughing now, even as I think of it! Give my love to Gayden. Your old shipmate,

     [K]

To BEVERLEY CROSS

15 August 1973

My dear Beverley,
Deep joy in the eyebold to see your letter this morning and to know that all is going well with you and Gayden and Shaun. Here it is sweltering and they say the temperatures are continuing to soar to record heights. I just about manage to totter along to the odd social engagement and savour the drink-ette before reeling back to bed for the afternoon. I was built for comfort not for speed and the years have not treated me kindly. Your friend is becoming a derelict and no mistake . . . I have been doing these TV shows – What's My Line – from Birmingham studios. What a dreadful town! even as you approach it, the heart sinks at the sight of such endless filth and appalling planning blight. Nothing but horrible buildings marooned inside networks of upraised roads and endless flyovers. One wrong turning and you start going round the whole mad set-up all over again. The chauffeur said to me 'I hate this bloody hole! I'm always getting bloody lost!' When I asked what he'd done during our trans-

mission, he said he'd been to the pictures to see the 'Last Tango In Paris' with Marlon Brando & I said 'O I hear that is marvellous! apparently there is a blow job with the two of them and you actually see the cock and everything, it must have been fascinating.' He was derisive and said 'You don't see nothing like that . . . there's just this bit where she sticks her finger up his arse, that's all.' I said 'O what a frost! I was totally misled by the notices! These critics should be shot. They don't know an arse from a blow job and that's a fact.' The panel on the TV show is me, Isobel Barnett, Anna Quayle, and Bill Franklyn. Our celebrity guest last week was a cricketer called Illingworth.[1] Far too much make-up on I thought. He said that when he wasn't playing cricket he had this job going round selling greetings cards. I was amazed that he actually admitted it. I mean. A Captain one minute and a salesman the next. Ludicrous. But there, I suppose I'm the same. The woman in the flat below said 'I was amazed to see you cleaning your own windows!' and I said airily 'That is nothing! You should see Ingrid Bergman washing the walls down' and got into the lift with aplomb. Of course I've only seen Ingrid doing the washing up, never the walls, but I thought it sounded effective. I attended an incredible banquet thrown by Barbara Windsor's husband for her birthday. Didn't get away till 5 in the morning and fell off the taxi seat twice before arriving back at the flat. And there is no health in us!

[K]

To BEVERLEY CROSS

15 September 1973

My dear Beverley,
. . . The EEC have given permission to Rome to place an embargo on the export of all kinds of pasta as from September 8.[2] This restaurant we were in (Peter Mario's) were telling us that they can't get the spaghetti or anything. There is all this talk about the world food shortage. I watched that Herman Kahn[3] speaking on the subject at

[1] Raymond Illingworth (CBE, 1973), b.1932, sometime England cricket captain and Manager, Yorkshire CCC, now (1994) Chairman of Selectors.
[2] These exports had indeed been banned 'to avert a shortage of spaghetti and other forms of pasta in Italy' (*Times* report, 14 September). There had been riots in Italy in July, during a bread shortage.
[3] American mathematician and futurist (1922–83). Founder of the Hudson Institute, 1961; author of *Thinking About the Unthinkable*.

the Royal Institution. One ecologist said to him 'With population growth as it is, we simply will not be able to grow enough food to feed people' and Herman said 'You're crazy! We'll feed 'em with chemical protein which we can produce in factories – so it won't taste as nice – so that's too bad – but they will stay alive – then there is hydropones which will enable us to grow anything we like, under any conditions anywhere – so we'll need a lot of greenhouses and if we don't get them built in time some people die – so? – a lot of people die all the time – O K? – so what else is new?' All the people in the Royal Institution looked slightly dazed, and the sheer speed of his delivery left them reeling. All the questions afterwards were antipathetic and one man said derisively 'All your theories will be useless extrapolations if it comes to nuclear war' but Herman riposted 'So will yours buddy. Look! we have been told for so long! – God is dead – remember Nietzsche? – well I got news for you! he ain't dead. He's none too well at the moment – right? – O K – so he's a bit sick – but brother, dead he is N O T.' Before he left the rostrum, he thanked them and said that he felt 'kinda wonderful to have spoken in the same place that Faraday had lectured' which was a very nice touch I thought. Then my programme came on – 'What's My Line' – and you were suddenly plunged into the absurdities of what people actually do for a living. The prettiest contestant of all, in a very chic outfit, turned out to be a S A N D B L A S T E R. I never knew sand could be blasted. Apparently it is the way they clean the grime off all the dirty buildings. She said 'I am up there on the scaffolding blasting away and making these places look lovely again' and when they asked her if she enjoyed her work she said 'I love it' and you knew she meant it . . .

[K]

To SAM SMITH[1]

24 September 1973

My dear Sam,
I hope you opened this carefully and did not destroy the work of a genius. You understand? Thank you so much for such an enjoyable evening on Sunday. I enjoyed our meal together and I am glad that

[1] A young chance acquaintance to whom K W had shown some of the sights of London. They obviously argued about several topics, including English spelling, as they walked.

I said what I did about the great American films because I don't think you realise how wealthy you are. I also hope that you will come to reassess Garland. You must stop insisting that people behave in a FASHION YOU APPROVE OF. That is not what America is about. It is about the triumph of the INDIVIDUAL. Garland was intensely individual. Of course she wasn't a 'professional' as you kept saying. She wasn't supposed to be a professional. Just look around you – they are myriad! – there are hundreds of professionals around, but there aren't any Garlands. Not this time round. I have this correspondent in Beachwood, N.J.,[1] and he wrote to me some time ago about the Watergate business and I replied saying that I'd heard the latest line going round was that 'Nixon should have used Japanese (not all these Germans like Erlichman and Haldeman) at the White House because they're better at electronics and if they disgrace themselves they commit hari kari' and today he has replied and said that he has just heard that very line spoken on a live TV show. He seems surprised. He shouldn't be. The joke obviously has its birth in America. Not Britain. Jokes are like people. They go back and forth. I hope you were not too worn out with all that walking we did on Sunday afternoon. I was exhausted. My feet are still blistered. I haven't been round the city for years! It was quite extraordinary coming upon the London Symphony Orchestra in the middle of the practically deserted Barbican! – and fancy you not knowing that St Margaret's Aldermanbury has been lifted stone by stone and re-erected at Fulton, Missouri!! I can't understand that. I said to you 'Haven't you heard of Westminster College at Fulton?' and you replied 'I've never heard of Fulton' – the nonchalance was incredible. There is an ible you see! As in perfectible. Which reminds me! – if you read this line 'he pandiculated all over me' what would you make of it? How does pandiculate strike you? – I mean – do you like the sound of it? It is a legitimate word. In my edition of the Oxford it says 'to yawn, or stretch the limbs in drowsiness.' I don't know what it will say in yours. I suppose you have Webster's. I am using pandiculate a lot now. Saying things like 'this siccative creature pandiculated all over me . . .' which is very useful because eyebrows are raised immediately. I went to the BBC to do this broadcast this morning, and afterwards the producer took me to the BBC Club for a drink. We met two theologians there. Very knowledgeable and all that. I said something about the validity of the Ontological creed and there was a pause and one of them said 'What does ontological mean?' which rather surprised me coming from a

[1] Andrew Hathaway (see appendix, p. 291).

broadcaster on religious affairs. Well I have gone on too much, I simply intended to write a thank you letter and to convey my address, and the result is a very badly typed letter which looks like, and probably reads like, a mess! – nevertheless it comes with affectionate remembrance from

> your old chumm (only one M)
> [K]

To ANDREW HATHAWAY

24 September 1973

Dear Andrew,

Now I know the year is dying because I have to type this with the light switched on and it's only six in the evening; for so many months one gets used to the light staying and then suddenly, it's gone. I always forget. In the heat of summer I forget how bitterly cold the winter was, and when I am shivering in December I forget about the languorous heat of summer. I don't really forget. I mean I could, if pressed, recall these things, but the fact is that there are still these moments of surprise – that awful 'Oh it's like THIS' feeling – which experience should have prepared you for . . . I don't like the sound of your sarcasm about Sam Ervin's eyebrows.[1] Don't you denigrate that man. He is the most impressive thing in that hearing. On the one or two occasions I saw the Committee on TV satellite I thought Ervin was a man of sense and a man of honour. He is the kind of man America goes on obstinately producing, year in and year out; a man of steadfastness and stature. In a world that has largely discounted heroes, America goes on producing heroes. That is why the best films in the world have ALWAYS come from America; especially the Western. The Western embodies the heroic. Understand what you say about your Mama. Mine lives next door. I moved here (as you know) last year when the adjacent apartment became vacant, so that I could be handy if she wanted anything in the event of illness. So far it's me who has been ill, and it's Mum who does all the work! She once said to me 'I wouldn't want to live with you. I would rather have a bed-sitting room on my own than live with you. I couldn't stand all the pettifogging ways you have and we would get on each other's nerves.' Well it's all true. So we have compromised with separate flats which

---

[1] Senator Sam Ervin of North Carolina (as Judge Ervin) was the Chairman of the Senate Select Committee appointed to investigate the Watergate conspiracy.

are next door to each other . . . My line to you about the exhaustion of everything – 'there is the toothpaste to be squeezed . . .'[1] etc etc. was an attempt at a joke. It obviously misfired, because here you are replying and telling me to switch to bicarbonate. Perhaps humour in letters IS a bit difficult, between countries. However we will have to go on trying. I remain, your old chum,

    [K]

To the EDITOR of the *Listener*[2]

Peter Eade Ltd,
9 Cork Street,
London W1X 1PD
n.d.

Dear Sir,
I fell about laughing at that letter you published (4.10.73) under the title 'Nixon at Lime Grove' – with all that stuff about 'I strongly deprecate the allocation of space to backstairs gossip . . .' But then as I read on through the collection of cliches and cant I began to suspect the authenticity and by the time I got to the name Pollard and the bit about Teddington followed by Middlesex, I thought 'Hallo! they're having us on!' Nevertheless I welcome this diversion and write to tell you how much I have enjoyed all the letters on this subject which you have printed, especially those from Sir Hugh Greene. These delightful anecdotes have been both entertaining and illuminating, and will provide future historians with the same kind of indebtedness they

---

[1] KW's favourite evocation of humdrum daily routine, used (generally as a concluding thought) in many letters, e.g. 13 January 1975, p. 200. Hathaway later explained that he had not misunderstood this reference; he really did use bicarbonate of soda to clean his teeth, and recommended it.
[2] This letter was published by the *Listener* on 11 October (they confused matters by interpreting KW's '4.10.73' as '4 September'). Mr D.E. Pollard's complaint, published on 4 October, referred at least partly to Sir Hugh Greene's anecdotal piece 'Nixon at Lime Grove' (published 2 August 1973). Greene recalled the time when, as newly appointed Director of News and Current Affairs, he welcomed then American Vice-President Richard Nixon to the BBC studios in 1958. The availability of a hospitality room was suggested, but Nixon's Security Officer declined it, saying 'Between you and me, alcohol tends to impair the Vice-President's workability.' After the appearance of KW's letter, Mr Pollard wrote in to say: 'It was clever of Kenneth Williams (the comedian, I presume) to suspect that I do not exist. A shadow of doubt on the question does cross my mind occasionally.' Teddington, when not classed as part of Greater London, is in Middlesex.

presently owe to Suetonius, Saint Simon, Boswell, and of course your loyal correspondent,

Kenneth Williams

To ANDREW HATHAWAY

4 October 1973

Dear Andrew,

Well I am sorry about misinterpreting your words about the bicarbonate of soda but, in truth, it all sounded so UNLIKELY! Thank you for the clarification apropos the lavatory show.[1] I am not so sure it is a good idea. Ordure and urine have never been staple ingredients in humour for one very good reason: they are not in themselves very funny. Doubtless in the hands of a genius they can be side splitting, and sometimes the exasperated anguish of the themes in correspondence are very funny indeed. All that stuff from Coleridge on the voyage to Malta – 'OH! the endless flatulence!!'[2] does make me burst into laughter albeit grudgingly. Glad we are in accord about Sam Ervin. I think he is marvellous. I see in the paper today that the committee hearings are being televised again. I am not at all surprised. They make fascinating viewing. This Segretti sounds outrageous![3] Our papers also say that confidence in Nixon is at 'a low ebb' in the United States. I am not surprised. I think it is amazing that he continues to occupy the White House AT ALL. Interesting to read all your comments on UFOs and superstition generally. As Shakespeare properly observes 'There are more things in heaven and earth, Horatio, than

[1] Hathaway had explained that a whole episode of a comedy show ('Lotsa Luck') had involved the efforts of one character to get her foot unstuck from the 'storage box'. He took this as the TV networks' first admission that 'the American people ever did anything in a bathroom (water closet) *except* wash their hands'.

[2] In 1804, Samuel Taylor Coleridge sailed to Malta in the *Speedwell*. He suffered gravely from seasickness and from a constipation so severe that a surgeon was called from another ship to administer aperients. His agonies recall many similar passages from KW's diaries, viz: 'Pain without gloom & anxious Horror, & from causes communicable openly to all, rheumatism etc., O it is a sport! – but the Obscure, or the disgustful – the dull quasi-finger pressure on the Liver, the endless Flatulence, the frightful constipation when the dead Filth *impales* the lower gut – to weep & sweat & moan & scream for the parturience of an excrement with such pangs & such convulsions as a woman with an Infant heir of Immortality . . . O this is hard, hard, hard!' (Notebooks of S.T. Coleridge, item 2091, dated 'Sunday Midnight, May 13th, 1804'.)

[3] Donald Segretti, under the name Simmons, recruited infiltrators of the Democrat Party on behalf of the Republican President, Richard Nixon.

are dreamed of in your philosophy . . .' O yes, I am willing to go along with all of this. I think the sum total of knowledge DOES find completion SOMEWHERE, perhaps in infinity itself, and I believe that man has portions of this TRUTH revealed to him at various stages of history, but that he never finds out the whole truth. He can't. Because the TRUTH is outside of man. That is why the TRUTH is incorruptible. A lie was a lie in Babylon just as a lie is a lie today in London. It makes no difference. Eternity makes no haste. If men choose to call this TRUTH by the name of God I find that preferable to most of the silly ISMS at the end of words with which we are beset. DeterminISM is one of the most foolish of all. It makes nonsense of all the normal human concepts of language – especially the concepts of praise and blame. The criminal is not really wicked, he just represents the natural result of an unhappy background. Once you alter the background, you won't have any more criminals. Specious rubbish. It doesn't explain why so many criminals come from affluent backgrounds, nor why plenty of god fearing and decent citizens have grown up in poverty and deprivation. You can stick determinism up your arse as far as I am concerned. Your words about all those unwanted pets having to be destroyed were very moving. I know the sort of anguish this arouses in us. One visit to our own Battersea Dogs' Home was enough for me. If they are not collected within 3 months, they kill them painlessly. When you walk round the cages and see them looking up at you with such love and trust – they seem to be saying 'Take me home with you, please!' and you walk away feeling like a shit. O it is the same with all love. It represents a terrible burden. Once you choose to love you choose to start crying. And the crying will never be done. All sensitive men spend their waking lives wrestling with their conscience and sometimes they can never reconcile the thought with the practice. When the crisis is profound enough it can lead to suicide. I think it is your countryman Thoreau who says 'All artists lead lives of quiet desperation'[1] – something like that. It is the sort of line that reverberates in the memory.

Your old chum,
[K]

---

[1] Henry David Thoreau (1817–62) actually said (in *Walden*) 'The mass of men lead lives of quiet desperation.'

To CARLETON CARPENTER

9 October 1973

Hilda Bracegirdle ached all over; her arm was numb from the weight of the shopping bag and her feet were damp in the ill-fitting shoes she'd got cheap at the jumble sale. As she crossed Bedford Square she shuddered with the sudden gust of cold wind and began to think longingly about the warmth of her bed-sitting room – even if the oil heater DID smell of paraffin – and decided she would have her boiled egg in the blue egg-cup: that would be something to look forward to. She concentrated on the vision of azure pottery from Poole and it was almost with reluctance that she turned into Caroline Place and fitted her key into the lock. There were two letters addressed to her on the hall table. She knew the buff coloured envelope contained a bill, and sighed inwardly at the thought of her meagre bank balance, but her spirits rose when she picked up the other missive: it was a colourful blue air letter from America. As soon as she could dump the shopping, kick off the shoes and find the letter-opener, she sat down to read the contents avidly. The opening line 'What's up with you?' made her smile bitterly. This was how he always wrote to her. He always managed to make it sound as if she'd been remiss. That was a particular flair of his. Ever since she'd first tip-toed across the ward to his bed in the Charing Cross Hospital and seen his tousled hair and sulky mouth upon the pillow, she could never forget the reprimand as he took the proffered paperbacks from her – 'these are quite the wrong things Hilda! an invalid doesn't want to read about travel! don't you know about the kind of frustration it induces? God! do you ever use that pinhead of a brain?' She had bitten back her tears then, and found herself doing the same now, as she read on, the next line said 'Don't be vulgar, sitting there staring at your knobbly knees.' O yes! he knew how to hurt all right. It was all true her knees were knobbly. He'd always said her legs were the most unprepossessing thing about her. She'd even affected long dresses because he'd made her so self-conscious about them. She read on past the banter and the mockery, and she knew there must be a sting in the tail. He never wrote unless he wanted something. Yes – here it was, in the last paragraph, 'Could you please check the adagio movement from the original score of the "Bohemian Girl" – see if it is F sharp – you can do it in the Reading Room of the British Museum . . .' O dear, she thought, as if I haven't got enough to do without trundling all round there! Then she saw the postscript – 'incidentally why don't you change your name by Deed Poll? – I have never thought Bracegirdle suited you. Try using your mother's name.' That was another twist of the knife. He knew her mother's name very well. It was Woodywhist. Everyone laughed at it. Especially him. When he'd first heard it, he'd thrown back his head, roared with laughter and said 'sounds like a tree at a card game' and he'd known it had hurt her. It had hurt her mother too. She cried so much her wig fell off. Even that didn't touch him. 'Use it for a tea-cosy!' he said cynically, and crashed out of the house leaving them both disconsolate. She felt the rebellion surging up inside her. Fuck him! she thought, and his bloody BOHEMIAN GIRL! She was damned if she was going to tramp round to that stinking Museum with its smell of bees-wax and those awful drears wearing half-moon testicles – no – spectacles . . . or was she right the first time? She fell back on the chair musing. Then she took up the pen and replied – Dear Carleton, I got your airletter of October 3 today and was delighted to hear from you. I read your last two novels with delight. I replied and said so, at the time, but I never heard anything from you. It seemed eons ago. Lackaday and rue. You ask after 'The Bohemian Girl' in the most affected fashion. I suppose you mean Nora [Stapleton]. She is working for Thames Television and I don't know whether she does it in F sharp or not. She is always out. This work she does for Thames Television must be very exacting. I thought I would tell her about my Hilda Bracegirdle saga. Hilda Bracegirdle was the name of a rather unfortunate lady who was always in the outer office of a tatty theatrical agent called Miriam Warner. She really did exist. Hair drawn back in a terrible bun. Make-up was horribly white, and the total effect was distinctly discouraging. She used to have her desk by this spluttering gas fire and was forever blowing her nose. I could hardly believe it when she changed her name to Woodywhist. It was received with incredulity by everybody. Well I have rambled on for too long. I can see that I have bored you – no – don't protest! – I can see quite clearly that I am right. Why else would you have yawned. I have never witnessed such pandiculation. I shall prevail upon you no longer. I shall take myself off. I shall wish you au revoir as our friends across the channel put it,

> your lod (old) chum,
> [K]

To W.R. ELTON[1]

11 October 1973

Dear Mr Elton,
I saw that interview on television when John Osborne spoke about the foreign tourists as 'human rubbish' and I remember being quite staggered as I ached (that should have come out as watched but this machine is playing very odd tricks) anyway I was shocked because I thought 'he is an author, he knows very well he is being watched by millions and he has had enough experience of the media to know that there will be a disgusted reaction to this ill-considered and stupid remark.' I was even more shocked to find that there was practically no reaction at all. All I found was your letter in the Listener. I nearly wrote then, straightway, to say that I applauded your sentiments wholeheartedly and to express the hope that you would not regard Osborne as typical. If you look back on that interview you will realise that he was coming on at a rather tricky moment. We began with Russell Harty trying to get some conversation out of Jill Bennett[2] and heard this halting stuff about her getting drunk and cycling round with her dog in a basket and being (very properly) apprehended by a policeman. Then she admitted that she opened tins of potatoes taken from the fridge (kept in her bedroom) during the sleepless hours. Then Osborne came on. Well I ask you! how would you feel if you had to follow all that banality? – you would feel pretty desperate. He has been an actor – an unsuccessful one – and so he can feel when an audience is becoming lukewarm, and this one had been patiently sitting through some very soggy rubbish indeed. I think he felt he had to liven it up, and all these foolish remarks came out as a consequence ... Johnson once remarked that the oral tradition was like a meteor which eventually falls and cannot be rekindled and he added 'Written learning is a fixed luminary, which, after the cloud that has hidden it has passed away, is again bright in its proper station' so I suppose

---

[1] W.R. Elton, writing from City University, New York, had said (*Listener*, 6 September): 'One of the most memorable experiences of a happy research visit to Britain this summer was to hear, on television, John Osborne categorise summer tourists, especially German, Japanese and American, as "human rubbish".' Mr Elton asked in what sense 'different from Hitler's' Osborne was employing the phrase. Osborne himself had replied in the next issue, describing New York as a 'tottering slum', and appending the p.s.: 'My plays may be rubbish, but at least they're good British rubbish.'
[2] Actress (1930–90); John Osborne's (fourth) wife from 1968 to 1977.

one has the consolation of knowing that things spoken are not so dangerous as things written ... I don't think you quite realise the extent to which Osborne's views are disliked in this country. He is a very odd creature. I always find the writing most discouraging. I sat patiently through 'Inadmissable [sic][1] Evidence' but eventually had to admit defeat – and boredom. I don't think he writes plays so much as diatribes. I am an actor and have appeared on a number of television chat shows – including the Russell Harty one – so I know about some of the pitfalls of hasty pronouncements. I did one programme with Parkinson on BBC-TV (with Maggie Smith and John Betjeman) and had to go back twice! cos there had been such a furious reaction to my remarks about the selfishness of strikers who only really hurt their fellow men and NOT the entrenched power they were ostensibly protesting against ... I am not much good at writing and (as you can see) not much good at typing either, so you will have to forgive all the literary errors – just wanted you to know that I am a born Londoner who loves to see his city full of human beings from any part of the world, but especially full of Americans.

> sincerely yours,
> [K]

To BEVERLEY CROSS

16 October 1973

My dear Beverley,
... I did this 'Any Questions' programme with Baroness Stocks, and Richard Marsh – the Minister for Transport – and Lady Barnett. They gave us a terrific dinner first with a different wine for every course so when it came to the broadcast I was pissed. It was LIVE. They said to me after 'There will be a lot of complaints about the language you were using'. All I did was say 'show us your winkle' apropos barrack room life. Died the death Don't fancy I shall be asked again.[2] Bloody awful journey anyway. Takes you two hours to get to Bristol and you know how the bum sticks to that PVC. I do not understand why car manufacturers continue to use that stuff I really don't. It is disgusting ... Isn't it frightful with another Israel/Arab conflict? and all this

---

[1]   KW was not infallible on his 'ibles' (see letter of 24 September 1973, p. 185).
[2]   A correct assumption.

corruption in the US and dear Spiro pissing off like that and admitting to evading the tax.[1] Just got mine in. Felt like doing the same.

> your old shipmate,
> [K]

To ANDREW HATHAWAY

29 October 1973

Dear Andrew,

. . . Interesting to read your account of the interview with Katharine Hepburn. One of the great actresses of our time. I was told by some acquaintances who are homosexual that she stayed once in a house next door to them, by the river, just outside London. Apparently their landlord had always told Hepburn that she could come over from the garden and use their swimming pool whenever she wished to do so. But these boys didn't KNOW any of this. Well they were all sitting round this pool in an entirely male gathering and having a lot of laughs when they suddenly saw what they thought was an old lady cycling up the drive with swimming costume and towel under her arm, and they cried out in horror 'Who the hell is this?' until she got near and they realised who it was. They stuttered 'Hallo!' and said she was very welcome etc., but she wheeled her bicycle round and said 'No thank you – I saw that look of hate . . . it was cold, cold hate . . . I'll just be getting along' and went away. They said they felt awful. They said 'We thought it was just some awful old woman trying to use the pool, we never realised it was HER! . . . of course if we'd known . . .' When their landlord returned from abroad and learned how his distinguished neighbour had been treated, he was furious. Shows that one should be more careful about the treatment meted out to old ladies. Especially those on bicycles . . .

> your old friend,
> [K]

---

[1] United States Vice President Spiro Agnew resigned after pleading 'no contest' to Federal charges of tax evasion.

To ANDREW HATHAWAY

5 November 1973

Dear Mr Hathaway,[1]
I begin to wonder if you have taken leave of your senses or whether you are not being affected by your country's malaise. What on earth do you mean about have I ever stripped shale? How dare you. I am thankful to say I have never stripped anything. Or indeed anyone. I am not in the habit of indulging in that kind of pastime and it's highly improper for you to make such lewd suggestions. In future I'll thank you to keep your big mouth shut. And don't repeat don't write out any more of those ghastly apocryphal 'stage stories' to tell me. I have heard them all – in slightly varied and generally better versions. Actors hear those sort of stories when other people are cutting teeth and they don't want them repeated to them by laymen. Do you hear? I never want to hear that kind of crap again. 'Wait till you see the Duke of Buckingham' indeed.[2] Ugh! I thought it was lousy in '46 when I first heard it. These dreadful hackneyed old stories don't have anywhere near the same value as the anecdote which has some roots in reality. The account I gave you of the incident with Hepburn is true. The Carradine story is far too long a tag to be practical. All good jokes depend on an economical tag. After a colossal build-up by Jack Benny about the unfairness of him performing for nothing in a charity programme when he later found that Eddie Cantor had got five thousand dollars for the same show, Benny did this agonised pause & said 'Eddie Cantor needs five thousand dollars . . . ? . . . like a reindeer needs a hat-rack.' Now, that is what I call a tag. The whole theatre practically fell in. You've never heard such laughter . . . If you get a film over there called 'Don't Look Now'[3] avoid it like the plague. I went last night and it was terrible. It was so boring I let my hand wander into the crotch of my companion and the only reaction was the line 'Any diversion is welcome.' O! it was the worst thing I have seen for ages. Truly decadent rubbish. You kept looking around the auditorium wondering why the audience wasn't going hysterical with the utter boredom of it all, but in the half empty house you could see they

---

[1] The letter to which this is a reply is missing.
[2] Theatrical chestnut usually ascribed to the fine but intemperate actor Wilfrid Lawson (né Worsnop, 1900–66), who is said to have interrupted himself on stage by saying 'If you think I'm drunk, wait till you see . . .' etc.
[3] British film based on a Daphne Du Maurier story set in Venice, starring Julie Christie and Donald Sutherland, directed by Nicholas Roeg.

were all either eating ice-cream and nuts etc., or doing the other thing . . .

sincerely,
[K]

To CARLETON CARPENTER

8 November 1973

Mon cher Carleton,
Merci blow through for your letter which did not come a wink too soon. Tardy, dilatory, or just plain sluggish, are all reasonable words to describe your literary responses . . . Last night I was the guest speaker at the annual meeting of the Harveian Society[1] in London. The opening address was given by an Oxford don. He was followed by a prelate . . . Then there was a Trade Unionist who called vaguely for 'more quality in the way we spend our leisure' and after some desultory hand-clapping, I went up to the podium. I told them that my arse had practically dropped off with the boredom of it all and said that as doctors of medicine they should all be ashamed of themselves. I said 'When I had this boil on the bum they pumped me full of anti-biotics for weeks and nothing happened. The boil remained and so did the pain. Eventually I took the advice of a crank herbalist who told me to rub in root of marigolds. It sounded like a load of rubbish but I was desperate for any remedy and so I found myself rubbing in the root of marigolds one night and thinking what a pretty pass the modern intelligence had come to, but lo and behold, in the morning it had gone! the awful inflammation had vanished. The boil was no more.' This speech was received with a sort of stunned silence. When I got to the word 'bum' I sensed a feeling of antagonism, and at the end there was a bit of giggling. After the President had made the closing address and the meeting broke up, I was surrounded by people who all asked 'Where can you get this root of marigolds?' and I began to wonder if I'd taken leave of my senses. They were all doctors and surgeons! – some of them are among the most distinguished in the world. Root of marigold indeed. Heigh ho.

We are told very loudly and often to lift up our hearts,
We are told that good humour will soften fate's deadliest darts,

[1]   M.G.M. Smith, MA, MB, MRCP, Honorary Secretary, described the Harveian Society as having been 'founded by doctors in memory of William Harvey who, as you know, discovered the fact that blood actually circulates around the body'.

So however bad our domestic troubles may be
We just shake with amusement and sing with glee,
Heigh ho, mum's got those pains again
Granny's in bed with her varicose veins again,
Everyone's gay because dear cousin Florrie was run down on
    Saturday night by a lorrie,
The whole world's light as a bubble
The family's thrilled because Elsie's in trouble
'Cos now she's had seven, so God's in his heaven
And that is the end of the news.

Nora Stapleton has acquired a primus stove and was recently seen in the back-yard of her apartment building, trying to light the thing with spirits of tartar and an assortment of cloves. I must bid you adieu. Perhaps in some other place we shall meet in more propitious circumstances and thou will cling to me and claim me thine, not Lancelot's nor another's, but thine own . . . till then I remain,

       your old shipmate,
       [K]

To JANET BURNS[1]

13 November 1973

Dear Mrs Burns,
Thank you for your letter apropos the problem of leisure discussion. The argument you use – 'many people are prevented from doing what they would like, by lack of money or knowledge of available facilities' – is one which is continually advanced in modern society. It is a fallacious argument. It goes back to the ancient controversy between Socrates and the Sophists, and these latter, as you know, maintained that all knowledge and teachable skills were saleable commodities. They are not.

    The truly cultivated mind is concerned with a sense of quality rather than measurable quantity, and of meaning rather than explanation, its business lies in a task which would appear impossible by the standards of the scientific laboratory: to teach what, strictly speaking, what cannot be taught, but only 'caught' like a passion, a vice, or a virtue. This impossibility is the inspiration of all art. It brings us to

---

[1] This, and the following two letters, are KW's answers to typical items in his professional postbag. This one arose from his Harveian Society address.

the observation of the Greek nobleman about the education of his children: 'Let them be instructed in what they will never learn.'

The evidence of our senses shows us, in the world around us, that people are not all talented. Doubtless if they were the world would be a very different place. In our society there is an abundance of institutional teaching and extensive further educational facilities which those people who require them can easily obtain. To assume that people don't know about them is to assume a state of illiteracy in our country which is belied by the facts.

All the Utopian concepts – Hegelian, Marxian, etc., are impracticable because they assume a possible conformity and as long as man possesses free will, conformity is the one thing against which he will continually rebel.

> sincerely,
> [KW]

To WESLEY R. COLDHAM

14 November 1973

Dear Mr Coldham,
Thank you for your letter. In my talk with Russell Harty on television where I discussed my religious upbringing, I mentioned the Wesleyan church. This was the one that I attended at Crestfield Street in London.

In 1784 John Wesley established the legal status of Methodist Societies, and though he had not thought to establish a separate church he made plans for the society to go on after his death.

You will note the entry in the Columbia Encyclopedia under the title METHODISM where there follows a discourse on the derivation of the title, i.e. 'a group derisively called methodists for their methodical habits of study and religious studies.'

The further entry under WESLEYAN CHURCH states: Wesleyan Church, a branch of Methodism founded in England by followers of John Wesley. At the conference of 1791, they engaged to 'follow strictly the plan' he had left them when he died.

As further testament to the validity of the title of WESLEYANISM you doubtless know of the Wesleyan University in Middletown.

I am sorry that I spoke too fast for your liking, but would point out that it was extempore conversation, unscripted & unrehearsed, and most of this kind of talk is ill-considered, hasty, and often needs to be qualified, or even 'called back' so to speak. I therefore ask your indulgence.

yours faithfully,
[KW]

To M.B.L. GERAKIS

16 November 1973

Sir,
Your letter with its story of Barrymore and the comments on the performance at the Playhouse Theatre[1] recently arrived this morning. There is praise for what you call 'the beautiful exposition of the poetry of Wordsworth' and there is complaint about my vulgarity. It seems that what you give away with one hand, you take away with the other. I think it is you with your references to 'nether regions' that is being vulgar. I told the audience about my suffering from a boil on the bum. Shakespeare did not disdain the use of the word 'BUM' and gives it very effectively to Puck in The Dream. It is also used well by Jonson and Webster, and in our own age by Mervyn Peake ... For the most part, audiences have extended faithful hands to me, and they have shown me the breath of kindness. For all the carping letters I receive in the post there is always another which expresses this generosity and for which I am always grateful.

[KW]

To MAGGIE SMITH

13 January 1975

My dear Mags,
I went out to Greenwich to see Peter Nichols and met the family: his wife and children. Had a very pleasant evening and he told me all his news. Do you remember the Avery twins? one was called Sam and the older – no the other one – was called Wilfred. Well Wilfred lives just round the corner from the Nichols house and they are often bumping into him. He has had no success with his paintings and Peter's wife Thelma said 'They are all the same ... always drawings of huge cocks ... the only difference is that they seem to get bigger

---

[1] KW's poetry recital 'The Crystal Spirit', recorded for BBC radio on 9 November.

all the time' and then she added 'the canvases not the cocks!' which made me laugh. Peter said that Wilfred was forever reiterating 'well bugger it, I didn't ELECT to be another Van Gogh but that is what has happened . . . I mean . . . I didn't bloody choose it . . . but there it is . . . I can't help myself . . . I am another Van Gogh . . .' Thelma said they had tried to help by offering to buy one of these drawings of yet another cock and [she] was staggered when Wilfred said 'You can have one for fifty pounds' but I pointed out that I paid that sum for one of his efforts in 1960 or thereabouts, so the price hasn't inflated. Peter said that when his play[1] was done in New York — 'contrary to what I expected, there was no bally-hoo at all! in fact, no one came near me . . . I wandered around the city alone like any other tourist . . . all this talk of them making such a fuss of you and the endless invitations just didn't happen . . . the telephone never rang.' We talked for ages and I was quite surprised when it was approaching midnight and time to go.

Went out to have dinner with Gordon and Rona last night at Hampstead. Gordon had been on a quiz panel at Salisbury (fund raising for their new theatre) which had included Evelyn Laye, Honor Blackman and William Douglas Home.[2] He said that Evelyn was very sad & indistinct. Said her favourite piece of music was 'Jesu Joy of Man's Desiring' and told the audience 'I am really a very religious woman' and there was dead silence. William Douglas Home said 'Did you know that Pontius Pilate was born at Pitlochry?' and seemed almost demolished when Gordon said truthfully 'Yes'.[3]

Well as I told you in my last letter, I am having lunch with Chris Downes[4] at Peter Mario today and he will tell me all the news of you. Then I have got to collect my stuff from the cleaners and get the haircut so it is a busy life. The laces to be tied and the toothpaste to be squeezed. It all takes time.

> lots of love from your old chum,
> [K]

---

[1] Probably *A Day in the Death of Joe Egg* (Brooks Atkinson Theatre, 1968).
[2] Evelyn ('Boo') Laye, b.1900; Honor Blackman (b.1926), actress; William Douglas-Home (1900–93), playwright.
[3] This improbable legend actually belongs to Fortingall on Tayside. Pilate is said to have been the offspring of a Roman soldier and a Caledonian woman.
[4] Dresser, later friend and confidant, of Maggie Smith.

To MAGGIE SMITH

27 January 1975

My dear Mags,
Had to go up to Manchester for this television show called 'Password'. There was a train accident so we were all shoved on the aeroplane instead. At Heathrow, I met the others, Moira Lister, Tony Britton, and Yootha Joyce.[1] Moira said she had known Bev years ago – 'Oh! he was so good looking my dear! that lovely skin! – I really rather fancied him, but of course he married that Princess from the Cocos Islands and I didn't have a chance . . . actually I was left a map by an old pirate . . . it shows the location of the treasure which is buried in one of the caves in the Cocos Islands . . . I must get hold of Bev and a geiger counter and we could go out there and find it . . . shouldn't be too difficult because there can't be THAT many caves out there . . .' On the plane, she was handing round photographs of her huge villa in the South of France with the inevitable vast swimming pool etc. 'Any time you are out that way, you must come and visit me' as if it were the sort of journey you did as a commuter or something. I sat with Yootha Joyce. She was clenched in the seat like a terrified mute and admitted to being scared of aeroplanes. I said 'They have the lowest accident rate of any transport' and she said that was no consolation to her. She told me she was in a series called 'Man About The House' – 'it is doing very well in the ratings and of course they have had to up the money to get us all back for the next series . . . it is ITV not BBC . . . so I am surprised the BBC have asked me to appear in this "Password" show . . . after all, I do work for the opposition . . .' When the hostess or stewardess or whatever you call her came along, she ordered a large brandy and was obviously enjoying it when they suddenly announced the descent for landing (the journey is very short) and she had to leave half of it, put the fag out and fasten the safety belt. We got to the Manchester studio by midday. When it came to the run through I was surprised to find that the old casting was altered. Eleanor Summerfield[2] used to chair it,

---

[1] Actors, usually in light comedy: Lister, b.1923; Britton, b.1925. Joyce, successful actress in TV sitcom, died in 1980. The Coroner's verdict on the fifty-three-year-old star of 'George and Mildred' was that she died of chronic alcoholism. A liver specialist, Dr Iain Murray-Lyon, gave evidence to the effect that Miss Joyce 'had been drinking half a bottle of spirits a day for ten years, and recently very much more'. Murray-Lyon treated KW in the last two years of his life.
[2] Character actress and comedienne, b.1921.

and now it is a girl called Esther Rantzen.[1] She was nervous and had sloppy diction. Eventually they let the audience in – mainly geriatric – and we started. Everything went wrong. There were about six false starts and stops. The machines for clocking up the scores all went haywire, someone got the dialogue wrong, I was stopped for cheating (perfectly ridiculous) and the retakes were endless. Luckily we made the plane all right, and Yootha settled down to another double brandy and I heard more excerpts from the biography 'I was in Fings Ain't Wot They Used To be . . . but the really happy days were in rep . . . you felt you were really achieving something . . .' I thought of Edith Evans' line 'How touching' but said nothing. The searching, going on and coming off the aircraft, was very thorough. The security men feel your legs and crotch and everything. I said to Yootha 'if we hang round here long enough we could all get very worked up' and she told me that they were squeezing her tits 'as if they were inflatable'. Well I have got to start writing this column I do for the Radio Times[2] so I will have to stop. I suppose that by the time you receive this, you will have opened in New York[3] – the city which you don't really like – and I hope that you will have an enormous success . . . whatever you want . . . but I don't think you should stay away from England too long . . . after all, home is where the heart is . . . somewhere in your heart . . . a late lark singing . . .

> love from your old chum,
> [K]

To MAGGIE SMITH and BEVERLEY CROSS[4]

1 February 1975

My dear Mags and Bev,
When I went in to see Louie this morning she said 'Have you heard the news on the wireless? Richard Wattis collapsed in a restaurant last night and died in hospital afterwards.' I was staggered cos I had seen him at the Terry Theobald party just before Christmas and he was looking fine. Later on, the BBC telephoned and asked me to speak about him on radio tonight. I said 'Why don't you get Hattie? – she and Eric Sykes did the series with Dickie Wattis' and they said

[1] Mrs Desmond Wilcox, b.1940. TV presenter, producer, campaigner.
[2] KW wrote a regular 'Preview' column for the *Radio Times*, 1974–7.
[3] In Noël Coward's *Private Lives*.
[4] They married in 1975.

'Yes well Hat's not the best interviewee in the world' and I went along and did it. I suddenly thought – why do they all connect us? – after all, I didn't know Dickie all THAT well, and often we didn't see each other for months on end. I knew at that Christmas party that he wasn't SUPPOSED to be drinking. Apparently his doctor had said he should give it up, but Dickie had simply switched to wine – 'O my dears, one must have something!' and I recalled Lauren Bacall saying 'I have never met a man that was interesting who didn't drink' and I sympathised. One taxi driver told me 'He often comes round the cabmen's caff about three in the morning! He just sits there and chats! He can't half jaw that bloke! Told us that he had insomnia all the time' and none of it surprised me. This has been a period for dying I think. Only a week ago it was John Gregson[1] and John Slater[2] and they were on the SAME DAY. O yes, and the Duke of Norfolk too. He's gone. Always remember that interview he had on the television with Dimbleby. The latter had eulogised about the picture gallery at Arundel and said 'How much are all these paintings actually worth?' and Norfolk drawled 'Mind your own business' and the camera had to follow as he moved away to another part of the castle, with Dimbleby following quickly and rather embarrassedly. Well I must stop now cos it is time for me to go out now. It is a lovely evening. No doubt of that.

Warm embraces to you two lovelies,
⌊K⌋

To MAGGIE SMITH and BEVERLEY CROSS

10 February 1975

My dear Mags and Bev,
I went with Rona to the Equity[3] meeting at the Cambridge because there had been a great appeal to the moderates to attend and stop the Communists introducing a motion to stop the use of the postal vote and the referendum. Roland Culver got a big laugh with 'Some of you here today have written yourself longer speeches than you would ever get in a theatre' . . . Elspeth March was sitting on the aisle surrounded by picnic paraphernalia – 'I have got enough here to feed an army my dear, have some home-made paté!' and she had flasks

---

[1] Leading man in British films of the fifties (b.1919).
[2] Character player, on stage, films and TV (b.1916).
[3] British Actors' Equity, the union for actors, founded in 1929.

of coffee & everything – 'I am with Ambrosine Philpotts but she's gone to the loo . . . how are you my dear? Have you heard from Maggie? She has had wonderful notices in New York you know! It has been a triumph!' and Emlyn Williams was behind her smiling benignly & looking as if he found the proceedings as intriguing as the Moors Murder[s].[1] Michael Denison said that people should remember that it was stars who had formed Equity in the first place and mentioned 'dear old Marie Tempest'[2] and an elderly gentleman called William Mollison rose and thundered 'Marie Tempest was not the founder!' and then there was a loud cry of 'fuck Marie Tempest' and someone else shouted 'and you too!' so it was all very elevated I can tell you. Then there was a motion that Provisional Members should be allowed to vote and the mover was unbelievable. 'Ar fink everyone in the feeyeta should av a say like in what we're doin' like an ar fink too many posh blokes like an all vat are avin like too much of a say in the runin of fings like . . .' he began to fade away as cries of 'O get off' and 'illiterate fool' were bawled at him, and he retreated muttering 'yeah well all right I just wanted my say like' and the motion fell to the ground. Edward de Souza came up and said I was looking marvellous and I replied 'really? well I don't feel it' and he said 'well you should' and Alfred Burke shouted 'How's Louie? Still in Marchmont Street?' right across the stalls. I went back with Rona to Hampstead where I reproved Gordon for not attending and he said 'O I hate all that union stuff' and I said 'You will hate it even more when the communists take over because people like you never attend!' and he said he'd got enough on his plate with lines to learn for 'Upstairs & Downstairs' and he is doing THAT play[3] with the RSC (no, I'm not superstitious but I don't like writing the name) and he certainly looks very tired these days. I went to Remenham on Saturday & the countryside was looking lovely and the cherry trees were in blossom but I ain't got room to go into all that on this airform so I send you lots of love my darlings – your old chum,

[K]

---

[1] About which he had written the book *Beyond Belief*.
[2] Dame Marie Tempest (1864–1942), elegant comedy actress.
[3] i.e. *Macbeth*.

To BEVERLEY CROSS

12 February 1975

My dear Beverley,
Your letter arrived this morning. I am delighted to hear about the great success Mags enjoyed on the opening night. It is balm to the hurt mind. The ego massage will do her a world of good. Had to go the entire way to the studio last night on foot, cos there wasn't a taxi in sight and it was raining, so I wasn't pleased. I got a newspaper (first time I have purchased one this year) and saw that Margaret Thatcher had won the Tory leadership. The headline was 'They All Love Maggie' and of course I thought your girl had won an Oscar or something. It will be a terrible blow to Norman Mills.[1] He can't stand Thatcher. He said 'Every time I hear that woman speak in those carefully modulated tones . . . ugh . . . it sends shivers down my spine.' I don't react that violently. Although she does rather tend to do the 'sweet reason' stuff softly and monotonously. Spreading light and joy from the top of a very moral Christmas tree. Shouldn't think Ted [Heath] will serve in her cabinet; and it will be a real sock in the eye for poor old bumble [Willie] Whitelaw.

The chairman of the radio show ('The Year in Question') was Sheridan Morley. He is the best chairman I have ever come across. He keeps it all bouncing along. First game was awful for me cos I didn't know ANY of the answers. The opposing team, Isobel Barnett and Terry Wogan, knew them all. They pushed the boat out afterwards and gave us sherry and some old sandwiches curling at the toes. That Stonehouse[2] came up in conversation and Isobel confessed that he had tried it on with her! – 'My dears I was judging the Miss Telephone of Great Britain contest when he was Postmaster General, and he kept on about giving me a lift home after the proceedings . . . of course I didn't dream! – though everyone was looking apprehensive as he bundled me away . . . then in the car he said he'd got this little pied a terre in Charles Street and would I care for a night cap . . . I had to lie very smoothly about friends awaiting me at my club . . . I suppose he was a snob to have picked on me; there were plenty of dolly birds about without a title' . . .

> love from your old chum,
> [K]

---

[1] KW's dentist.
[2] John Stonehouse (1925–88), former Labour Minister, disgraced after a business scandal and a faked suicide; died a few hours before KW.

To RAE HAMMOND

24 February 1975

Dear Rae,
It was kind of you to remember my birthday but judging from the hair recession in the mirror this morning, I think you had better ignore it next time. It seems that age is moving in very fast as far as I'm concerned; if it's not the teeth it is the back and if it's not the sinus it's the scalp. Heigh ho, if love were all, I would be lonely.[1] Thank you too for sending me the Leacock but I have already got it (in another form) so I will send it back to you because I know you value it, and will not want it wasted. Can't think what you mean about Nichols being 'sinister'!! Oh dear no. That is not the word I would apply to him at all. He is far too vulnerable and tender. You should see him with his children and with his wife. Lovely family. I think courage is the word for Peter; when I think of all the travail that has been meted out to him, from the period in London when I visited him in hospital when he had the collapsed lung, and thereafter for about ten years (during which he had the spastic child) he faced appalling adversity. We talked about you at great length and he was staggered when I told him that you were SIB and had been planted in the unit to ferret out the corruption.[2]

> your old chum,
> [K]

To MAGGIE SMITH

27 February 1975

Darling Mags,
I had dinner with Beverley last night at Peter Mario's and we had a marvellous evening. He was looking splendid, a good colour in the face and clear eyed, and in very good humour. I fell about when he told me the story of the theatre manager informing you about the impending demolition of the theatre, and your reply: 'find me a pick-

---

[1] 'If Love Were All', from Noël Coward's *Bitter Sweet* ('Heigho, if love were all, I should be lonely'.
[2] As Hammond hastened to explain to KW, he was never a spy for 'Stars in Battledress', but a member of Field Security (Intelligence Corps). He also made clear that it was not Nichols whom he considered sinister, but the magician in Nichols's play *Forget-Me-Not Lane*, a character based on Hammond – or at least on his act in the CSE troupe.

axe and I'll give you a hand.' And I heard the saga of the invalid chair
parked in the aisle, and the consequent rumpus. I said to Beverley
'the moment you leave, things start to go wrong.' Gloria was all over
Bev. When I booked the table, she said on the phone 'O isn't he a
dish?' and he was wearing this superb jacket made of cashmere and
she kept feeling the material and saying 'lovely and soft' and when
Bev told me the price I nearly choked over me campari. I said it looked
very sprauncy and Gloria and Romano began to giggle, and then
explained that, in Italian, that means shit[1] . . . I told B about Peter
Eade trying it on with the raising of the percentage. I said that I didn't
agree with the principle and that I thought it established a dangerous
precedent. Eade then retreated and said that it would stay at ten
percent. B said 'You were quite right to take that attitude' which
pleased me greatly, and I enlarged on the subject – 'yes well you see,
it is all a TRY ON . . . they tell you the costs have gone up and how
the VAT takes half the morning, but seem to forget that MY COSTS
have gone up as well.' I had to go down to the BBC Bristol studio
to do this literary quiz thing, and the chairman was Patrick Kavanagh
– there is a very good poem of his in the Larkin Oxford Book of
English Verse (and a very good one by Coward too, in that volume)
– and when I talked about this to Beverley, he said 'I know him. We
were in a play together', it was extraordinary. One of the excerpts
which was read out in this quiz was a speech of Christoforou from
'Public Ear & the Private Eye'[2] and so I launched into an account of
how Shaffer never had a final curtain till you suggested the business
of the sour grapefruit and the search for the sugar, on the final lines.
I said 'She has a genius for strengthening comedy by linking it with
idiosyncrasy' and they all nodded sagely. Apparently, this Kavanagh
fellow wrote a brilliant book about his marriage to Sally Lehman[3]
who died tragically young. He looked as though he'd had his share
of tears. Beverley made me laugh when he said you had to grapple
with nail files and things, to open the air mail forms of mine! It
conjured up a vision of you plunging about! O I loved it. Terribly
funny. The weather here is being superb. Sun all day and mild air.
Masses of daffodils in Regent's Park which makes you think of Wordsworth . . . extraordinary when you think that it was HIS poetry that

[1] They must have had in mind 'stronzi', meaning 'turds'.
[2] Properly The Public Ear and The Public Eye, the Peter Shaffer plays, starring Maggie
Smith and KW, from 1962. KW did not recognise the speech read out, which had
been his own.
[3] Sally Philipps (d. 1958). P.J. Kavanagh's book was The Perfect Stranger (1966).

got John Stuart Mill OUT of his horrific depression and put some meaning back into his life.

    love from your old chum,
    [K]

To RICHARD PEARSON[1]

29 February 1975
I mean 1st March of course!

My dear Richard,
I was staggered to receive your letter because it seems ages ago that I wrote to you, and I had assumed that mail was not being received, or that you had moved to some other location. If my letter took a fortnight, I just hope that Pat has better luck. I read a piece in the paper about Mona Washbourne[2] talking about the film and she certainly made it sound like an experience one never wants to repeat. I must say, the idea of you bringing tit bits to her from the canteen made me laugh, though I think it's a bit much, her going on about 'indignities' I mean, she isn't the Queen Mother or anything is she? Well I think that Mags hearing from you and me, plus Bev being in New York, did the trick. She had a triumphant reception with flowers from the auditorium nightly, and waiters fawning and genuflecting in all the restaurants. Of course she never writes letters, but Bev came over last week – 'I have got to work on this script for Charlie Schneer who is doing this science fiction picture; he wants his monsters motivated . . .' and he told me all about Mags being apprehensive about NY. The original intention had been to play Los Angeles and one or two other towns and then go to Toronto and finish, but it was so astonishingly successful everywhere that they persuaded Mags to agree to NY and then she went back on it. There were endless phone calls to the agent – & 'get me out of it' etc., but Bev calmed it all down, got her there, and the rest was fine. Honestly Richard, Bev looks just the same as he did when we were all in the Shaffer plays. He talked at length about his children (two daughters by the first marriage to that princess in the Cocos Islands and the boy by Gayden

---

[1] Character actor (b.1918) who had appeared in the Shaffer plays (1962), and whose wife (Pat) and children were also friends of KW's. Pearson was then filming in Leningrad with Olivier and Katharine Hepburn, in *Love Among the Ruins* (made by George Kukor for TV).
[2] A senior character actress of the day (b.1903).

whom he has just divorced) and said what a job it was about the education etc. He sighed and said 'Yes, we do all this for our children . . . and is it worth it? – they get married, or hitch up with someone, go off, and forget it . . .' Yes, sad about Dickie Wattis. It is all happening. Dick Crossman's son hanged himself. And Dennis Goodwin (used to work with Bob Monkhouse remember?) was found dead yesterday. They said a letter and pills were found by the bed. Police rule out foul play. He was only 44. Tony Whitby (Controller Radio 4), who was very kind to me, died of cancer. He was 44. It's been quite a year for death. Mags did 'Travels With My Aunt' with Cukor and said he was nice. He wanted her to do something about Virginia Woolf. I should mention it all to him. Makes for conversation doesn't it? I mentioned it to Bev. He said 'I think all that Virginia Woolf stuff is dreary . . . I think she was a dreary cow . . .' and I said 'Yes so do I . . .' Love from your old chum,

|K|

To RAE HAMMOND[1]

5 March 1975

Dear Rae,
. . . I always remember Woodings[2] addressing us before we left for Burma and saying 'You are going on the toughest assignment in SEAC . . .' The burden of his speech was that it was going to be tough, not only because of the nature of the country, but because ENSA had been FREE but now, CSE was charging fourpence a show and the troops resented it. Thinking back on it, one can hardly blame them. As to the inscribing of names![3] – seems that I did it on everyone's gear – I honestly don't remember writing yours – mind you, I was a bit taken aback when Peter Nichols told me that I had done HIS. I have always thought of myself as a selfish sod and little given to acts of helpfulness or consideration for others. Incidentally, do you remember Arlen[4] coming backstage somewhere we were never

---

[1] Hammond at this time was helping Peter Nichols recall details of the CSE period for his play *Privates on Parade*.

[2] Major Woodings, who met new CSE personnel at the docks and oversaw their performance in the company, terminating some entertainment careers with the dread notice 'R.T.U.' (Returned To Unit).

[3] KW's calligraphic skills were in demand for the drawing of posters and, evidently, for the marking of kit.

[4] Albert Arlen, CSE producer, who predicted a successful professional career for KW.

expecting him to be, and telling us all that we had disobeyed orders by not wearing the forage caps in the opening chorus? – we had left them all off, cos we hated wearing the bloody things anyway. I think it was Rangoon, and we never thought he would come all that way. I think he did it by Sunderland Flying Boat. That was how Baxter arrived in Singapore, alongside a load of VIPs. I saw him last year, in a restaurant. He was going on about all his illnesses and kept muttering 'it is as though the room was going round' and I said I was sick of the hypochondria and he took offence. Haven't seen it since. Did you know there was a Captain Ohms at CSE Neesoon? He came to the docks and met me when I was posted to CSE from Ceylon (I had sailed from Colombo) and he had this car waiting. He said 'What do you do?' and I said 'Impersonations' and he said, very tiredly, 'They'll be getting performing seals next.' When he was demobbed, he changed his name from Ohms to Vaughan. Peter Vaughan. He married Billie Whitelaw. They have since separated though, cos she's now married Robert Muller. He used to be a paper critic but has since tried to do playwrighting I believe. Ah well, they all do, don't they? I noticed, when Peter Nichols got his album out, there were loads of him and Les Wilson taken together. I think they did some sort of double act when I left on the Devonshire. We did a song about the Devonshire. There was a bit about 'The ship's M.O. blows through the keyhole every half an hour, in Devon, glorious Devonshire . . .' It was done as a sort of Western Brothers parody. Or is it Weston Brothers. Yes, I fancy it is.[1] The other marvellous thing which Peter & I laughed over: the opening chorus originally ran: 'We're boys of the service' and Woodings told Arlen it was all too sibilant and poofy and to change it to MEN of the service. So we all came on singing: 'We're men of the service' instead. Didn't make a blind bit of difference, but Woodings cried out 'Ah! – there! – now, that's more LIKE it!'

> your old chum,
> [K]

---

[1] No it isn't: Western Brothers was correct, and KW's CSE partnership, Hammond reminded him, called itself the Far Eastern Brothers.

To RAE HAMMOND

10 March 1975

Dear Rae,
How on earth do you remember all their names? As for 'Theirs is the Glory' . . . oh! yes, I remember Geoff Deakin doing all that 'Ye mariners of England who guard our native seas . . .' and Baxter doing something that ended 'R.A.F., the Royal Air Force, Britain kneels, in pledge to you . . .' And the pause after pledge was long, with the last two words spoken very dramatically. I told him I thought it was very hammy & he said that the whole tableau was anyway. My piece was something about El Alamein. Arlen was mad about that. He wrote the El Alamein Concerto; I think he thought it was going to enjoy the same success Addinsell had with the Warsaw[1] but alas there was no Anton Walbrook to push that image in Singapore . . . So you see nothing really changes. Schopenhauer was quite right. Only the FORM but never the content. The sceptic finds refuge in irony, and camp is the JUNIOR version. I telephoned Peter Nichols on Sunday. He said his work was coming on apace and that you had been wonderfully helpful. I said 'I don't know how he remembers it all . . . I really don't.'

> Your old chum,
> [K]

To ANDREW RAY

29 March 1975

Mon cher Andrew,
I have started the film. It is called 'Carry On Behind'. The trailer is 'we gave you loving, we gave you Dick, and now we give you Behind' and ostensibly the title is apropos the towing of the caravan. We are supposed to be on an archaeological dig. Of course it is really an excuse to do anything which is similar to Carry On Camping cos that was a money spinner. They've got this girl called Elke Sommer. The driver said to me 'We had to go out to London Airport and meet her; they were all there, Peter Rogers in his Rolls, Gerald Thomas in his Jensen, the press, the red roses and the boxes of chocolates, the lot. She came off the plane and they all took these photographs of her

---

[1]   Richard Addinsell's most famous composition was the 'Warsaw Concerto', featured in the wartime film *Dangerous Moonlight*.

and there was all this bally hoo but I saw nothing in any of the papers about it.' I said 'Well of course not. She isn't news. The only thing in a Carry On that is news is ME. They don't want to know about some Kraut they've brought over. They don't want foreigners in these films anyway. They are always disaster. When they had Phil Silvers he didn't understand a word of the idiosyncratic dialogue.' When I saw Gerald Thomas I twitted him: 'all that trouble you went to, and for that German girl, and not one paper printed it!' and he said defiantly 'O yes they did! it was in Cine Weekly!' as if that were a paper! O it is pathetic. Nothing alters at Pinewood. Still the same old crowd at the bar. Trevor Howard down there (on this musical 'Tom Jones') and stoned out of his mind. Two of them were holding him up in the corridor. He doesn't know what time it is. The driver said 'I begged him to sit in the back of the car but he insists on sitting in the front. He is so pissed he keeps falling forward and banging his head on the windscreen . . .' On the set, the publicity people (reeking of whisky) bring on various journalists — 'we want to write about the funny things that happen when you are making these films. What are you really like . . . as people?' and Connor says 'bleeding tragic mate' and walks away to chat to the electricians he finds far more interesting.

You say in your letter 'You can't keep an indigenous population down by force' and then you add, 'I know we argue on this subject.' Oh no, we don't. I am in complete agreement with you on this issue. Vietnam and Northern Ireland are both tragic examples of the truth in your postulation. Yes the Whites in South Africa — Oh! all these dreary expatriates living it up at the expense of other people . . . they make me sick. O! the ego of it all! Love from your old chum,

   [K]

To CONSTABLE J. DENNEY (Muswell Hill Police Station)

7 May 1975

Dear Constable Denney,
It was good of you to send the photograph of me with the children at the presentation ceremony.[1] So often, people say they will let you see the pictures, and then promptly forget about it. I don't know if I told you but my flat was burgled on the 22nd April, and curiously, they took travellers' cheques and four pairs of shoes. After leaving

---

[1]   It's not clear what activity this ceremony was celebrating, but KW attended another one later in the summer, when prizes were given for road safety.

Muswell Hill on the 25th, I had a call from the CID at Albany Street asking me to go round to identify some shoe trees! they were the same make, but alas, not mine. I flew to Malta the next day and in the market at Valletta I got a pair of sandals for £1.50 and a nice pair of blue socks. I was congratulating myself on these bargains till I found (when I undressed for bed) that the dye from these cheap socks had turned my feet blue. I've heard of Tories, but this is ridiculous.

Sincerely yours,
Kenneth Williams

To STEPHEN GRIFFIN[1]

Peter Eade Ltd,
9 Cork Street,
London W1X 1PD
8 May 1975

Dear Stephen,
Write to Spotlight at 42/43 Cranbourn Street, London WC2H 7AP and ask for their booklet called 'Contacts'. It's probably best to ring them first and ask the price, so that you can send the money with your letter. The book contains a list of all the provincial repertory theatres and their directors. You have to write to all of them and say you want to be an ASM (Assistant Stage Manager) with a view to becoming an actor. I always said 'I want a job as ASM with small parts'. In all your applications you are supposed to send a photograph and details of any acting work or theatrical experience like school productions or amateur companies. 'Contacts' also has the list of all Television and Radio production centres and you must write to them as well. I was told to 'pester everybody'. You say that you reject the idea of a Drama School. I wonder if that is wise. By mixing with a lot of aspiring actors you might learn a lot. If you have second thoughts on this try writing to Hugh Cruttwell, The Royal Academy of Dramatic Art, Gower Street, London WC1 and ask for an interview. They may ask for auditions — all these sources — so it is best to have a couple of speeches up your sleeve which you can take from any parts you would particularly like to play. I always used to do Enobarbus's barge speech till Laurence Olivier pointed out that the role was for a big man and I would never be offered such a part. After that, I did bits from Feste, or Puck. I got my first job in rep by putting an advert in the Stage

---

[1] An aspiring actor.

newspaper. I did AS Ming and small parts in Newquay Repertory Theatre, in Cornwall. I thought it was best to make all my mistakes Outside London. I spent about seven years going round the various reps. I think I learned most when I graduated to the better theatres like York (when then linked with Scarborough) and Birmingham. The only provincial theatre I have visited recently was the Everyman at Cheltenham. They do very good work, and keep a remarkably high standard.

Most people will speak discouragingly about your desire to make the theatre your career because of the deplorable state of an industry in which only about 20% are gainfully employed during the whole year. There is only a small number of actors (outside the star range) who actually manage to PAY THEIR WAY. Most of them have a spare time occupation which they practise when they are out of work. I know one actor who does Mini Cab driving. I know another who is an upholsterer. Both of them are talented and both of them cannot earn a living from the theatre.

None of this deters the egomaniac who wants to act. He confidently asserts at every interview that he is a potential genius, and, if he convinces the prospective employer, this latter imagines that he WILL be able to assert himself on a stage and that he will hold the audience's attention and he gives him a job.

> Yours sincerely,
> Kenneth W.

To D.M. DALY (MRS)

16 July 1975

Dear Sir [sic],
Thank you for your letter regarding the honorary presidency of the Saints Youth Club. I am sensible of the compliment you pay me, but I have to decline. If I agreed to these sorts of requests my name would be on more notepaper than you've had hot dinners. It is a rule of my life that [I] belong to no club or organisation of ANY kind. I bitterly resent being forced to join the Actors' Union. Nevertheless, if I can help you in any other way I shall do my best to comply. If you think my coming along one evening to meet your members is a good idea, then write giving me a couple of dates, and correct address etc.

> Sincerely yours,
> [KW]

To BOB GRIMES[1]

30 July 1975

Dear Bob,

I was among a group of people entertaining some War Veterans yester-day; many were in wheel chairs and surgical appliances of some kind or another. The entire occasion was daunting, and one actress left because she was so overcome by the depression of it all. It certainly wasn't easy to be funny. During my spot, I think I heard all of two laughs in about six minutes. The evening was really intolerably hot and the sweat was pouring from the faces. When I got home, I had to change everything. I woke up this morning with the whole thing vivid in my memory and the morale was literally round the ankles, and then, among the letters on the doormat, I found your missive. I must have read it about three times. I was saying to myself 'this sort of thing doesn't happen by accident' because I don't think it does, and I suddenly remembered the last lines of a beautiful poem by Francis Meynell . . .

> . . . when your love's flight shall falter
> And fall like a wounded bird.
> You too cannot alter
> The said or unsaid word.
>
> So this is the sum of it, this
> Say not: 'it is not much'
> You cannot unkiss that kiss,
> You cannot untouch that touch.[2]

and I recalled how, in a period of grief, they were lines of enormous comfort to me. Of course it isn't given to us to know the extraordinary complexities and nuances which underlie affectionate relationships but even if we can offer no practical help, as Johnson says 'Heaven demands our tears . . .' and these have a reciprocity of their own. I am so glad that something of the work I've done on radio has afforded

---

[1] Mr Grimes, a freelance artist living in Kentucky, had written to thank KW for helping him to get over the death of his twelve-year-old daughter Laura in an accident. He and Laura had been in the habit of listening to PBS relays of 'Round the Horne', and hearing for the first time a broadcast of 'Just a Minute' had reminded him of Laura's pleasure in KW's voice.

[2] From 'Tissue of Time', by Sir Francis Meynell (1891–1975, son of the poet Alice Meynell). Meynell's own Nonesuch Press edition of *Poems and Pieces* gives 'Shall fall, like a wounded bird' in the second line, and omits the quotation marks in the last verse.

you diversion; it was tremendously rewarding to read your words. I am not a writer so I cannot send you a book I have written. I contribute the odd piece for the Radio Times but it is largely professional and esoteric. Certainly none of my friends seem to be aware of it (though they all buy the publication) and I'm beginning to wonder if it's worth bothering about. Humour is something we have to cling on to. Chesterton said that the man who maintained 'Faith is nonsense' would find, if he thought about it long enough, that 'nonsense is faith' and I know what he means. It is the same motivation in the Shavian correspondence, when Ibsen wrote despairingly 'What if life IS all without point or purpose . . . what if it is all a joke' and Shaw's reply: 'If it is, let's make it a good one . . .' Endless thanks to you for writing to me, for expressing such good sentiments, and for raising my spirits.

Sincerely yours,
[KW]

To VALENTINE ORFORD

29 August 1975

Dear Val,
Thank you for your letter;[1] yes, I agree about the disagreeable nature of this hot weather. It leaves me feeling exhausted. It is a good thing (in that sense) that I haven't got a lot of work to do. At the moment I am busy with scriptwriters and producers regarding the radio series[2] which begins in the autumn. It has been a bad period economically and I have had to cut down drastically as far as expenditure is concerned. You mention the programme about Homosexuality;[3] it was interesting because it pointed out that the law has NOT been changed to legalise homosexuality; the law has been changed only with regard to the co-habitation of men who are over 21. Even then, there is the anomaly of application to civilians but NOT members of the Forces, to Englishmen and Welshmen but NOT to Scotsmen. The position is ludicrous. As far as public places are concerned, the homosexual STILL has nowhere to go. It is illegal for men to dance together in

---

[1] Orford's letter was not in fact very welcome: 'there is one from Val Orford with AGAIN that withering patronage. "I'm afraid NONE of the things you said (in your last broadcast) stayed in my head . . ." One wonders "why bother?"' (KW's diary, 28 August.)
[2] 'Get on With it!' began recording in November.
[3] 'Homosexuality – The Years of Change', broadcast on 24 July 1975.

a public place, or show demonstrable affection. Of course it hasn't stopped men finding such places — clubs, sauna baths etc. — but the fact remains that these places get suddenly raided, and a number of people are arrested, and the same old persecutions go on and on. It is all a very sad business and of course it has given rise to a militant sort of protest which is represented by a movement like Gay Liberation — or Gay Lib as it's always called. These people believe in defiant demonstrations where they DELIBERATELY break the law: at one widely publicised Gay Ball, they had hundreds of men dancing together, tacitly inviting the police (who were present) to arrest ALL OF THEM. The police did not take the bait, but simply satisfied themselves that the proceedings did not 'get out of hand'. At the recent Gay Lib Conference in Sheffield (of all places!) the guest speaker was Angus Wilson, the novelist. Apparently he talked approvingly about his 25-year relationship with a man[1] — 'we are now celebrating our jubilee' — and encouraged the aims of their organisation.

The book you discuss by Paul Johnson[2] would not interest me. It sounds awful. That stuff about Charles the First is muck. Johnson is too much of a propagandist to be a good writer. There are political motives, of course, in say Tolstoy or Dickens, but both of them manage to transcend the polemical issue by constructing a WORK OF ART. Alas, this course is not open to Paul Johnson because his political enthusiasm is not accompanied by literary talent. No interpretation of the Stuart trouble is any use, unless there is a real understanding about the appalling inflation suffered under the Tudors (with Elizabeth ordering Gresham to reform the currency) and the comparative penury of the English monarchs. The dire necessity of something like the Ship Tax (for Charles) and the obstinate refusal of people like Hampden to pay it, is part and parcel of the dilemma. The Crown income had stayed fixed and feudal, while the wealth of the new merchant class, mercantile etc., was being colossally inflated. Maynard Keynes makes the interesting point that GREAT TALENT (Shakespeare for example) flourishes in times of PROFIT INFLATION. Of course, that is only part of the picture. The next thing one has to try and understand is the nature of the religious argument which so

---

[1] Sir Angus Wilson (1913–91) 'courageously revealed his homosexuality before it was common to do so, but was upset by the repercussions, particularly as they affected Tony Garrett. The latter had to leave his job as a probation officer when their relationship became known' (*The Annual Obituary*).
[2] Most probably *The Offshore Islanders* (1972), where Johnson's comments on the Stuarts ('set their faces against the whole dynamic trend of England's development' etc.) ran severely counter to KW's view.

preoccupied a man like Charles, and made him appoint someone like Laud to a position of such enormous power. It is very difficult for the modern intelligence to comprehend what is at stake here. (Stake is the word!) If one looks at the sort of argument which took place between Zwingli and Luther, one begins to see something of real significance concerning the DISPLACEMENT of the REAL to the MERELY SYMBOLICAL. From say: the Mass as a REAL and living experience to its celebration as a symbolic ritual, with no one BELIEVING in the idea of partaking of flesh and blood union with Christ, at all. As the REAL (real in the sense of spiritual and physical reality) got displaced by the SYMBOL so began the disassociation of sensibility and faith. They start to actually GO different ways, and centuries later you have Snow writing about TWO CULTURES and making a division between the Scientific (and supposedly Objective) Mind, and the Artistic (and supposedly subjective) Mind.[1] Much the same way that Forster sketches the two schools of thought in Howards End with the materialistic insensitivity of the Howards,[2] as opposed to the talent and generosity of the Schlegels. It follows all the way down, from this original collapse of REAL into SYMBOL, through Hölderlin, Kafka, to T.S. Eliot and the line – 'we have learned many words but LOST THE WORD . . .' again and again he returns to this theme. 'In the beginning was the word . . .' and 'words crack and break under the strain' and 'the endless search for the right words to say the thing which I no longer wanted to say . . .'[3] And now, this WEEK we have one of our most eminent scientists (Lovell) admitting that the claims made for science (in fact, for all the so-called Objectivity involved OUTSIDE of the Humanities) were fundamentally wrong.[4] The notion that science was neutral he showed was untenable. Of course it is. An atom doesn't SAY ANYTHING TO US but

[1] C.P. Snow, Baron Snow of Leicester (1905–80), novelist and critic. His Rede Lecture of 1959, 'The Two Cultures and the Scientific Revolution', argued that science and literary life were on diverging paths.
[2] Actually the Wilcoxes.
[3] 'Knowledge of words, and ignorance of the Word', from The Rock; 'In the beginning was the Word', from 'Mr Eliot's Sunday Morning Service'; 'words strain, crack and sometimes break, under the burden', from 'Burnt Norton'; 'Because one has only learnt to get the better of words/For the thing one no longer has to say, or the way in which/One is no longer disposed to say it', from 'East Coker' (Four Quartets).
[4] Sir Bernard Lovell, the radio astronomer of Jodrell Bank, had addressed the 137th annual meeting of the British Association for the Advancement of Science, saying: 'Exploration with spacecraft and ground-based radio telescopes seeking life on other planets might produce answers too overwhelming for the mind of people with an understanding limited to our small world' (Times report, 28 August 1975).

scientists (i.e. MEN) say something about the atom. And what they say is entirely Human, just as given to prejudice, bigotry, psychology, environment, politics, as ANY OTHER MAN. It may seem that I have strayed too far from the original contention about the Stuart Problem, but I think it's all bound up with this crisis of faith. The period shows CHARLES wrestling with revolutionary concepts of FAITH (Protest-antism) and POLITICS (a new class arising) with a bankrupt kingdom in a time of profit inflation, and he is a CHARLES who *believes* that the oil poured on his head at his coronation is HOLY and sanctifies his succession. He does not think it MERELY SYM-BOLIC. He thought that if it ever became that, it would be worthless, and the basic safeguards of ROYALTY (as opposed to Dictatorship) would be eroded. And, in fact, that is exactly what happened.

Only Faith could show that Truth and Goodness and Beauty are qualities OUTSIDE man. Man doesn't make the truth. God makes the truth. Man can come to know something of it, but he is Not its creator. If he COULD make his own truth we should have (for ever) to believe the lies of people as disparate as Adolf Hitler, and Genghis Khan; and both these people were mass murderers.

Once we dispensed with the Spiritual Truths of our Faith, we weakened it terribly, and gave rise to whole nations of emotional and intellectual cripples. Once we said 'we will keep the morality but we will do away with the Spiritual ethos surrounding it' we threw the baby away with the bathwater. The odd remnants that remain, and obstinately refuse to go away (like the Oath at the Trial, or the simple saying of Goodbye which means God Be With You) stay because LANGUAGE itself embraces certain deeply held convictions which no man made logic can attempt to describe. Such convictions are atavistic, and they are the expressions of Faith spoken in the very teeth of socialist materialism. They are heard in cries like 'God Help Me!' which come from all men when they are in deep distress; from the learned to the illiterate. They DON'T cry out for the Webbs, or Karl Marx, or Chairman Mao.

I agree with what you say about our present parlous state. The country seems to be actually voicing its despair. There is more crime, more drinking, more drug taking, more road and train disasters, more anarchy and terrorism . . . and now, hyper-inflation. And of course the worst hit (people on fixed incomes, the aged and the maimed) are mostly inarticulate. My mother said to me the other day 'Why are all these terrible things happening? . . . things weren't like this when I was a girl . . .' It is impossible to explain it all. She refers to the new currency as DISMAL MONEY. When told that she's speaking incorrectly and that, properly, it is DECIMAL MONEY, she replies 'it is still Dismal to me' and says that the pounds shillings and pence should never have been allowed to go. Heigh ho. She is 74 and, thank goodness, still unimpaired. Goes to her dancing club every week, and does the WVS voluntary work at the Hospitals. More energy than I've got!

> yours,
> [K]

To SARAH HAMSHERE[1]

17 September 1975

Dear Miss Hamshere,
The exact date of the dream is immaterial. The picture of the hotel and me sliding down the stairs is indicative of the morale falling to zero in alien surroundings, i.e. the flashy hotel is the world of entertainment. The fact that I was proceeding head first means that intellectual activity is the cause of my undoing and the facts would testify to that. The odd socks show a disregard for convention and a natural dichotomy; a being 'torn in two directions' so to speak.

   Thank you for writing to me, and for expressing such encouraging sentiments about my work.

> Sincerely yours,
> [KW]

To the EDITOR of *The Times*[2]

c/o Peter Eade,
9 Cork Street,
London W1
27 September 1975

Dear Sir,
There is something absurd about someone of my stature having to reply to your radio critic's cheap contumely about my work in 'Just A Minute', but pip squeak circus ponies masquerading as thoroughbreds

---

[1] A young fan from Harborne, Birmingham, who had written requesting explication of a dream she had had, featuring KW in the odd circumstances implied by his response.
[2] Carbon copy annotated by KW: 'Sent to Times. They replied. They didn't print it.'

seem to be part of the contemporary scene, and it is proper that someone should distinguish between the braying and neighing. Your writer appears to be confused. He says: 'We've all played "Just A Minute" in some form at a party for an evening'; this is news to me because I have not. He goes on to tell us: 'and gruesome fun it was; that's what it was meant for.' Indeed! It certainly leads us to question his definition of fun; it seems to have more in common with Sacher-Masoch than Ian Messiter.[1] But if we take him at his word, and accept that deliberately gruesome fun is possible, what are we to make of his complaint: 'we did not enjoy ourselves'? Judging from his dolorous description of the programme, he should have been having a ball. He has no conception of architecture because he maintains that I was playing to the gallery all the time; the Paris Studio has only one floor. Albeit, if he spoke metaphorically, and meant that I was continually appealing to the commonalty, he should have said so plainly, and reported the fact that they found it amusing, which is more than you can say about Mr Wade's column. There is little excuse for him: he is a writer. The player in 'Just A Minute' is a speaker, and extempore at that. The difference between writing and conversation has been described by Johnson thus: 'Remotely we see nothing but spires of temples and turrets of palaces . . . but once we have passed the gates, we find it perplexed with narrow passages, disgraced with despicable cottages, embarrassed with obstructions, and clouded with smoke.' If your critic doesn't like the cottages, the obstructions and the smoke, he should leave them to those who do. There are many of them; they can be found in the audience at 'Just A Minute', they are the reason for the transcription sales overseas, they can be heard in Britain round that parish pump which Mr Wade professes so much to admire.

> yours faithfully,
> Kenneth Williams

To ANDREW HATHAWAY

21 October 1975

Dear Andrew,
Got your letter of the 15th October today. You say 'Roger Bacon is the only name that comes to mind' as a likely collaborator with Shakespeare. He'd have had to extend his life several hundred years to do so. Roger Bacon is thirteenth century (Shakespeare is in the

---

[1] Prolific adaptor and inventor of parlour games for radio and TV.

sixteenth). He was in the Franciscan Order; he wrote something which they considered rather shocking and they shoved him into prison. He seems to have languished there for an unconscionable time. I really don't know very much about him, except that he invented the Magnifying Glass.

I think you really meant Francis Bacon. Lovely writer of extraordinary pull. Take the following passage from his essay OF RICHES: 'I cannot call riches better than the baggage of virtue. The Roman word is better, impedimenta. For as the baggage is to an army, so is riches to virtue. It cannot be spared nor left behind, but it hindreth the march; yea, and the care of it sometimes loseth or disturbeth the victory.'

It is a superb passage; the line about riches hindering the march is wonderfully apt. It reverberates in the memory. We do well to ponder the outpourings of great minds on such weighty subjects.

Daphne du Maurier has got a new book out,[1] about Francis Bacon's brother, Anthony. Apparently he was homosexual. He certainly looks very handsome. He and his brother carried out various diplomatic tasks for Essex, and when that foolish Earl fell from grace, and Elizabeth put him to death, the Bacon brothers both suffered in the process. I had thought vaguely of buying the du Maurier book, then, I saw the price and thought 'do me a favour!' which is a cockney expression signifying 'this is an untenable and unacceptable position' or 'I don't wish to know' and can be very useful on occasion; especially to puncture pomposity. I have been very busy reading over a hundred and fifty essays by children for a Television Competition at the BBC. The winning entries actually get read on TV by professional actors. It has been an exhausting task, and there is a depressing sameness in their themes. There is always some castle and a wicked knight, or a dragon, or a prince, or a lonely princess. But of course, I am wrong to decry this. If children think these things up, there must obviously be a need for them. I suppose the modern world has starved the romantic imagination. The result of starvation is stunted growth. Trouble is, it's easier to recognise it MENTALLY or perhaps I should say, Spiritually. That's what it comes down to, in the end. Finally, man is dealing with Faith . . . yours ever,

[K]

---

[1] *Golden Lads: A Study of Anthony Bacon, Francis and Their Friends.*

To WILLIAM McRAE

27 October 1975

Dear Mr McRae,
You have written to me about a broadcast called 'Year in Question'[1]
in which you attribute to me remarks which I never made.

I did NOT say that the Stone of Scone was nicked by Scottish
Nationalists. I did not say ANYTHING about the Scottish Nationalists.
I have never mentioned the Scottish Nationalists in public in my life.

I do not use the word 'nicked'. I believe it is slang for STOLEN. If
I thought that thieves had been at work anywhere, I would say (in
speaking of it) that they had stolen something. I would never say that
they had 'nicked' something.

Since you appear to be in legal practice I am surprised that you
should commit rash accusations to paper, without having first satisfied
yourself as to the accuracy of the allegations.

I suspect you are confusing me with Gordon Clough.[2] He was next
to me on the panel, and DID speak on the subject; I did NOT.

Since you seem to be concerned about authenticity I should telephone Broadcasting House (if I were you) so you can have these facts
substantiated,

    [KW]

To BARBARA[3]

1 November 1975

Dear Barbara,
... Got your letter of the 27th yesterday. You are one of the few
correspondents who uses the first class stamp. And WHAT NEWS
YOU CONVEY. Getting married indeed. And you drop it quite casually! I was staggered. Had to have the fag and a glass of Andrews and
then re-read the whole thing. You had better get someone to tell HIM
that he is very lucky to be getting you. Get them to lay it on thick. It
would not look right coming from you cos they would think it big
headed. Well of course you are right about marriage being an invasion
of privacy but then that is what sharing is about. Apart from love in
the high romantic sense of the word, most people marry because it's

---

[1] A quiz show.
[2] b.1934, writer and broadcaster, especially on current-affairs topics.
[3] A correspondent in Hull, otherwise unidentified.

the sort of thing that 'everybody else does and I don't want to be left out' or because they simply do not like the idea of living alone. Solitude is all very well if you can express it as superbly as Duke Ellington but for most of us it's just miserable. Most men are clever enough to see that the economics are in their favour: the wife does everything from laundering, cleaning, cooking, child-bearing and breeding, to mending the fuses and being a counsellor. Most men know which side their bread is buttered, but few of them are willing to acknowledge it. The great unanswerable (for the man) used to be 'I provide the income' but nowadays, a lot of wives are providing a considerable amount of income themselves . . . Incidentally, you hear a lot of criticism about the NHS, but I was put down for the operation in March, seen by the surgeon in May, and given the bed in October. The service and attention throughout was superb. I don't think anyone can complain about that, do you?

> [K]

To GILLIAM FROOM (Social Secretary, Students' Association, Royal College of Music)

20 November 1975

Dear Gillian Froom,
Thank you for your kind letter,[1] but I never appear outside the professional media. The cabaret series on television was a simulated affair by the BBC with an invited audience; it had nothing to do with the public. I have never acted in real cabaret in my life. I should die of fright.

> sincerely yours,
> [KW]

To KATHLEEN E. RITCHIE[2]

20 November 1975

Dear Miss Ritchie,
For a broadcast called 'The Time of My Life' the BBC made available their archive recording of King George VI speaking on Christmas Day.

[1] Inviting KW to perform at the college's May Ball.
[2] A radio listener in Aberdeen, asking for identification of the quotation specified by KW.

I had particularly wanted this recording because it included an excerpt from a beautiful passage which he quoted from Minnie Haskins.[1] It had a profound effect on me, when I first heard it, and somehow, every Christmas which comes round seems to re-affirm its message in my mind. I have typed out the passage for you, and hope that it answers the request in your letter.

> sincerely yours,
> [KW]

To DENIS GOACHER[2]

14 December 1975

My dear Denis,

I've been doing about three things at once and it's meant that I've been disorientated. Got all the dates wrong about when I'd written to you. I read your book again last night. 'Four Dead Friends' sent me spinning back over the years. Again and again, in my life, I have thought 'this is a fill-in, this temporary' only to find, afterwards: 'that was IT, mate! you're not getting it again.' Do you know what I mean? There was something of it in the Ackerley book 'My Father and Myself' – that endless turning down of what was thought second best, only to find at the end, there was nothing else. But that's not quite it. I remember talking to Robert Bolt once, and he said 'the trouble is we have got hindsight and we have got foresight; in the process we've buggered the present' and he talked about a dog rolling about on the grass in total abandonment to the moment, adding 'you can't do that, back of your mind you are thinking about the next week's rent or something'. I saw Michael Harald before he died. I was on the top of a bus. It was passing the Ivanhoe Hotel, and I saw him running from this huge motor-coach ushering in a load of tourists. I saw him quite clearly, and he looked emaciated.[3] Then I had the letter from Richard West telling me of his death. Another day, I was walking in the Inner Circle and suddenly a jeep stopped with a screech of

---

[1] From 'God Knows': 'I said to the man who stood at the gate of the year . . .'
[2] Actor, poet, later teacher, etc. For KW's introduction to Goacher, see letter to Erich Heller of 30 April 1952 (p. 22).
[3] '. . . a man called Wilson had rung to say that Michael Harald (Cotton) had died of cancer and was to be buried today. It was only a few months ago I saw him doing courier work in Gower Street' (KW's diary, 31 December 1970).

brakes and a lady leaned out calling me. She was in mackintosh and wellingtons and it was Margaret Vines![1] I could hardly believe it! At one point in my life I had this compulsion to break with the past, and I was perfectly foul to lots of old chums. I met Hugh Manning in a restaurant and he said 'it's been so long! we really must meet' and I said 'for what purpose?' and he stuttered something and I turned on my heel and left.

Do you remember that night at Museum Street when Hugh got into such a lather cos you said that an actor with no money should get the job in preference to the actor who had plenty? He went right off about talent being more important than economics. And that incredible night when John Vere started raving about queens being perfectly 'natural'! he was a riot. O he did make me laugh so much. That haughty indignance. In that Hancock episode where he played the Bishop, they none of them realised that HE was the real original in it. Not Tony. Well I don't agree with you about the poems.[2] I don't agree at all. D.H. Lawrence was right – 'the artist doesn't have to attend the lectures' – and there must be loads of examples of fine writing that has nothing to do with the sort of meticulous scholarship of which you speak. I haven't the ability to write about this kind of thing. I wish I had. But poetry begins as TELLING A STORY. That's what it's about. All the rest is variation and it may be extraordinarily complicated in its forms, but if it DEPARTS totally from that original concept, then the poetry isn't as good. Poetry should talk to US and tell us something. It shouldn't be talking to itself. It's got to interpret life for us. I don't want real life. I want the artist's vision of life. That's why the poem 'The End'[3] is so good. A lot of what you say about your early work is like a writer objecting to the childish nature of some diaries he kept when he was seven. The essence of them is being seven. I cannot explain. I know my collection is full of things which have colour and light. Story and illumination. Soon as I read them I wanted to say them. When I was rehearsing at those awful rooms the BBC have at Acton, I saw Gordon Jackson in the canteen. He said he had been lunching with the Queen the day before. When he congratulated Princess Margaret on Snowdon's documentary about midgets – 'The Little People' – she replied 'not my cup of tea at all.

[1] Former partner of this letter's recipient.
[2] Goacher had shown his own poems to KW in the early days of their friendship, and continued to send newer ones. At this point, KW's opinion of them seems to have been higher than the poet's.
[3] One of Goacher's earlier poems, dated 1954.

Bit too near home I'm afraid' and he said 'I suddenly realised, they're all TINY! the Queen, and Margaret, and the mum . . . !'

> love,
> [K]

To BEVERLEY CROSS and MAGGIE SMITH

15 December 1975

My dear Bev and Mags,
. . . I have had this operation on my hand. My left. And I am left handed as you well know. It was agony. They removed a fibroid neuroma. My hand was in this elephantine bandage and sling for two weeks. You didn't even send me a get well card. I had it done on the National Health. It was dreadful. Communal ward, and all these men in the other beds shouting the odds – 'Carry on Kenny!' and 'How's your bum chum?' and other ribaldries.

When I recovered in the post-operative ward, I was laughing uncontrollably. Totally without mirth. Just an endless daft cackle. All the rest were looking bemusedly at the bed. I couldn't stop at all. Went on for over an hour. Eventually a surgeon came and said 'you've had too much nitrous oxide' and I was given another injection and that quietened me down. It was quite an experience NOT to get a bill on the departure I can tell you! Everything done for nothing. Tomorrow I've got the dentist. There's always something. Love,

> [K]

To HENRY FENWICK (*Radio Times*)

8 January 1976

Dear Henry,
Thank you for your letter which came this morning. Yes, it is odd, my using 'indignance' instead of indignation;[1] I think it's because I think of the former plurally and the latter individually. On the other hand, I use malignity rather than malignant or malignance. Johnson uses malignity, it has a good sound to it. Quite a scene last night at dinner, when an actor spoke of Greene's having written 'The

---

[1] In his 'Preview' column. Neither 'indignance' nor 'indignation' appears in the piece Fenwick was editing, though, oddly enough, KW had recently used 'indignance' in his letter to Denis Goacher of 14 December 1975.

Complacent Lover' and I said there was no such play. 'What do you mean?' he cried, 'I saw it!' and when I said that he'd seen 'The Complaisant Lover' he asked 'what's the difference?' and the rest accused me of pedantry. I am back from Tenerife on the 25th January all being well.

yours,
[K]

To the Hon. GEORGE BORWICK

8 January 1976

Mon cher George,
I finish the radio series[1] on Friday and that leaves me with practically everything free, so am taking Louie to the Canaries for a fortnight . . . I had this letter from John Bratby[2] saying that he'd painted Alec Guinness and Lord Thomson and now he wants to do me. When I mentioned it to Gordon, he said 'Well! that is a great compliment' but I heard that when Bratby did Margaret Thatcher she was furious with the result and cried out 'Where have my blue eyes gone?' and answer came there none. We had a great shindig at the Odeon Marble Arch for the opening of Carry On Behind. I was pleased with the screening cos (apart from the grey hair) I came out of it very well, and there are some very funny moments in it. Kenny Connor is hilarious as a randy old colonel who can hardly walk cos of the hard-on; I fell about. I have had a tremendous response to the Christmas poetry broadcast I did.[3] There have been loads of letters to answer, and many queries about sources . . .

[K]

---

[1] 'Get on With it!'
[2] John Bratby, RA (1928–92) painted KW on 4 October 1976. He offered the portrait to KW for £350, but KW claimed he couldn't afford it. He later saw it at an exhibition of unsold Bratbys in Bristol, priced at £500.
[3] In 'Woman's Hour', 23 December 1975 ('Christmas Anthology: Kenneth Williams with his own selection of seasonal music and poetry'.

To MAGGIE SMITH and BEVERLEY CROSS

28 January 1976

My darling Mags and Beverley,

Funny me protesting about not hearing from you! cos you wrote on January 19th, and I was away! Went to Tenerife with Louie. Got back on the 27th. Hateful to have to put up with cold London after the languorous heat of the Canaries. I had a marvellous fortnight at Puerto de la Cruz. Most of the people in the hotel had the children with them and we used to lark about by the pool and I played badminton with them and clock golf and it was riotous. I was exhausted at the end of the days. But O aren't they marvellous? When Children look at you and tell you something confidential, it's almost heartbreaking. When one little boy put his hand on my wrist and said 'I wish you were my daddy' I had to talk very quickly indeed to keep my countenance and remain self-possessed. I know what you mean about not being able to get it into your head – the idea – that you are going to WORK. I am planning this Feydeau[1] at the moment, and I can't really believe I am going back into the theatre. Helen Montagu at Tennent's is being very kind and understanding and Christopher Hampton has done a very good translation and Patrick Garland is directing, so it should be all right, but it seems a bit too good to be true. We still haven't found the mother in law. Physically it's Hattie Jacques, and orally it's Martita Hunt. Where do you find it? I ask you? The picture you draw of Bev trying to write while children hurtle about made me smile! I think he could write on a railway station. Keats did Endymion in a coffee house. And I don't mean the Kardomah. Do you realise I shall be fifty shortly? it don't seem right does it? O yes, my hand. I had it done at the Orthopaedic at Gt. Portland Street, so I only had to walk over the road. All lovely now. You can hardly see the scar. I had the best peripheral surgeon in Europe. All for nothing! Lots of love,

[K]

---

[1] *Signed and Sealed*, with KW as Barillon.

To ANDREW HATHAWAY

29 January 1976

Dear Andrew,

Apropos your question about nadgers,[1] well, I shouldn't think they exist, but the words occur in a song which was recorded on a disc entitled 'The Best of Rambling Syd' which was largely a lot of rubbish satirising the flok – sorry – folk song. I think the idea is that you put your own interpretation on the sound of the words. Now I come to think of it, the Rambling Syd record is published in USA by something called STANRECORDS or something like that; it is a company under the banner of Rod McKuen, the song writer, singer and poet. But in the USA the record is not called 'The Best of Rambling Syd'. It is called something else. I can't remember what. It came out ages ago. Somewhere around '67 I imagine. Yes, I know all about the Goons and was an enthusiastic admirer of the radio series. It represents a mile stone in anarchic humour, and so much of it is ephemeral so it couldn't last. A lot of the jokes are esoteric, and in any case, the idiom is so thoroughly English that I shouldn't think it would translate well. In one programme there was a voice thundering MORE BROWN POWER at regular intervals. People thought it was a reference to negroes but when I met Harry Secombe he told me it was simply about farting – or breaking wind, as they put it in polite parlance. Then there was the sound of an explosion after a lavatory chain had been pulled, and an anguished voice crying NO MORE CURRIED EGGS FOR ME! All very English – they're obsessed by bums and tits and jokes about lavatories – probably due to the puritanical ethic which has been dominant for so long . . .

      yours,
      [K]

---

[1]   KW often had to explain British references in exported comedy programmes Hathaway had heard. 'Nadgers' did occur in Rambling Syd Rumpo's songs, but as 'the nadgers' (an affliction causing virtually unlimited symptoms) it had appeared on the earlier 'Goon Show'.

To the HEAD POSTMASTER, EDINBURGH[1]

21 February 1976

Dear Sir,
I write to beg a favour. During a holiday spent in Tenerife, I had the good fortune to meet some very kind people from Edinburgh and we passed some very happy days together. Before we parted, they gave me their address which is now, inexplicably, lost. I have searched everywhere and cannot find it.

They recently sent me a birthday card and some photographs taken during the holiday and I would very much like to write and thank them, but they have put no address on the envelope, so I don't know where to write to. I am wondering if you can help me?

The first couple is Ian and Janet Blackie, and they have a pub in Edinburgh – I don't know its name. The other couple is Charles and Margaret Martin, and Mr Martin is in business on his own – I think in plumbing and sanitary fittings, bathrooms etc.

If you have any chance of tracing the address of either one or the other, it will do, because I can then thank them both.

[KW]

To the HEAD POSTMASTER, EDINBURGH

25 February 1976

Dear Sir,
I would like to convey my delighted thanks to you for the prompt efficiency and kindness with which you dealt with my enquiry regarding the address of my friend Mr Blackie in Edinburgh. I certainly never expected to receive such a successful reply so quickly.

I have said it on radio, and I have said it on television, and at the risk of becoming repetitive I say it again: the Post Office is one of the most marvellous organisations we have in Britain, not least because of the humanity of the people who run it.

Gratefully yours,
KENNETH WILLIAMS

[1] This letter was published under the heading 'Bouquets' in the Post Office staff magazine. KW's follow-up letter of thanks was included as an Editor's Note.

To 'FRED'[1]

26 February 1976

Dear Fred,

The matron has written from Dunromin at Cromer Road, to say that we've got to get Phoebe out of there. It's the old story I'm afraid; she's got through three mattresses in the last month. She says she can't help it and that it's the 'laughing that brings it on' but as you know, exactly the same thing occurred at Bellview and goodness knows, there was precious little laughter there. Ernestine has suggested we try the Distressed Gentlefolk, she says you would have the contacts through your association with the Twittering woman whom you knew at the Institute. I know it is not an easy task (you with your trumpet and all) but if you could make some tentative enquiries, it would be a great help to us all. I would go down there myself, but alas, I've pulled a muscle in the calf whilst running in the Inner Circle. No, it was nothing to do with any training programme. It was to get away from a great hulking brute of a man; he'd been stalking me, all the way from Baker Street, after the sewing class. It attracted considerable attention because he kept brandishing this huge cucumber and making lewd noises. I won't go into any details. I just thought 'it's coats girls' and flew. It wasn't till I got home that I realised what a strain I'd given myself. Gertrude Knoblock has been wonderful. She's come every day to do the rubbing. She's got a marvellous touch and no mistake. After she's got going for a bit, you actually forget there was anything wrong in the first place. She always asks after you, and says she will never forget your pneumatic douche and the Spanish mantilla! She still wears them both! such a quaint old fashioned thing. O! I almost forgot, will you send the cheque to Dunromin this month? it is your turn I fancy.

   yours truly,
   Doris[2]

---

[1] Although K W did have more than one correspondent of this name, it is unlikely that a real Fred was the recipient of this fantasy. K W's diary mentions only the typing of the George Borwick letter on this day.
[2] The carbon copy is signed thus.

To the Hon. GEORGE BORWICK

26 February 1976

My dear George,
Thank you for sending me the cutting about that poor boy Sal Mineo.[1]
It is scandalous that such a talent should ever have been in such
appalling jeopardy; he was a very good actor . . . The radio series 'Get
On With It' has had stinking reviews. In the Sunday Times it said
'appalling old jokes and dirty double entendre' and the Times said
'pathetic' and the rest have ignored it. Into every life a little rain must
fall and it looks like your friend is drenched. I have been struggling
to write my column for the Radio Times. When I rang the BBC and
asked who was to give the Lent talks, they told me it was Bishop
Trevor Huddleston,[2] so I telephoned the Bishop to ask for something
to put in the column about the content of his speech. The secretary
said 'The Bishop is very busy at the moment but I will ask him to
telephone you' and promptly at 9.30 the next morning he was on the
line. O! such a kind and delightful voice. I said 'What are you going
to talk about?' and he said 'I don't know. I never do until the day'
and I privately thought 'That's a lot of help!' but he went on to give
me some general views about communication which I can incorporate
into the column. I said to him 'You must be reflecting very wryly on
some of the evil chickens which are now coming home to roost in
Southern Africa' and he sighed and said 'I warned them again and
again' and goodness knows he did.
They have sent out Lord Greenhill to talk to that traitor Ian Smith.[3]
I see no point in it whatsoever. The stupidity and bigotry of the
Rhodesians is insurmountable. They will only learn the lesson the
way Angola learned it: in blood and anguish and tears. Did you read
that Harry Oppenheimer[4] has transferred all the company assets and
trusts to Europe? already, he has seen the light. After Rhodesia goes,
the RSA will be utterly alone on that continent, surrounded by the
very people she's persecuted for years. And thus, the whirligig of time

---

[1] The death of the Hollywood actor Sal Mineo (b.1939), formerly a specialist in
troubled teenage roles (e.g. *Rebel Without a Cause*), had been reported on 14 February.
He was stabbed to death outside his West Hollywood apartment. His wallet was not
taken. A homosexual background to the case was suspected.
[2] Most Rev. Trevor Huddleston (b.1913), then Bishop Suffragan of Stepney.
[3] Who had made a Unilateral Declaration of Independence on Rhodesia's behalf in
November 1965, and had since feinted to return his outlawed country to legal
status.
[4] Chairman, Anglo-American Corporation of SA Ltd, 1957–82, and De Beers
Consolidated Mines Ltd, 1934–85.

brings in his revenges[1] . . . This little island still remains one of the most civilised places in a barbaric world.

    love from your old chum,
    [K]

To the Hon. GEORGE BORWICK

2 March 1976

My dear George,
. . . When you asked me in Peter Mario's five years ago 'How long do you think the RSA set-up will last?' I told you, five to ten years, depending on the emergent nations surrounding her. Certainly I never envisaged then such a rapid development in Mozambique, let alone Angola. But these events have moved faster than anybody predicted BECAUSE of something. They didn't happen by accident. They happened because the indigenous people in these places WANT their freedom, and are going to get it. As for this rubbish about 'They are not ready for self-government' oh dear oh dear. Was Europe ready for it? It took endless wars (including the 100 years one) and slaughter, and the collapse of the Holy Roman Empire and two WORLD wars to define the national boundaries we've got NOW. And it don't look as though we'll have them for long. Europe has produced bigger and better villains than Amin. Indeed, the man after whom Rhodesia is named was one of the most corrupt scoundrels ever to come out of England . . . Love,

    [K]

To FRANK WILSON[2]

4 April 1976

Dear Frank,
Your account does not tally with mine. I left Ruabon for Northolt where I was stationed with an MRS[3] group. From Northolt I was sent to Liss, Aldershot and from there, a train took us to Greenock where we got the troopship which took us to Bombay. From thereafter, your account sounds like mine. I too was at Kalyan, then Dehra

[1] 'And thus the whirligig of time brings in his revenges': *Twelfth Night*, V, i.
[2] An 'ex-sapper in 66 [Map] Reproduction Group'.
[3] Map Reproduction Section.

Dun, and then I was sent to 62 MRS at Kurunegala. Think we merged with 66 MRS later. I have looked up the photograph and recognise you. The point is, however, I was never in Halifax, and there is no memory of a night out, let alone a piss-up. I was friends in Kurunegala with a sapper called Ted Underwood, but if he was from Millwall, I didn't know it. He was certainly a Londoner, so you may well be right. Dark curly hair and deliberate speech. I was extraordinarily fond of him and was deeply disappointed in his behaviour which I will explain soon. After Kurunegala I farted about in a transit camp in Colombo, and then went to Singapore where I joined CSE (Forces Entertainment) at NeeSoon. After a few months of this new life I got three stripes and was made a local acting unpaid sergeant. I learned that a number of men in the old MRS at Kurunegala had also arrived in Singapore. It wasn't far from NeeSoon, so one evening I went over the way to their camp. I asked for Ted Inwood. That was his name, Inwood. Not Underwood. Anyway I asked for him, and they directed me round a barrack-room which was very makeshift, and eventually I found him behind a mosquito net, and we had a talk. I didn't need a house of bricks to fall on me. It was obvious that he didn't want to know me. I was certainly not mistaken by that one occasion either. Sometime afterwards, I saw him with some other RE's in a cafe in Singapore and I went over and spoke, but it was the same reception. Ostensibly polite, but the undercurrent was sneering . . . The friends I made in CSE included Stanley Baxter, Peter Nichols and John Schlesinger.[1] All of them proved to be exceptional talents. They made up for the loss of that shit Inwood. I often remember Kurunegala and the heat & humidity of that coconut plantation, and Captain Hardman, quite a dandy wasn't he? looked like the sort of good looking officer in the advertisements. Were you there when we had that party? put coloured lights in the trees and a notice saying 'The Coconut Grove' and invited a crowd of ATS girls. When they got to our camp in the lorries they were all dying for a pee and no one had thought to build a ladies' loo and of course our facilities were men only. Some bright spark had the idea of using a portable commode in Hardman's bunga-low and sticking a red light sign outside. Hardman was in Colombo seeing his girlfriend in the WRNS. I was supposed to be a litho draughtsman but I KNOW I was never any good at that job. It is really amazing that I conned anyone into believing that I was any good at it. I think Hardman must have had an inkling though, cos I know I spent a lot of time in the office at Kurunegala. I used to type

[1] John Schlesinger (b.1926), film director, former actor.

and do odd clerical jobs for the old man. When I was anxious to get into CSE and go to Singapore for the audition I remember asking Hardman if he would write a commendation for me. He did. It said 'I think that L/Corporal Williams will be of more use to CSE Singapore than he has ever been at 62 MRS Kurunegala.' Really quite acid. I was very offended. I went up to his hut. He was in the shower. I shouted my complaints. He laughed and shouted 'the real letter is in the IN TRAY' and I went back to the office and found it. He'd written a charming letter saying how good I'd been in the impromptu cabaret things we'd organised in the mess.

O! something else I've remembered. I went from Dehra Dun to Ceylon with Corporal Denzil Sherwin. Just the two of us went. A horrendous journey. The Americans started us off with a lorry lift to a station and then train to Delhi. We were stuck in the Wavell club for days before getting a train to Madras, and then boat to Ceylon. Denzil was always smoking fags and being unconcerned. I was frightened to death and saying 'we must get ON' but he felt no such compulsion. He was a fastidious creature and a SUPERB draughtsman. Come to think of it, all the really good draughtsmen I've known have been neat and clean individuals.

My mother's sister is in hospital at Skegness. My aunt. She is a Mrs Rose Cracknell. I suppose she must be eighty or so. Haven't seen her for years. Met her grandson accidentally cos he was the purser on the Canberra when I went on this cruise with P & O. Quite a coincidence meeting him. Of course he was half my age, very young and immature, but I could see all the arrogance of the FAMILY coming out. Perhaps it was that quality in me that decided on a theatre career. If I had the choice over again, I would go all out for a degree in the Humanities and specialise in teaching. Heigh ho. Too late to change now.

> regards from your OLD army chum,
> [KW]

To MR CHAMBERS[1]

21 April 1976

Dear Mr Chambers,
I think all the labels are wrong. Motorist and Pedestrian sounds feasible, but what does the motorist become when he gets out of the car?

---

[1] Mr Chambers's letter is lost, but it is evident that one of his questions was, more or less bluntly phrased, Are you homosexual? (See third paragraph.)

and what does the pedestrian become when he becomes the driver of the vehicle? The true answer to this shows that both the labels are wrong and that the two categories do not, in fact, exist; only one thing is constant, and that is the human heart; lose sight of THAT and you have lost sight of everything.

You say that you find it 'difficult to think that actors really mean it . . . that they know the spirit within as well as the appearance without . . .' I should accept their declarations of faith if I were you. If you sit on the fence long enough you might split yourself right up the middle.

As to your question about my private life, the proper answer would be to tell you to mind your own business, but I am not desirous of rebuffing you, and I think you asked the question in a genuine spirit of enlightenment, so the answer is, mentally yes, spiritually yes: physically, no.

You're wrong about Christ only caring for the outcasts and sinners: He cared (and cares) for us all. And we are all sinners. That's why we need him. Do try and forget the labels.

> sincerely yours,
> [KW]

To DENIS GOACHER[1]

30 June 1976

My dear Denis,
Your letter was a joy. You must be one of the few people left in the world who knows how to correspond. I am so glad that things are progressing with you and that the teaching looks promising! that is marvellous news. Hope all the pupils are prosperous. The Feydeau has been a disaster. Every single critic panned it. The management moaned 'There isn't one quote we can use!' and bad reviews PLUS the heat wave (it's been averaging 95 degrees) has emptied the auditorium. Couldn't even fill it on the opening night, and the second was unbelievable, they took about 20 pounds . . . I had been expecting bad notices but, quite honestly, I had never dreamed that they would go for me! I thought it would be stuff like 'Kenneth Williams does his best with a thin little play' etc etc. Instead, the play has been only slightly attacked, the supporting cast praised, and yours truly

---

[1] Goacher had moved from Devon to Greece, where English-language teaching promised to be his best source of income.

SAVAGED. The gist of their message is that I totally fail to pull it off. Judging from the reaction in the barely occupied theatre, they're absolutely right. I forgot to tell [you], when we played Newcastle, the manager came into the dressing room and said: 'I have written this speech which I would like you to read from the stage, in the interval' and I asked 'what is it about?' and he replied 'It is a tribute to Sybil Thorndike.' When I said to hell with that, he protested 'She died yesterday!' and I screamed 'I've been dying for five fucking weeks and no one's giving a funeral oration over me!' and chucked him out of the room. He got his way in the end. After we'd taken the curtain at the end of the evening, he went on and read this speech, talking about 'how wonderful she was in CANDEEDA by Mister Shore . . .' and the pianist (in a dreadful toupee) played 'I'll See You Again'. It was something between a seance and a recitation for illiterates. The sort of thing you just can't believe is happening! Yesterday I had the phone call from Gordon Jackson. He is doing Malvolio at Chichester and has had awful notices. He said 'I know what you're going through . . . at least I am finished in July . . . I can see the light at the end of the tunnel . . . it's been hell here . . . I never want to tread boards again as long as I live . . .' He said that Barbara Windsor (who is playing Maria) keeps coming into his dressing room with all the bad notices she gets from a press agency – 'she came in the other night with the Sussex Gazette and said here is another bad one for your Malvolio! they say you are awful in this! ain't it a shame! you and Kenny in the shit together . . .' Stanley Baxter gave me lunch yesterday and he told me 'Your only hope is to get out of the country: my advice is that you go to America . . . you'd go very well on the chat shows . . . you could take a revue over there with some old sketches you've done in the past . . . get a few dancers together . . . you'd go like a bomb.' I thought 'yes, and disintegrate in the process' but heard myself saying 'It's a very interesting idea' and he cried 'It's your only chance, and if you don't take it, you will just ROT . . .' I staggered home through streets as hot as an oven, feeling like a pariah. According to the Met. Office this MAD weather is going to go on and on. London is actually hotter than Honolulu.

[K]

To MILES KINGTON (*Punch*)

9 August 1976

Dear Miles,
It was very good of you to write such a reassuring letter.[1] You need never worry if you haven't got my address to hand; if you send it to the BBC it's always forwarded, or my agent, Peter Eade. Failing that, just put Kenneth Williams, London. The post office always deliver letters to me – some of them bearing the vaguest address. I got one such missive from Havana bearing over thirty signatures and asking for autographed photographs; one wonders what Marxist Cubans want with actors from decadent Western Carry On films! Seems incomprehensible to me.

Thank you for asking me to do a piece on the James book and nineteenth century verse,[2] but I have to decline cos I'm not competent in that direction. I am not a writer you know. If I had any talent in that field I would have left acting years ago . . .

Since seeing you, I had an unfortunate experience with some tinned food. The body was covered with blisters and the stinging was intolerable. Rushed to the doctor in a panic and he prescribed these tablets, saying 'they will be effective but they will make you feel low.' I said 'that'll be nothing new dearie' and shot over to Boots and took three straightaway. The dispenser told me 'these'll make you lethargic' and I thought 'what rubbish!' and got the bus home. The rash went away and so did I. Didn't wake up till the terminus.

> yours,
> [K]

---

[1] KW had worried that his appearance at a *Punch* lunch (14 July) had been uncontrolled and characterised by too much 'smut'.
[2] 'Sadly, people aren't writing much nineteenth century verse these days,' Kington had written, offering instead Clive James's latest narrative poem, *Peregrine Prykke's Pilgrimage Through the London Literary World*.

To the EDITOR of *The Times*[1]

c/o Peter Eade Ltd,
9 Cork Street, W1
28 August 1976

Sir,

There are occasions in life when the unwary spectator is dazzled by the meretricious, and is inveigled into watching a propaganda masquerading as an entertainment; this happened to me when I saw the film 'Rosemary's Baby'. It is an unpleasant perversion when the clever use of technique and dramatic resource serve to obscure the barren nature of a product, but it is even worse when such methods are deliberately employed to exploit and depict human suffering. This latter should always arouse our compassion, but cruelty practised upon a pregnant woman should provoke our anger: it does mine.

It is on those grounds that Mrs Whitehouse is right to seek its proscription from our television screens, and in so doing she deserves the support of all people of conscience. The peculiarly nauseating version of witchcraft which it peddles incurs no wrath, only revulsion and sadness; one is conscious of a bleak misuse of talent and a childish obsession with cruelty.

Like all propagandas disguised as art, it will always find ready defenders, and liberally minded people will deplore the attempt to stifle work on which the commonalty should be allowed to form its own judgment, et cetera. Alas, the commonalty has no such ability; that is why we have the BBC Board of Governors. Mrs Whitehouse is right to appeal to them. They are custodians of an honourable tradition and should show the same concern as she does about things which do violence to the human spirit, and wound the conscience, not in the cause of art, but of making money.

> Yours faithfully,
> KENNETH WILLIAMS

---

[1] This letter was (eventually) published by *The Times*, on 13 September.

To BARRIE KENYON (Hon. Chairman, Campaign for
Homosexual Equality)

9 September 1976

Dear Barrie,
Thank you for your letter[1] which was sent to my agent; I received it
this morning. Yes, well most of the information it contained made
me feel very out of touch. Of course I would be willing to help you
in any matter which causes alleviation of suffering, but quite honestly,
I am not qualified to talk about things like 'the proper age of consent'
or about the practicable aspect of homosexuality 'cos I don't have
knowledge of the first or experience of the second. I mean, I don't
count masturbatory experiences with others equally immature, and
as far as adulthood is concerned, I'm very Lady of Shalottish. I tell
you these things in confidence. But if you think these reasons do not
invalidate my endorsing a document intended to help your cause,
then I will certainly append my signature. I don't share your conviction that my views would give 'special weight' as far as the committee
is concerned, but it's a very pleasing idea and I'm sensible of the
compliment you pay me.

    sincerely yours,
    [KW]

To PAMELA ROSS[2]

29 September 1976

Dear Miss Ross,
Thank you for writing about the article in Radio Times. It was kind
of you to take the trouble. I am sorry you found my comedy crude
and 'full of easy innuendo bringing easy laughs' but frankly I have
never found the latter 'easy'. What do you think of this line: 'These
her C's, her U's, her T's, and thus maketh she her great P'? In the
Temple edition, it says 'this joke can be explained to the actor by any

---

[1] A request for KW to put his name to a letter to the Policy Advisory Committee
of the Criminal Law Revision Committee (reporting to the Home Secretary), seeking
equal treatment before the law for homosexuals and heterosexuals, i.e. effectively
an age of consent of sixteen for homosexual men.
[2] Miss Ross had written, from Angus, in appreciation of 'your review of the
"Generation to Generation" programme in this week's *Radio Times*'. She particularly
liked his observation 'It is in the clash of wills, not in their acquiescence, that our
attention is compelled.'

common sailor.' Well I didn't need to have it explained to me. It is certainly a rude joke and I don't think you can term it 'subtle', but it is written by our greatest poet. I shouldn't bother with labels if I were you; they're generally misleading. Like Pedestrian & Motorist: what happens when the latter gets OUT of the car? It is the human heart we should be concerned with, and its intense vulnerability. I'm sorry about this dreadful typing.

Yours,
[KW]

To FRANCES MEREDITH[1]

8 October 1976

Dear Frances,
I should cancel the Tatler if I were you; I got a copy on Tuesday and was appalled at the price. It is ridiculous to pay ten shillings for this kind of thing. It is years since I looked at all these silly photographs of daft people at daft parties. It used to be in the dentist's waiting room but it's been supplanted by Woman's Own. My own piece is squeezed in between pictures of these awful parties and the type is too small[2] . . . Interesting about your chaplain seeing me in Tangier. I hope I gave a decent account of myself. I used to go to Morocco a lot. It all began in the period when you were not allowed to take more than fifty pounds out of the country. There was this friend who owned a property business out there. One would go out for the holiday and he would give one car trips and meals; then when he was in England one would do the same. One felt it was reciprocity of the most welcome kind, and an ethical way of getting round abominable fiscal laws. Of course that was the period when I was earning money. I was averaging 15 to 20 thousand. Now, I am lucky to scrape 5 to 6. That's another thing. For the 'Just A Minute' recordings I get £35 and Parsons gets MORE. I mean! it is infuriating. The BBC said it was policy to pay the chairman a higher rate . . . Last week, at the recording, he kept pronouncing Bavaria as BARvaria. I said 'Why do you keep saying Barvaria when everyone knows it's Bavaria' and he replied 'Because Barvaria is correct' and I said 'Well we learn something every day don't we?' to the audience, and in the next sequence

[1] A 'very aged fan' (her own description) from Yorkshire.
[2] KW was providing a monthly column called 'Ad Lib' to the *Tatler & Bystander* magazine.

Alfred Marks said 'When I was walking through HARNover Square the other day . . .' and got an enormous laugh. Parsons was furious. I tackled him about it after the show: 'Do you really believe that Barvaria is correct?' and to my astonishment, he replied: 'Of course I don't, but I had to say that after you had drawn attention to my mistake in public.' If you can understand THAT, you can understand Parsons . . .

No Frances, I wasn't born in Wales! I was born in London. On the afternoon of February 22nd in the year of the general strike, 1926. My mother said: 'I remember the time because your father had the afternoon free cos of the early closing day.' It all happened in a house (one of those terraced affairs) in Bingfield Street off the Caledonian Road. Three or four families in one house. It was a slum all right. The houses have all gone now, and dreadful high rise blocks have replaced the erstwhile dwellings. The place is as barbaric as ever. Significantly, a beautiful Nash-type church which once stood on the corner has been replaced by Woolworth's. When my father got his own hairdressing shop, we moved into rooms above it, in Marchmont Street. That was near Russell Square and much grander. We all thought it was quite a step up. My mother came from a large family called Morgan. The Morgans all lived in Sandwich Street which was quite near to Marchmont Street, and my mother used to take me round there, walk past the house, and say: 'that's number seven, where my father, Henry Morgan lived; the front parlour there was beautiful! the furniture was all red leather and mahogany . . . it was lovely there, and it was a happy house till our mum died . . . then he married Eliza Cod . . . she was in service in a very big house in Bayswater . . . she came to look after us. I didn't like her. She used to make me carry her bag from the station at King's Cross. I told her I didn't like her and she shoved my head between the iron bars of the bed. I was stuck there till my brother Sonny came and released me . . .' There were a lot of stories in this vein. Anyway, my mother was a Morgan, and my father was a Williams, so I suppose the ancestry can be said to be Welsh. But I don't like nationalism. The very IDEA of devolution is mad. I don't even like the sound of the Welsh language, and I think their insistence on retaining it is barmy. All those signs to be re-written! can you imagine? I see, in the Fraser book on Cromwell,[1] that his name was Williams! isn't it horrifying? that disgusting regicide. Thoroughly agree with you about the lowering of standards in English

---

[1] Antonia Fraser, *Cromwell, Our Chief of Men* (1973). Cromwell was descended from Thomas Cromwell's sister Katherine, who married a Welshman, Morgan Williams. To make it worse for KW, Morgan was his mother's maiden name.

usage on the BBC. 'At this moment of time' instead of 'Now' is outrageous. The one I can't stand is 'personally speaking'. Stupid. Every time you speak it's personal. Why comment on it?

> yours,
> [KW]

To MILES KINGTON (*Punch*)

20 October 1976

Dear Miles,
Your scepticism about my ruling on the use of inverted commas[1] sent me to my copy of Fowler's 'Modern English Usage' and he says:
   There is no universally accepted distinction between the single form ('. . .') and the double (". . ."). The more sensible practice is to regard the single as the normal, and to resort to the double only when, as fairly often happens, an interior quotation is necessary in the middle of a passage that is itself quoted. To reverse this is clearly less reasonable.
   This is, as I am sure you will agree, advice from a distinguished source; it would seem to indict you as 'less reasonable'.
   Of course you will probably think: 'all this comes from his fury at being told how to spell excerpt'. And you'll be right.

> yours,
> [KW]

To NIGEL TURNER[2]

1 November 1976

Dear Nigel Turner,
Thank you for your letter. I am totally unable to help you however, because I don't employ anybody. I am simply an actor, who occasionally gets offered work. The work is controlled by casting directors and theatre managers. I have no say in the matter of casting, and I never get involved in this field. If your ambition is to be an actor then you must seek auditions with producers and directors. The list is in SPOTLIGHT which you can get from their office . . . That's how I started. Frankly, I wouldn't bother with impersonations of me; you

---

[1] Kington had received from KW a review of Barry Took's history of radio comedy *Laughter in the Air*, and this wrangle followed.
[2] An aspirant from Welling, Kent, who had written requesting an audition, to 'help me to carry on your style of acting'.

will find that the best work comes from being yourself. The manner-
isms of others always attract us when we're young, but on maturity
they should drop off like dead leaves.

      Yours,
      [KW]

To ROBERT LIGHTFOOT (*Tatler*)

1 November 1976

Dear Robert,
I wrote 'with your known face' in the reference to Robert Mitchum;[1]
it appears in your magazine as 'with your brown face', and since he
is neither red indian or african the whole thing reads ruinously.

    When I saw the October issue, and found my stuff sandwiched
between other items in such a way that it was practically camouflaged
in the process, and in a type-setting that forced me to use a magnifying
glass, I thought 'O well, perhaps it will get a better lay-out next time!'
but my spirits sunk to zero when I saw this month's issue.

    It looks even more orphan-like when I see the sort of spread given
to the other contributors; there, the layout is clear, eye-catching, and
you straightway identify with the authors.

    No offence, but let's forget it after December.[2]

      yours,
      [KW]

To MAGGIE SMITH and BEVERLEY CROSS

11 November 1976

My dear Mags and Beverley,
The Equity meeting at the Coliseum was disgraceful.[3] The left turned
up in force, and the shouting and obscene threats were hurled through
the air. Miriam Karlin[4] said 'I agree with the audience here today, I
don't want to be on this rotten council any longer' and resigned from

---

[1] In his 'Ad Lib' column.
[2] Peace was later restored, and KW carried on supplying his column to the *Tatler*.
[3] This meeting occurred at the height of the left-wing revolt against the elders of
the Equity Council. Local representation and South African policy were constant
sources of bitter dispute.
[4] One of the few left-wing actresses with whom KW was on friendly terms.

the platform, taking eight councillors with her. As they left the stage, they were cheered to the echo. We were left sitting there, visibly depleted and trying to look unconcerned. They all rose in their seats and began chanting 'RESIGN' with such elongated syllables that it sounded like Sieg Heil. The whole thing was Nurembergish. Stanley Baxter told me: 'I was up in the circle; it was full of Workers' Theatre Group down from the Midlands and Scotland by the coachload. Their language and tactics were appalling. I can't see things going on like this. We will have to split & form another union.' Stanley said that the only light moment was provided by the designer who told him: 'I'm doing the Queen Elizabeth costumes for Patience Collier to wear; she is very difficult. She keeps screaming at me: "I must be able to PEE in it, you understand? You will have to fix it so I can pee whatever happens! Fix a trap door inside the skirt or something. If I can't pee it is death! You must do the fitting while I'm sitting down so we can allow for peeing."' He said 'She was absolutely manic about it! it's barmy. I can't fix a loo inside a skirt! she is not supposed to pee during the action. Why does she keep on about urination? and how can I do a fitting with a woman sitting down all the time? O dear! it is MAD.' When I saw Gordon & Rona they said to send you their love. Gordon said he'd seen Gracie Fields on TV singing 'When I Grow Too Old To Dream' and admitted: 'I just burst into tears, it was so moving! took me right back to my childhood!' Rona said: 'I thought it was boring. I went to bed.' Louie has been to the consultant specialist and he says: 'You're very healthy; you'll live till you're ninety.'[1] Lots of love to you both, and the children,

[K]

To IAN COSENS[2]

12 November 1976

Dear Ian,
I don't know what dictionary you are using, but mine is the two volumes Shorter Oxford, and it states: 'DISASSOCIATE, 1603, to free or detach from, sever; so Disassociation', so, far from your allegation that no such word exists, it is actually printed in heavy

---

[1] She died in July 1991, aged eighty-nine.
[2] A correspondent from Halifax. The press cutting – a piece by KW – which caused this dispute is lost.

type. I am truly bewildered by your apparent desire to find fault
with me.

> sincerely yours,
> [KW]

To IAN COSENS

17 November 1976

Dear Ian,
The Shorter Oxford defines DISSOCIATE as: 'to cut off from association, or society' so it seems to have something in common with
proscription or banishment. Under DISASSOCIATE it says: 'To free
or detach from' which is the sense in which I wanted to convey the
alienation which Eliot refers to in the poem I quoted. The children
aren't sent to Coventry or anything, they voluntarily choose NOT to
mix with the older generation. That's what I meant. And it doesn't
help when you get your letters saying 'there ain't no sitch word'. The
slang PLUS the didacticism was vexatious to me. We're here to love
each other, not to annoy, mislead, or try to score points. Oh, I find it
all so petty.

> yours wearily,
> [KW][1]

To JOHN HUSSEY

16 April 1977

Mon cher John,
As I told you in my first hurried note, I got back from that appalling
stay in Tenerife on the 13th. The desk was piled high with mail &
there were a couple of broadcasts to do. Louie paid for the holiday
(out of her savings) cos I haven't been doing very well. The odd bit
of work here & there, but no more films (Rank have withdrawn the
Carry Ons) no offers from telly and so I fall back on the odd bit of
radio, and have had to turn to writing . . . Yes, George B[orwick] told
me all about your TV series.[2] Delighted to know that it has ensured

---

[1] Mr Cosens again wrote, this time apologising. KW's pencil annotation on his
letter reads: 'Replied in conciliatory fashion 'cos this is really a generous letter.'
[2] Hussey had found fame in South Africa as Mr Dingley in 'The Dingleys', a family
serial set in Pietermaritzburg.

you are before the public eye. That's the real secret really. STAYING THERE. Having them see you so often that you become a part of the scene. Talent isn't important. It's the staying power that matters. O! I have missed you greatly. Alas, no understudy could play your part. Sometimes when I feel like crying my eyes out, I fancy I hear you making one of those cracks, and I recover the poise. All my love, dear chum, yr. devoted:

[K]

To BEVERLEY CROSS and MAGGIE SMITH

24 August 1977

My dear Beverley and Mags,
What a superb photograph!! – I took one look at it and thought 'Oh! I'll have this for myself!' and then of course I realised the inscription forbade it. I will take it round to Wimpole Street. John[1] will be delighted with it. Since I wrote to tell you of his indisposition I've found out the real cause. He was in the operating theatre, using an aerosol can, and the thing exploded. He had the good sense to cover his eyes, but he inhaled the stuff. It was chloride gas. He was out of circulation for a year. It has obviously damaged a lot of vital tissue. I saw him last week. He speaks with difficulty and says he's now had to give up working at the E. Grinstead Hospital, which is a great shame cos he was their ENT consultant. He is allowed to work so many hours and then has to rest. He admitted to me: 'It's just ruined my life chum' and I must say I felt terribly sorry for him. You know how brusque and efficient he always was. He is the sort of man who loathes weakness and debilitation of any kind. The film I was on, 'The Hound of the Baskervilles',[2] was suspended cos the director, Paul Morrissey, went down with Hepatitis. I thought it was all too good to be true. I haven't enjoyed work so much for years and years. Cannot get over this photograph of Mags. Looks so beautiful. Thank you for sending the Stratford programme. Loved the picture of Mags kneeling with that hat on. Fancy M going 'up the Nile' as you put it! how marvellous! and then back to Britain in October! Lovely. Hope to see you both and have a proper talk. Baxter is busy: 'I'm trying to learn the lines for this show I'm doing with Bing.' He is in this Crosby TV programme. The 'Bing' stuff is dropped all the time. 'They said I needn't

[1] Musgrove, KW's doctor.
[2] A zany version starring Peter Cook and Dudley Moore. It was not well received.

learn it cos they'd put it on autocue, and I told them that I'm blind and can't see anything.' I told him: 'Yes, and your legs are not what they were.' Gordon is on a 13 episode series[1] which he says is an imitation of 'Starsky & Hutch' and is exhausting. Loved the Groucho Marx crack when he was asked 'Don't you want to play Hamlet?' and he replied: 'I don't even want to SEE it.' It was in the Times obituary.[2] I fell about. And the lovely line: 'I wouldn't live my life over again for a million dollars. Unless it was tax-free.' Love from yr old chum,

[K]

To the ENVIRONMENTAL HEALTH OFFICER, CAMDEN BOROUGH COUNCIL

5 November 1977

Dear Sir,
There have been many occasions in the past when the residents of this block of flats (Marlborough House) and those adjoining (Regency House) have been kept awake in the early hours of the morning, or late at night, by the burglar bells of Henly's (Motors) in Osnaburgh Street. You have only to ask the Albany Street Police Station to find out the number of times they have been telephoned by tenants driven to screaming desperation by the endless clanging. The police always say: 'We are trying to get the key-holder' and everyone waits for hours until the racket is eventually silenced. One has endured this for years but now I read in the Times that the Borough of Islington have stopped such offences by serving notices to the owners, under Section 58: Control of Pollution Act, 1974, telling them to cease caus-ing the nuisance and prescribing ways in which this can be achieved. Notices require, with alternatives, the installation of a cut-out device in an intruder alarm system to automatically turn off the alarm bell within twenty minutes of it beginning to ring. Mr Pritchard, Environ-mental Officer at Islington Town Hall, says they are using the Act with success. Why can't you serve Henly's with such a notice, under the Control of Pollution Act? Many of the residents of this block are elderly and their sleep is shattered by the Henly bell which is situated close to their back windows, and consequently they are forced to

---

[1] 'The Professionals'.
[2] Groucho had died on 19 August.

endure this torture. The flats are small, and there isn't another room to go to.

>   yours faithfully,
>   [KW]

To JOHN CURTIS (Weidenfeld & Nicolson)

28 January 1978

Dear John,
I am dropping the idea of doing the book.[1] It has become a nagging worry for me – always at the back of my mind – and when my doctor recently asked: 'Is there anything wrong?' and I told him, he advised me to give it a rest. And that's what I am going to do. Nevertheless, I assure you that if I ever do get anything substantial down on paper, I will certainly send it to you.

>   yours,
>   [KW]

To GERALD THOMAS

16 March 1978

My dear Gerald,
Goodness knows you should be aware that it gives me no pleasure to say I don't want to be in the picture.[2] All my life I am conscious of how much I owe both to you and to Peter [Rogers]; you have sustained me in a personal as well as a professional sense. I want to be left out of this piece because I don't like any of it. It isn't a question of what can be cut, or what scenes can be modified or re-written. The very essence of it is offensive. In the old days, the Carry Ons had something with which people could identify: in 'Sergeant' there was humanity as well as saucy fun. Every time I have been interviewed & asked: 'What about the rudeness in your films?' I have always been able to defend them on the grounds of honest vulgarity, and morality; one could say that the villains got their come-uppance. This piece depends for its

---

[1]   KW did abandon his projected autobiography at this stage; but it is clear from details he gave of it in his diary that the work he had done for Curtis was incorporated into *Just Williams*, published in 1985 by Dent.
[2]   *Carry On Emmanuelle*. After script revisions, KW did appear in this, his last Carry On.

success on an audience accepting promiscuity; I think most people are becoming increasingly nauseated by it. The fun in 'Abroad' came from this very sense of decency & the foiled attempts of would-be seducers PLUS the spoiled holiday with which ALL people can identify & sympathise. In this script, I don't believe in anyone. Nonetheless I remain,

> your old chum,
> [K]

To HORACE CUTLER, OBE (Leader, Greater London Council)

5 May 1978

Dear Mr Cutler,
I got my mother and one or two others to make their reluctant way to the polling stations but we had a pathetic turn out in Camden and the borough remains in Labour control; the overspending etc. will go on. Nevertheless, I was delighted to read in the Times this morning that there have been swings to the Tories in many places, and Wandsworth is certainly a turn-up for the book! This is the vindication of all your stated policies. Incidentally I must congratulate you on your television appearances; you're one of the few that can marshal an argument and remain good humoured in the face of rudeness. Anyway, you've got a fan in

> your enthusiastic,
> [KW]

To EMMA SAMMS[1]

3 August 1978

Dear Emma,
It was good of you to write expressing such generous sentiments, and I am delighted that one of your ambitions has been realised. But in the

---

[1] Young actress, née Samuelson, later to come to international prominence in the TV series 'Dynasty'. She had been seeking permission to appear (which she did, as Princess Zuleira) in *Arabian Adventure*, produced by John Dark and directed by Kevin Connor. The film featured Christopher Lee and Peter Cushing; KW had also been invited to take part (as Khasim), but declined on grounds of discomfort. 'The idea of a turban wound right round my head drives me up the wall' (KW's diary, 5 June 1978). Milo O'Shea took the part.

interests of probity, please remember that I was only ONE member of the delegation of Equity councillors! Since the matter is confidential I cannot give you chapter and verse but I can assure you that someone other than myself was eloquent on your behalf, especially recognising the dedication involved in your early training. The FPA and Equity meet not as litigants but as agencies with mutual interests: the desire to resolve problems with professional sagacity and human understanding. So, my dear, in any future discussion on this subject, please acknowledge the collective institution – employers & union – working on your behalf, and not me, the individual. I am sure that, with John and Kevin, you will enjoy a very happy film – they know what they're doing, so just relax and trust them. You have all my good wishes,

     love,
     [KW]

To JOHN LAHR

3 September 1978

Dear John,
My old chum Stanley Baxter [is] in St Thomas's Hospital with a fractured pelvis caused by an accident at the television studios; some scenery fell on him while they were filming. I sat by the bedside chatting to him. Conversation came round to the news of a new charge 'incitement to murder' levelled against Jeremy Thorpe[1] and then we talked about Joe Orton. I walked out of the hospital and across Westminster Bridge thinking it presented a different spectacle today than it once did for Mr Wordsworth. Got home and found your book[2] had been delivered. I just sat reading and reading. I found it utterly compelling. The biographical element is fascinating, the analysis of the plays enlightening, and the recreation of the past astoundingly vivid. Scenes which I had observed in a blurred fashion suddenly assumed clarity. It was as if a camera lens had been adjusted so that everything was brought into sharp focus. You have woven all the disparities together and given them symmetry. Every single clue, like a piece of the mosaic, is eventually part of a thoroughly authentic picture. It's like someone who's had to keep diving down to the sea-

---

[1] Jeremy Thorpe, leader of the Liberal Party 1967–76, stood accused of incitement to murder Norman Scott, a male model, who claimed to have been his homosexual partner. Thorpe was acquitted.
[2] *Prick Up Your Ears*, Lahr's biography of Orton.

bed and come up with enough evidence of the original craft to make us see how it was put together, and how it actually floated. It is a great eye-opener. No one could have served J.O. better. I can see what you mean about it being a 'long and lonely slog' because all that garnering must necessarily have led you into a hundred by-ways and cul de sacs, the paradoxes and the ironies abound. What is wonderful is the way you have gathered all the dissonance together and given it harmony. The book is a whole. It must have been a gargantuan task.

I am particularly grateful that you so thoughtfully arranged to have a copy sent to me straightway. I shall send this to the publishers, asking them to forward it to you, cos I don't know where you will be in America. I hope that you will be able to take a holiday, because, having put together such an extraordinarily complicated jig saw, you deserve it. And it all reads so flowingly, so effortlessly! Labour of love must be right. The affection shone through the book about your father,[1] and it is here too. That's why you were the best one for the job. Endless congratulations to you.

> your old chum,
> [K]

To KENNETH HOARE[2]

22 September 1978

My dear Kenneth,

I've got one of those earnest correspondents who tirelessly works for Youth Clubs; overtly hearty but obviously a raver who sublimates it with work for the lads crap; his letters always bear the Sudbury post-mark and when I saw your envelope this morning I groaned aloud, crying to myself 'O! why don't she shut up?' and then I opened it and found your letter! horror turned to delight. It is extraordinary cos I had seen the 'Faith Brown Awards'[3] and had quite a few chuckles I can tell you! But how intriguing about Miss Shubik![4] and what an unlikely name! something between footwear and KitKat; one expects a dog with a slipper. Your account of the interview and the mooting

[1] *Notes on a Cowardly Lion*, on Bert Lahr (1895–1968), who played the Cowardly Lion in *The Wizard of Oz*.
[2] Writer with whom KW had been working up a comedy idea.
[3] TV comedy show starring the comedienne and impressionist.
[4] Irene Shubik, b.1935. Historian turned TV drama producer, best known for her involvement in the BBC's *Play For Today* series.

of the chat show subject was very funny to read! We had the right idea, but obviously it wasn't the right time. It will all be done eventually. Probably by someone else with material just far enough away for them to be guiltless of piracy. I certainly thought that 'Nitty'[1] was right at the time, but we have to face the fact that nobody else did. For some reason or other, they don't see it in terms of a series. Every time Gerald spoke to me it was always: 'they can't see it going on . . . the gaff is blown in number one you see . . .' etc. My only worry was that it had to go outside the studio. My original theory was about something all taking place within the confines of the studio, with the run-thro done with the house present just as warm-ups are done, and the supposedly real thing continuing after. I can see why they want to include the 'phone-in' element. Terribly funny some of that! 'Hallo hallo – are you there? is that Irene of Clapham? – no? you're Ruby from Romford? – ah yes – well go ahead!'

'I heard what you were saying about wheelchairs earlier on.'

'O yes – the mad granny from Chipping Sodbury?'

'That's right!'

'Yes well she certainly has a lot to put up with!'

'Not as much as me.'

'How's that?'

'My legs were blown off in the blitz.'

'O dear! that's a very different kettle of fish.'

'Both my arms were blown off as well.'

'How d'you get to the phone Ruby?'

'They've rigged up these wires and pulleys like the old change in the draper's shop; I'm on this meat-hook.'

'What is your problem?'

'Keeping cheerful.'

'You should take something up.'

'I'm up already.'

'No Ruby, a hobby . . . you should take up a hobby.'

'Hm. Well I have learned this touch typing with my navel.'

'That's terrific!'

'Yes I can push it right out! I could come over and show you –'

'Not just at the moment Ruby! the public are not quite ready for that sort of thing, but you keep right on pushing in Romford cos I've got Irene of Clapham waiting on the other line, all right? thank you for calling Ruby! and more power to your elbow – er – I mean navel – Hallo? is that Irene of Clapham? hallo? –'

---

[1] Their pilot project, 'The Nitty Gritty', based on a chat show.

It's all such meaningless rubbish you can't believe a word of it. I think it has something to do with the fact that it is all happening late at night. I don't think any of them would be able to go blabbing on in that fashion if it were morning.

love,
[K]

To ANDREW HATHAWAY

25 September 1978

Dear Andrew,
. . . If I ever told you – 'the trouble with acting is that you can never leave it'[1] – I must have meant it in the economic sense; once you have become established in the business you can command a wage which isn't available for an unskilled person in any other profession. Yes, I know there are people who maintain that acting is a skill, but I mean that it C A N be done by people who are not versed in the art of drama: you can get a child who comes along and acts marvellously, or you can get some pop singer who has had no stage experience becoming an overnight success. It is a business where the rules are there to be broken, and there are those who come along and break them again and again. One fundamental truth about theatre: 'conviction convinces'. Anyone who appears to be confident succeeds in convincing others. You don't have to be confident at all. You have to APPEAR to be confident, which is another matter entirely. The art of acting lies in the ability to create an impression. If you appear in front of any casting director, trying to convince him you are right for the role, it is HIM that needs reassuring; so the clever actor doesn't say 'use me, I will be great in the part' he says 'you must be an extraordinarily clever and discerning person to have your kind of skill! what are the qualities you look for in casting?' etc etc., so by a subtle process of flattery and intuition, the roles are reversed and the applicant is doing the interviewing. The first impression I remember when seeing ACTING was the thought that I could do it better. Of course that wasn't (and isn't) always the case, but I found myself thinking 'I could do that better' for an awful lot of the time. When I did get the opportunity to act, I found I couldn't do it better at all. The first time I ever got on to a stage and spoke lines in a professional company, I was lousy. Forgot lines, made the wrong moves, and ruined several

[1] See letter of 15 January 1972, p. xvii.

scenes. It was only the professional expertise of the others on the stage which made continuance possible.

[K]

To ALASTAIR REID[1]

10 November 1978

My dear Alastair,

Hope you got my note thanking you for 'Weathering'[2] and sorry I have been so long telling you about my reactions, but the work has taken me to all the dreary provincial cities of England, and it's been a daunting experience I can tell you. Anyway, I got back from Sheffield yesterday and there was a call from Helen Fry at the BBC: 'Have you any books which you particularly wish to talk about on radio? I am doing this programme about the literature you'd like to recommend for Christmas . . .' So I said 'yes, I'd like to talk about the Reid poems in "Weathering"' and she said all right. Then she rang back and said 'No we can't do that because it has to be about books published in England, and that is Dutton's of New York' so I told her 'No – it is published simultaneously over here by Canongate' and that shut her up. I went to the studio and did the recording all right. Went very well with no fluffs at all. I said that I found a lot of modern poetry dispiriting and esoteric, that it seemed to be talking in a private language half the time, and that it was a delight to read your stuff because it didn't cheat. I said 'he never treats of despair despairingly but seems to be urging us continually to take not only the second chance but the third, fourth . . . the hundredth chance . . . his work is an affirmation of life and he celebrates a thousand aspects of it . . .' I talked about the 'cat and dog' similes, the two sides needed to make the whole coin so to speak and used a couple of quotes, and then did a verse from 'Curiosity' from 'Dogs say . . .' to the end. Helen said 'that was a good excerpt to choose because you got the humour from the first bit about the wives and the dinner tables before the seriousness of a "cat minority of one" . . .' so I was pleased about that she is a good producer and has a perceptive ear for the right nuance in reading. I am off now to Television Centre for five episodes of 'Jackanory' I'm doing. You stare at that autocue till your eyes are like gobstoppers; suppose it'll have to be specs soon, but I keep trying to do without

[1] Scots poet, long under contract to the *New Yorker*.
[2] His latest collection.

them. Tottered out of the studio yesterday saying to Helen 'My legs are not what they were' and she retorted 'They never were much anyway' which left the morale round the ankles.

yours,
[KW]

To the EDITOR of the *Spectator*[1]

25 November 1978

Dear Sir,
I wish we weren't beset by a thousand misapprehensions but alas we are; the Spectator recently referring to Dorothy Parker's dismissal of a Broadway production: 'there's less to this than meets the eye', says that she found the show portentous; in fact it was the total lack of portent which prompted her observation, so perhaps the Spectator meant pretentious. The following week there was an article by Mr Mosley referring to 'the Cretan riddle: All men are liars' which entirely misreported the legend. The truth is that on one side of the paper is written 'All Cretans are liars' and on the other: 'I am a Cretan'. Reading this sort of thing in the Spectator, I was reminded of President Ford in a television interview talking about 'the Protestant Ethnic'. One felt he knew the sound but not the sense. Of course misinterpretation is sometimes wilful: I once heard the manager of the Manchester Midland Hotel describing the vandalism and theft on his premises: 'One day a group of men pretending to be a removal gang actually stole the grand piano!' Somebody laughed and remarked: 'I've heard of the Lost Chord but that's ridiculous!' and I reproved them roundly, pointing out that any sort of wickedness was little short of scandalous. The Spectator should pronounce against solecisms and uphold standards. When I heard someone recently pronouncing Syndrome with a long O sound, I told him: 'The O is short and the final E pronounced as it is in epitome or Penelope.' A few weeks later he gleefully told me about his holiday flight to Italy: 'We landed at Pisa where they've got a lovely aerodromy!' and he added triumphantly: 'Your ruling is faulty!' I kept my countenance, retorting with some asperity: 'One bad doctor does not invalidate medicine' and departed in a flurry of talcum powder. These occasional victories are like tackling a properly boiled egg: you cut off its head with a sharp whack and feel every bit

[1] Printed in the *Spectator*, week ending 8 December.

as satisfied as learning that another nationalised industry has been restored to its rightful owners.

yours respectfully,
Kenneth Williams

To DENIS GOACHER

2 December 1978

My dear Denis,
. . . At the moment I am rehearsing for the Jackanory Children's Television writing competition. Over nine thousand entries. All of them literate, readable, extraordinary. One poem from a four year old had to be checked cos they thought the parents had cooked it up! but it was genuine. Some kids' minds are extraordinarily fertile, but the lit. editor said 'Have you noticed how sad all the poems are?' & I had to admit there wasn't a happy note in any of them. The short stories are weird. One which I am doing, from a nine year old, is about a diver fearing he might drown & ends — 'Who would have cared? there probably wouldn't even be a line in a newspaper.' The whole piece has the feel of despondency & terrible inevitability. O dear I keep feeling, hm . . . how are we going to follow that? . . . I have been going from there to the Paris Studio to do 'Just A Minute'. Clement Freud coming straight from Minehead where he has been keeping Thorpe's spirits up. He has been very close and loyal to his ex political chief throughout the entire period. A rock, no less. He was surprisingly good humoured and seemed to think that they should let this shit Scott talk and talk so that he could hang himself. All this humbug about his ill treatment etc. And this ghastly suburban dialogue: 'I don't think your client is a very nice class of person' to Sir David Napley. All this tripe! — 'He came into the bedroom with a tube of something. I can't mention what because it might offend some people (SIC) and I just lay there, biting the pillow.' Stupid queen. Should have known he wasn't going to see much of the ceiling . . .

your old chum,
[K]

To MYRA De GROOT[1]

25 January 1979

My dear Myra,
You seem to imagine that I am in touch with everyone, and can give you the low-down on their activities; nothing could be farther from the truth. Haven't seen Maggie Smith for years, nor Fenella Whatsit [Fielding]. Haven't seen anyone. I live like an anchorite and hardly stir to forage abroad. Don't think I would get past the picket-lines anyway. Are you aware of all the strikes that are going on here? The pickets are everywhere. You can't enter hospital (not even if you're sick) the refuse piles up in the streets. The lorries are at a stand still cos they're refusing to work, the ports are paralysed & imports and exports remain rotting on the quayside. All the guff about 'you must keep a sense of humour' etc. is only valid if one is facing true adversity (like a war or something) but this strike is not true adversity: it is manufactured by Communists and Left-wing groups with the avowed aim of 'bringing down the government' . . . I don't do much in the way of work. I am not fashionable any longer. If it wasn't for radio and the odd TV appearance I'd be on the bread line. As it is, I get by, and help comes from the commercials, voice-overs etc. Had a letter from John Hussey (he used to be with the RSC at the Aldwych) saying he is producing for some South African set-up in Johannesburg and would I like to do a play over there! 'They'll pay anything you like and you can choose whatever piece you want to do!' and it was very embarrassing having to decline without mentioning apartheid . . . I suppose you read about Sir Eric Miller (he owned that huge Park West set-up where you got me a flat, through Phil Berger, remember?) shooting himself?[2] It was extraordinary! A rep at Cheltenham has sent me 'The Love of Four Colonels'[3] and offered me the Ustinov part so I had to read it. Tedious stuff. Wrote saying 'It's not my cup of tea'. The agent said 'I think you should do it, at least it would keep you occupied' as if I were a lavatory cubicle . . .

[K]

---

[1] Singer in KW's second hit revue, *Pieces of Eight* (1959). For her later career, see the last letter in this volume (p. 286).
[2] Miller was found shot in his own home in September 1977. His will showed him to be bankrupt. Writs were outstanding against him from Peachey Properties, off whose board he had been voted. A Fraud Squad investigation followed.
[3] By Peter Ustinov (1951).

To PEGGY MAKINS (EVELYN HOME)[1]

27 January 1979

Dear Peggy Makins,
In such spiritless times as these one can draw comfort from the
thought that in the Dark Ages the candle of civilised Faith was kept
burning in the monasteries by ever faithful hands, and it is interesting
to find Chaucer writing: 'Man hath made a permutation from Right
to Wrong, and all is lost through lack of Steadfastness' about the
society of HIS time. We can shrug our shoulders and say that nothing
much has changed, that men are indeed base, that there was only
one Christian and he died on the cross, and that the schisms among
his would-be followers are appalling examples of pettiness and wasted
aims. As an actor I have only found Spiritual Truth in the realm of
Art – God speaking to me vicariously through the works of men –
looking at the Guercino canvas in the National Gallery (Doubting
Thomas) is to have the sublimity of Faith truly brought home to me.
I don't want life: I want the artist's vision of life. And when that
vision is suffused with Faith, it has the power to ennoble, to enlighten
and to recreate us.

yours sincerely,
Kenneth Williams

To the Hon. GEORGE BORWICK

19 February 1979

My dear George,
Had the most awful bout of bronchial flu; longed to be away from it
all, but there were a thousand fiddling jobs to do. Had this voice
over commercial with Betty Marsden and Hugh Paddick. She arrived
looking like Olga Palovsky[2] with the long black cloak and the Russian
hat. He didn't come at all. He is in the Middlesex Hospital. Gallstones
apparently. Place was taken by Barrie Ingham. The snow was whirling
outside while we recorded. BM looked fine and I was surprised when
she admitted 'I am over sixty dear!' at the end of the session. Walked

---

[1] Veteran agony aunt, as 'Evelyn Home', in women's magazines. She was then
collecting celebrity material for what she called a 'book of boost', or encouragement,
on behalf of the Society for Promoting Christian Knowledge.
[2] The reference is to the song 'Olga Pulloffski (the Beautiful Spy)' by Harris Weston
(from *Stop-Go*).

from there to Eade's office. Had to read two plays which have been sent for me. Both were awful. Peter E looked tired and said he'd had a horrendous journey going to Coventry to see a production there – trains dislocated, endless delays, no dining car, and so on. Walked back through the west end past piles of rotting refuse and whirling snow with Oxford Street practically deserted compared with the usual bustle there . . . All we see on the television news are endless shots of mobs rampaging in Iran and waving pictures of this bearded queen called Ayatolla someone or other, and burning other people's property, and showing all the capacity for cruelty which they used to condemn the Shah for practising! When the working classes don't work, they pillage. Other items on the TV news were: Housewives learning Belly Dancing in Hertfordshire (with pictures of them foolishly gyrating), Ambulance drivers refusing to work in the Blood Transfusion service, hospital patients given paper sheets (cos of laundry strike) to lie on, and complaining: 'by the morning they're in shreds under your bum!' and Queen Victoria's knickers fetching £250 at Sotheby's. It all unfolds on your television screen in glorious colour – a mad kaleidoscope of insane 'current affairs'. Roll on Armageddon.

love from your old chum:
[K]

To the Hon. GEORGE BORWICK

5 March 1979

My Dear George,
You should tell all your friends out there, who think they're in some way deprived by lack of imports on their television screens, that they are LUCKY. It is a blessing in disguise if they did but know it! The rubbish that is going out nightly on our sets is unbelievably rubbishy. The whole thing is comparable to the prosperity of the gutter press. All the good papers are vanishing, and these awful Mirrors and Suns proliferate, with huge photographs of ladies with big tits & silly cartoon scripts. The TV Sunday is atrocious. Scars on Sunday has all these daft women draped round pedestal vases singing Ave Maria or Bless This House, and James Mason intones bits from the Old Testament looking pained & perturbed. As well he might be. Last night on Credo there was a woman who'd been chucked out of the nunnery: 'It's a pity really because I enjoyed it there, but the Mother Superior said that I could not have communist literature. She made me kneel down and ask forgiveness of all the other novitiates. I didn't mind really. I

think they were more embarrassed than I was. So I went and joined
the British Communist Party and I am now their leading woman
spokesman. I encourage people to join the party. You can be a Christian AND a communist, that's what I try and tell them!' When someone pointed out that Communism was concerned with the
COLLECTIVE and that Christianity was concerned with the Individual she smiled like the blissfully ignorant cow that she was. Found
myself thinking 'No wonder those nuns chucked you out!' Have you
ever realised that the fervour of these people is always a measure of
their personal misery? All these political activists are fundamentally
miserable people – people who feel that the world has cheated them
in some way, that they have not had it good, and that someone else
IS having it good, and they are furious about that! . . . Oh yes! and
the changed telephone number goes on being a boon! The quiet since
it's been done! Miraculous.

>   Love from your old chum,
>   [K]

To NEIL COLLINGS (Abbey Chaplain at Westminster)

23 April 1979

Dear Neil,
A word of thanks for your kind hospitality yesterday; you made the
entire day memorable for us.[1] I was delighted that you remembered
the Saint Pancras story; I remember now, it was a radio programme
in which I spoke about Shaw's reference to the gay element in Christianity, he says 'the church was founded gaily with a pun' talking about
Peter saying 'on this rock I found my church' with the play on 'Petra'.
But the idea of an irate bishop of St Pancras calling outside the gates
'I am the Bishop of St Pancras!' and the boy leaning out of a turret
saying 'If it comes to that, I *am* St Pancras' struck me as delightfully
funny. I'm off to Bristol for ten radio episodes for the BBC.

>   yours,
>   [K]

---

[1]   KW and Michael Whittaker had visited the Turin Shroud exhibition at
Westminster Cathedral. KW had said 'Let's see how many there are at our place!', so
they went to Evensong at the Abbey. 'Afterwards the Abbey Chaplain gave us tea.'
(Details from KW's diary, 22 April.)

To JURY SUMMONING OFFICER (Greater London Jury Office)[1]

29 February 1980

Dear Sir,
Since I am an actor/comedian whose face is well known, and whose work has involved the role of a Judge in satirical sketches on television and in radio broadcasts and making quasi-legal asseverations on the BBC programme 'Just A Minute', I should have thought I was an unsuitable candidate for the anonymity and disinterested nature of Jury service.
   [K]

To ISABEL DEAN[2]

18 March 1980

My dear Isabel,
I'm having to wear the specs for writing now; did I tell you those bi-focals were no good? I took them back to Curry & Paxton. But they were understanding and changed them for the ordinary lenses without charging me. Remember that day I rushed you in there? 'This lady is in great distress and must have immediate attention . . .' etc. Oh! but your letter made me fall about! especially when I got to the stuff about actors' halitosis! It is disgusting but one DOES laugh . . . I had to go up to Wales for a mammoth recording of the Arthur Waley 'Monkey' stories.[3] The voice was like a foghorn cos of the aftermath of flu, the head full of rheum and the eyes swimming. In the recording studios they were all full of: 'We had Princess Grace of Monaco last week, doing this poetry recital with Alan Pascoe;[4] she had to be addressed as SERENE HIGHNESS the whole time. Very much on her dignity I can tell you! and an enormous retinue! with loads of luggage! we counted more than seven pieces, not to mention the hat-boxes!' After that, my zip-bag with pyjamas and tooth-brush must have looked pathetic . . . The agent has just telephoned: 'Mel Brooks

[1]   This letter survived as a handwritten rough, dated as shown (and 'posted 12.30')
[2]   Elegant actress and Equity Councillor, very popular in the profession. She and KW often took refuge in each other's company at Equity meetings.
[3]   Arthur Waley (1889–1966) published *Monkey*, his translation of a sixteenth-century Chinese novel, in 1942. KW recorded it for the Nimbus company at their country-house studios at Wyastone Leys, 8–11 February 1980.
[4]   KW means Richard Pasco (b.1926), the British actor, who had toured sundry festivals reciting poetry with HSH Princess Grace. Alan Pascoe (b.1948) was a British international 400-metre hurdler of the 1970s.

would like to meet you to talk about your being in his film "The History of the World" . . . would you go along to the Connaught Hotel?' When I said I would need to see a script she said 'There isn't one; I have already asked that and they say he gets the ideas as he goes along' so I said no thank you. Then there was a load of guff about 'you should do a film like this – you need to get out of the Carry On rut' etc. I have just caught another cold and the nose is streaming and the voice like a nutmeg grater and I hold the telephone receiver with my eyes closed thinking 'Shut up you stupid cow' but saying 'no I can't take part in these ad-lib creations; I think they are artistically invalid' and patiently listen to another load of hogwash. Sorry this typing is so lousy but I have got this awful cold and the eyes keep swimming & I can only do the two finger stuff anyway. I use the machine cos it helps me THINK. My handwriting isn't bad, but with a pen I tend to write a note, rather than compose a letter. Isn't that wierd (or is it weird? yes of course it is). Didn't go to Equity yesterday for the Council Meeting cos I had this job to do at Bush House. Chat show about Gossip with Elaine Stritch and two journalists. E S has got nothing to say really. She just burbles away. Everyone is extraordinarily obsequious towards her. If she were English they wouldn't bother, but always these expatriates command a ridiculous amount of attention. Dinner tonight with Gyles Brandreth;[1] he is doing this book I am writing, through an arrangement with Dent's. It is called 'Acid Drops' and it's about classic put-downs – an anthology of quotes, with some linking passages which he culls largely from one's own tape-recorded conversation. But there's rewrites, proof checks, book jacket designs, publicity plugs & loads of rubbish I could do without. Barbara Windsor on the phone 'Oh I hate living in Stanmore! it's all posh Kosher and I can't get anyone to do the cleaning . . . I have to pay this old queen to come all the way here from Peabody Buildings in Drury Lane . . . you can't get anyone round here . . . trouble is my Ronnie won't move!' Since he's on bail awaiting trial for murder, that situation may be considerably altered later on.[2] Meanwhile Stanmore is better than Brixton. But of course I didn't S A Y any of that.

>   love,
>   [K]

---

[1]   Later Conservative MP for Chester, then active as a writer and 'book-packager'.
[2]   'Ronald Knight, aged forty-five, the husband of Barbara Windsor, the actress, was cleared of a revenge killing by a jury at the Central Criminal Court yesterday' (*Times*, 20 November 1980). The case concerned the killing of Alfredo Zomparelli in a Soho amusement arcade in 1974. Nicholas Gerard was also cleared.

To SHEILA HANCOCK

4 June 1981

My dear Sheila,
Got to do a religious spot for Southern TV on Sunday with Roger
Royle & someone called Monseigneur Buckley![1] Phew! the grandeur.
Probably just as well 'cos I'm not one for Actors' Centres: when I'm
not working I think I prefer solitude. Saw a thing about a nature
reserve on TV & I thought 'How marvellous to live in such isolation!
not a soul about . . . just the puffins.' I thought I'd be all right till I
thought about the central heating and the dentist and bending down
to do the shoelaces. I'm working on a recording (mammoth) of a
series of stories and preparing a radio script & there's talk of going to
Sydney for [Michael] Parkinson[2] on 17 June but I'm not telling anyone (except you) 'cos the Australian High Commission ain't given the
work permit visa so it may all go awry. If it DOES come off, I'll be
back about July & we can go out for a snack & the chat.

> Love,
> Kenneth

To JEFFERY KEMP[3]

15 June 1982

Dear Jeffery,
I'm so glad you found the 'Sussex Stroll' diverting.[4] I was furious at
the ludicrous idea of rising at 3.30 in the morning for birdsong. I
pointed out – at 7.30 – we could hear all of 'em plainly enough at a
later hour, & was told 'Ah yes, but we'll be home much quicker!' It's
weird! the BBC says it's penniless etc. yet they do outside b'casts
which involve 6 hotel rooms, outside catering train fares & heaven
knows what else! Apropos what you say about DIARIES: the publishers of my last book have persuaded me to do another and it is

[1] Royle, b.1939. First known to KW as Senior Chaplain at Eton, later a broadcaster
of popular religious programmes on radio. Very Rev. Monsignor Michael J. Buckley,
D.D., a regular broadcaster on religious matters.
[2] On whose Australian chat show KW did appear that June.
[3] Retired teacher, composer, occasional broadcaster and journalist, resident in
France.
[4] Radio wildlife programme, principally about the dawn chorus (much to KW's
discomfort), with Johnny Morris and Percy Edwards, recorded 21 May 1982. The stroll
took place in Suffolk, however, not Sussex.

excerpts from the '81 diary. I think we've managed to avoid offence by fictionalising a few names & we're revising the typescript shortly. They hope to bring it out early '83. I've called it Back Drops 'cos of theatre scenes and going backwards & dropping in on the past.

>Yours,
>Kenneth

To STEPHEN REDMOND[1]

17 October 1982

Dear Stephen,
I fell about when I read the remarks apropos Welland![2] I did the TV thing with him on Friday at Granada in Manchester and I could hardly believe my ears when he launched into the army stories. He was making the sounds of marching feet, and military band noises as well! presumably to give flavour to the anecdotes. I kept thinking 'for heaven's sake get to the tag line' but alas, he never had one. He said that there was a party in America for Oscar winners and that the recipients were supposed to take the statuettes with them: 'I didn't have mine with me so the press ignored me.' They didn't know their luck.

I was in Manchester on my way back from Leeds where I did 'Countdown',[3] so of course I laughed again when I got to your description of Richard Whiteley. O! you are wickedly unerring. Mind you, I can't crow about anything as far as that show is concerned cos I don't think I was very good on it. Somebody said after that I struck one or two incongruous notes and they're probably right. I had the ear-plug with the producer's voice: 'interrupt – say something funny!' and it all got rather desperate. The audience kept groaning at Whiteley's puns. The canteen at Yorkshire Television uses beans in everything so I kept edging away for the farts. I left with a singed arse and a headache. The driver who picked me up outside the Leeds studio (to take me to Manchester) was garrulous. All I wanted was quiet. He went on and on about people being judged by their accents, and said that certain employers were prejudiced in favour of the ancient

---

[1] A young correspondent from Warrington.
[2] Colin Welland (né Williams) had won an Oscar for his screenplay for *Chariots of Fire*.
[3] Channel 4's letters-and-numbers game, the first programme broadcast on the channel, and still (1994) running. Richard Whiteley has been the host/chairman throughout.

universities etc. I didn't care if they were, so I kept grunting in a non-committal fashion.

I stayed at the Midland Hotel in Manchester. Suddenly realised when I was sitting in their restaurant 'I used to sit here every night with Isobel Barnett[1] for the What's My Line programme' — O! I felt very sad. And old. I got the 9.15 train to London on Saturday and sat next to two revolting creatures who entered carrying 12 cans of beer each. She had straggly blonde hair and a mirthless giggle, he had black stubble everywhere and a T shirt promoting some football team. I changed my seat after Doncaster. It seems odd to find so many of the great unwashed in the First Class. One never saw such filth in the old days. It's democracy gone mad. No of course I don't have one hand in a dictionary of quotes, but you're right about conservatism.[2]

   yours,
   [K]

To PAUL RICHARDSON[3]

26 December 1982

My dear Paul,
Endless thanks for such grand & generous gifts!! You really shouldn't have done it you know. Christmas Day was awful. Terrible people all sitting round overeating & farting surreptitiously. Got home about 12oc. Went for a walk today & heard (on return to block) fearful row 'twixt P. and his wife. They were screaming blue murder at each other. This holiday looks like stretching on & on don't it! All I've got is Gordon on Tuesday and M on the 30th. Do let me know when you get back.

   love,
   Kenneth

---

[1] Lady Barnett had committed suicide in October 1980, after being found guilty of shoplifting.
[2] Redmond had written: 'you either write letters with one hand on a dictionary of quotes, or else you've got a much better memory than I'; and 'you seem to express a conservatism (small "c"), even a stoicism in your letters'.
[3] A friend and near neighbour, and one of K W's legatees.

To PAUL RICHARDSON

21 January 1983

Mon cher Paul,
Going away early on the 25th January.[1] I've told the postman that if
he's got a package that won't go thro' the letter box to give it to you
'cos I don't want that idiot porter interfering, you know what she's
like. On Sat morning I've got to go to the Travel Agent to get tickets
& I've got Just A Minute on Sunday evening. Let me know if you're
free.

    love,
    Kenneth

To PETER ADAMS[2]

1 May 1983

Mon cher Peter,
Wandering round the airport at Singapore, I decided I couldn't stand
the humid heat and fled to the air-conditioned Qantas lounge. Sat
with an undersized fellow who told me: 'I am flying to Bahrain for
this horse-race. I am a jockey. I watched you in the M[ike] W[alsh]
Show. I thought it was marvellous!' I congratulated him on his perspicacity, and we re-boarded the plane together. At the next stop (Bahrain) I wandered round with a man who had a pronounced
mittel-Europa accent. 'I bet you cannot tell where I come from?' when
I said 'Bohemia – probably Prague' he looked amazed and said 'That's
right! – you obviously know about accents! you are brilliant!' I said
'tell me something I don't know' and we went into the Duty Free
shop where he purchased a lot of drink, cigarettes etc. Back on the
aeroplane with the new crew, I complained bitterly to the stewardess
'When the hell are we going to get something to eat? I am starving!'
and I was told 'It won't be long Sir Kenneth.' I did the double take.
'What's all this SIR stuff?' 'You are Sir Kenneth Williams aren't you?'
'No, I am plain Mister.' She looked mystified and went away, then
returned with a paper in her hand: 'The print-out from Melbourne
says SIR KENNETH WILLIAMS.' I told her that someone must
be having a joke and said 'Cross it out.' Eventually – one and a half

---

[1] To Tenerife, with Louie.
[2] One of KW's media minders on a second trip to Australia to appear on 'The Mike
Walsh Show' (April 1983).

hours out of Bahrain – we got the meal. Must say, I was surprised this trip with the quality of the food; it was rotten. All the bread like white blotting paper, and all the menus unadventurous. Onion Soup! ugh! I ask you! I found an extremely engaging youth with all the flesh bulging out of the jeans etc. Played a game of Scrabble with him. He won. I wasn't best pleased and my chagrin was obvious. 'I can see your chagrin' he smiled & I told him he shouldn't be looking. It sounded vaguely indecent . . . In the end, I was ensconced in the flat by 7.45 on Friday morning. Spoke to Michael Anderson[1] on the telephone. He asked 'How did they treat you?' 'Superbly.' 'Yes, well I must say Peter Adams struck me on the telephone as a thoroughly capable young man.' 'He's that all right. Looks like one of those senior boys from Eton. Very deceptive-looking. I thought he looked far too young to be any good but he was brilliant!' I've yet to peruse your Australian dialect dictionary; I was very touched you should have thought of giving it to me. Oh Peter! you were a godsend on that trip. Heaven knows how I would have fared without your perception. Hope your directing job is hugely successful. Love to you,

> your OLD chum,
> [K]

To STEPHEN CROPPER[2]

n.d. [October 1983]

Dear Steve,
Very pleasant surprise to see the unusual postmark and stamp on your envelope when it arrived this morning! You don't say how far Tamworth is from Sydney but since it is in NSW I fancy it cannot be very far. Your letter carries NO ADDRESS; just the date at the top of the notepaper. Just hope this gets to you all right. I have been involved with a one-man show for London Weekend TV.[3] A one-man show. I ran for about two hours and they've cut it down to 90 minutes and put in the editing pauses for the commercial breaks. I went to see this version last week and I was amazed at the standard they'd maintained . . . When I was doing a radio programme recently, it included playing requests for listeners and one old lady phoned in

---

[1] His agent (at the ICM agency) after the death of Peter Eade in 1979.
[2] Australian acquaintance from the staff of 'The Mike Walsh Show', later in local radio.
[3] 'An Audience with Kenneth Williams'.

asking for the song 'Edelweiss' and the producer received a letter of thanks which was full of malapropisms. She wrote 'thank you for my lovely Anal vice! all my neighbours thought it was the best thing in the show!' and obviously she is totally unaware of the error. Good job you didn't stay with the weird Sylvie. She sounds a bit frightening. This accommodation seeking can be off putting. I remember one land-lady in Bradford showing us the room and saying 'I had actors here last week, look at this!' and she flung back the bedclothes to reveal a stained sheet. 'What do you think that is?' she demanded. I was too appalled to reply but my companion showed great aplomb. 'Iron mould?' he asked smilingly but she enlightened him swiftly AND rudely . . . The publishers of the paper back of 'Acid Drops' – no, I mean 'Back Drops' – rang me and asked me to attend a literary dinner to promote it but I said I was far too busy; they want me to go all over the place next year, but with any luck I will find some excuse to get out of it.

    your old chum,
    KENNETH WILLIAMS

To ANDREW HATHAWAY

23 November 1983

Dear Andrew,
It is freezing here I can tell you. Temperatures down to minus 5 centigrade last night. Even the overcoat doesn't seem to keep out the cold when you're walking about the streets. A friend from Vikingstad in Sweden writes today 'I dream of going to the West Indies, away from all the cold of this country' and I can't say I blame him. Yes, Rupert Murdoch owns the Times and it seems to continue with a high journalistic standard but I must admit I don't take it very often. They went on strike for about ten months and I switched to the Telegraph and I have stayed with it ever since. Seems much more compact as a paper. The Times is sectionalised – and I don't care for that. I saw Rupert on television once. He comes over as a very likeable fellow I must say. And he paid for my trip to Australia because he owns the television station in Sydney that does the Parkinson show. I am going to the Television studios at Teddington tomorrow. We are doing this compilation of excerpts from the Carry On films. Me and Barbara Windsor talking in between to link the pieces. She goes on and on about 'I've never had it!' and when I ask 'What?' she says 'A white Christmas' and at the end, I become the fairy on top of the tree. I

wave the wand and she is covered in snow. They are using a poly-styrene stuff so she doesn't actually get wet. Don't want her going down with pneumonia . . .

[K]

To PAUL RICHARDSON

1 April 1985

Darling
Went over to Hyde Park & got your ticket for you. Cedric was WORN OUT after & said he walked back on his ankles!

love,
Monica

To JEFFERY KEMP

27 May 1986

Dear Jeff,
Your grapevine, as you call it, is full of misinformation. I'm not going ANYWHERE, let alone Paris. The last gastroscopy showed that the ulcer had receded. Now, they have given me ANOTHER bloody barium X-ray & I have to see the specialist next week to find out what other horrors they have in store. The radiographer seems to think it is a spastic colon. All meals are followed by pain of one kind or another. One LONGS to be able to fart. I told Gordon Jackson & he said 'Oh! my trouble is the desperate desire to BURP . . . of course, yours *would* be the other end, wouldn't it?' V. Freudian.

Yours,
Kenneth

To NICK LEWIS[1]

18 July 1986

Dear Nick,
I'm still laughing about that child's essay! 'I knocked on the door but the woman who answered it shit in my face.' Marvellous. It *shouldn't*

---

[1]   A Warwick University student to whom KW was acting as an epistolary mentor.

have been a mistake. It's exactly like the Pinter character (Tramp) in The Caretaker 'I knocked on the door of this monastery & this old monk come to the door and I asked him for a pair of shoes & he said PISS OFF...'

Thank you for your encouraging words apropos the book[1] – I have just done a children's book which involves me in an endless round of publicity events – signing sessions & talks etc. Liverpool tomorrow. Joan Rivers[2] Monday & then I start on the Galloping Galaxies series for children. Yes! pity you're not nearer – Redruth is a long way off – I did rep at Newquay & we were over there once but it's probably changed considerably since '48!

> Yours,
> Kenneth

To STANLEY BAXTER

30 December 1986

My dear Stanley,
After your TV show,[3] Lou turned to me & said 'Well, that's the funniest show I've ever seen Stanley do! He was marvellous!' She fell about over the Hottest Nurse In Town. It was a triumph for you. My favourites were the Queen at the Centre, and the Whicker section, but it's invidious to particularise. Even tiny items like the carpet-laying were superb. There is no one to touch you in this kind of show! Not a dull moment! The crack about Peter Hall[4] in the Western (a la Coward) was wonderful.

> Admiration & love,
> Kenneth

---

[1] *Just Williams*, his autobiography.
[2] The American comedienne was hosting a British chat show at this time.
[3] 'Stanley Baxter's Picture Annual', BBC1, 29 December.
[4] Sir Peter Hall, b.1930. Director, National Theatre, 1973–88.

To MICHAEL WHITTAKER[1]

4 January 1987

My dear Michael,
It was particularly kind & thoughtful of you to give me the Observer
piece on Maggie [Smith]. Read it when I came home & thought it
well put together. These profiles aren't easy things to do & in Mags'
case they're more difficult 'cos she hates publicity. My life as a sort
of mentor, jailer & male nurse is restricting. Even if it came to a
HOME, Lou would still be on my mind – visiting etc. – but I am
finding it more & more of a BORE. The thanks of the old are fulsome
at the time, but gutter as quick as a candle. But whenever you are
there, it's different again. She thinks you're wonderful. I will always
be grateful for your patience.

> Love,
> Kenneth

To NICK LEWIS

24 February 1987

Dear Nick,
Impossible to advise about 'cos friendships are matters for individuals
– there are no rules. The friends are those who take the chaff & grain
together, keep what's worth keeping & with a breath of kindness blow
the rest away. Emerson said his friends 'came to me unsought, the
good God sent them to me . . .' And that's a lovely thought for someone with Faith. Sometimes I think there is a benign influence for our
good & sometimes I don't. Sometimes I think this is a vast orphanage
where no one knows his origin & no one comes to claim us. The old
have no superior knowledge – if you'd read ALL the books they'd
read you'd only know as much as them. In the end, it comes back to
Rilke's 'only ENDURE' – we all have to find our own way to endure
& accept mortality.

> Your old chum,
> Kenneth

---

[1] Businessman and loyal friend to KW and his mother, particularly helpful in
practical matters like transport.

To JACK [?]

21 March 1987

Dear Jack,
I was fascinated reading your long and interesting letter. Symptoms seem to invariably match my own. I have had considerable rectal trouble over the years – including operations for fissure, fistula, and inflammation of colon – and it never seems to go away. Just some periods easier than others. I have never taken the food question seriously cos I always thought that the things you enjoyed eating were good for you, but after reading your letter I am beginning to think otherwise. Yesterday, I had nothing to eat until after a book signing session, the manager gave us sandwiches & tea in his office. When I got home, there were two blisters on the face. Looked in the mirror and thought 'What the hell gave rise to that?' and then tried to remember what I'd eaten. It was just the brown-bread sandwich with some sort of tinned fish, and the cup of tea.

   Last year I had such a pain & heartburn I went to a specialist. He sent me for every kind of test. Blood, urine etc. I had that sonic scan, the Barium X-ray (oral & anal) and the entire body scan. Nothing. Then, after a fortnight, he did a gastroscopy and found a stomach ulcer. 'That's been your trouble all along!' he pronounced. Put me on Zantac. Another gastroscopy after six weeks and he said it was gone. A couple of months later I went back to him and said I was still in pain 'like having a stitch pain – on the right side of the abdomen' and he sent me for ANOTHER barium X-ray. This was when he told me 'You have a spastic colon' and thereafter it was all talk of high-fibre diet etc. None of it has done any good. One dinner of raw vegetables, stalks and all, left me in agony afterwards. He put me on Libraxin, Colofac, Sucralfate, all no good. Went back to my own doctor. He gave me Nystan, then Colpermin, and then Fybogel. None of it works. All meals followed by discomfort, some meals followed by dreadful pain.

   After mentioning it on television I had LOADS of letters from people discussing the SAME symptoms. All of them desperate to find a cure. I think it is more widespread than anyone is aware. Of course there were weird letters as well. One woman offering to manipulate my feet 'Your trouble is in your feet' – but most of them were sincere correspondents obviously suffering. I think I'll ask my man about seeing Dr McEwen. I am v. grateful to you for the pointer.

      yours,
      [KW]

To JEFFERY KEMP

14 April 1987

Dear Jeff,

Your grapevine ain't v. reliable. I ain't had any operations. Haven't been near a hospital since those tests in Feb '86 (gastroscopy) and I certainly don't want to. More I hear about hospitals the more I distrust their efficacy. They're FULL of germs. The lavatories in University College Hosp. are unbelievable. The filth is quite disgusting. I keep getting loads of letters (10 more today) asking what I'm going to do next!! I ain't doing anything. You'd think when you get to my age (61) they'd leave you alone, wouldn't you? But no – what shows are you planning? etc etc. As tho' it's a sort of endless performance. Gawd 'elp us!

      Yours,
      Kenneth

To JEFFERY KEMP

14 May 1987

Dear Jeff,

Thank you for your letter of 6 May. Sorry my airmail took so long to reach you, but it's probably because there was a postal strike here. Several boxes were sealed up in this area! Yes, you're right about the ARENA programme.[1] Everyone has written asking why they don't USE the people involved instead of showing so many old clips. Oh! it is typical of TV. Recently they asked me to do a programme on Aberdeen! I was to be one of *three* guests invited to talk in a half hour show. Fly all that way for about 2 minutes' airtime! It is ridiculous. Told 'em to stuff it. The Clochemerle you mention was done over here but it flopped.[2] Sounded v. unsavoury to me. There has been a lot of publicity for ORTON, with a play about him at the King's Head,[3] and the film by Alan Bennett[4] and the publication of the Orton

---

[1] KW had not recently complained (in his diary) about BBC2's idiosyncratic arts programme. He had contributed, however, to an 'Arena' on chat shows (recorded in January 1987), in which a lot of old clips had been included. This was evidently the offending edition.

[2] French comic novel by Gabriel Chevallier, serialised on BBC TV without success.

[3] *Diary of a Somebody*, by John Lahr.

[4] *Prick Up Your Ears* (1987).

diaries. I'm getting sick of this saga. I think John Lahr has really MILKED this old cow till the teats are withered. Peggy Ramsay (Joe Orton's Literary Agent) was furious at being represented in the play! She wrote to me & said she'd taken out an injunction to stop it ever occurring again. Oh! now I've come to this bit in your letter about the photograph fading! and of course I can't put a photo in an airmail like this!! What are you doing in Cannes? You say 'arranging the film mob.'[1] What does it entail? Never did find out what your job was. You know mine of course. Not that it's *much* of one nowadays. I did a voice over for SONY but they said I lacked 'authority'!! So I got the elbow.

> Yours,
> Kenneth

To JEFFERY KEMP

24 June 1987

Dear Jeff,
Sorry you had such sad news apropos your mother. Mine still struggles on at 86 with failing powers, deafness, arthritis etc. and no quality of life. An endless worry & inhibition as far as I'm concerned. Funny you say writing is painful 'cos your handwriting is awfully good. Thank you for your flattering remarks about the Audience With KW. The original was 2 hours. They put it out originally in '82[2] on Channel 4 at 90 minutes (after a lot of cuts) and when they repeated it this year, they cut it down to 50 minutes. All the references to Moby Dick & Orson Welles vanished completely. Oh well. I always thought it was very pro'ey.[3] I had a phone call from Peggy Ramsay saying she was furious about how she's portrayed in the Orton play at the King's Head. 'I'm issuing a writ thro' my lawyers! Have you seen it?' I said no. 'You're in it! the actor plays you as a dreadful whining queen endlessly talking about cottaging & the size of men's cocks.' She said 'You should issue a writ! it's deformation.' I think she means defamation. I said that since it wasn't true I wasn't bothered. Then Bill Kenwright[4] rang. 'I'm thinking of transferring the Orton play to the

---

[1] Kemp had actually written '*avoiding* the film mob'.
[2] Actually first shown on 15 December 1983, on Channel 4. Later issued, in its shortened form, as a video.
[3] i.e. Overladen with material of interest only to fellow professionals.
[4] b.1945. Theatrical producer, entrepreneur, former actor.

West End . . . would you object?' I said no. Frankly I don't think it will LAST. They haven't got a NAME in it. It is raining here AGAIN. Seems to have rained all of June!

Yours,
Kenneth

To PETER CADLEY[1]

6 July 1987

Dear Peter,
Appalled to hear about the disgraceful ransacking of your post. The theft of the cheque book is horrible. I should instruct your bank NOT to post such items in future. Sounds as if the letter box facilities at Maybury Court are unsatisfactory. Worse than the Knightsbridge Safety Deposit.[2] Saw Michael [Whittaker] yesterday & we drove to Cambridgeshire – lunch at Elmdon. It's an enchanting sleepy village & one is slightly surprised to find such English tranquillity in the modern world, so near to London.

Yours,
Kenneth

To JEFFERY KEMP

17 July 1987

Dear Jeff,
The lines are from Thomas Gray's 'Ode on a Distant Prospect of Eton' which concludes:

> 'Since sorrow never comes too late
> And happiness where ignorance is bliss
> 'Tis folly to be wise.'

There are loads of quotes from him in general use, especially from the Stoke Poges 'Elegy in a Country Churchyard' but his name never seems to be remembered does it? And preceding lines, which so often give SENSE to a quote, are often forgotten. Think of Pope's –

---

[1] Latterly Deputy London Administrator, Royal Shakespeare Company.
[2] Report (*Times*) 14 July: 'Armed robbers escape with estimated £20 million worth of contents.'

> 'Fly to altars
> There they'll talk you dead
> Fools rush in where angels
> Fear to tread'

There, the first lines, with the reference to endless wrangling over theological arguments, is [sic] very sagacious. Thank you for the photographs. You look very good. And prosperous. As to pensions, well they're all a con really. You pay when money is worth something, and they pay when it isn't. The ones who have got a good deal are those who arrange to get it index linked, 'cos they're protected against inflation. Yes, Kenny Connor has aged considerably. I thought that, when I saw him on television. Probably worry. He is a family man, and Bacon tells us 'He that hath wife and children has given hostages to fortune.' I think Shaw was right. If you want to be single-minded it is best to be single. Philip Larkin echoed that with 'Don't have any kids yourself.'[1] Yes, Charlie Hawtrey is alive. He even survived a F I R E at his home in Deal. When the firemen brought him down the ladder, wrapped in a blanket from the upstairs window, they said 'You're all right now' and he told them 'No I'm not. My fags are upstairs by the bed, and my boyfriend's in it.' And it was true. I think there is something wrong with the ribbon on this typewriter. Don't like using a machine, but I thought I'd better type 'cos you asked for that quote you see. Dent tell me that they are going to re-issue 'Acid Drops' in paperback next year, so I'll put in about N's friend saying 'I am moving – I am going to Lower Sloane Street' & the reply was 'When you get there you will!'

> yours,
> Kenneth

To JEFFERY KEMP

9 September 1987

Dear Jeff,

The best anthology is Palgrave, so I will send you that. Thank you for your letter and the recording; heaven knows when I'll hear it, 'cos I haven't got a tape-recorder, only a gramophone. PLEASE don't send me ANYTHING. The flat is tiny and there is nowhere to put anything. Glad you heard the 'Desert Island Discs' programme.[2] It is so

---

[1]   Last line of 'This be the Verse', from Larkin's *High Windows* (1974).
[2]   Recorded 30 March 1987, with KW interviewed by Michael Parkinson.

much better without that oleaginous creature Plum Lee[1] – ugh! he made me want to throw up. I did it with him in the sixties and practically came out of the BBC gasping for air. You were not supposed to laugh about Charlie Hawtrey being hauled out of the fire, with the boyfriend languishing in the bed and the fags uncollected. It is supposed to have a tragic ring, like the 'Wreck of the Deutschland' or something. People are always writing asking me how they can get in touch with him. It is all otiose 'cos he never answers letters. When he first retired to Deal I went down there with some friends to visit. Banged and banged at the door to no avail. Eventually a window on the opposite side screeched open and a woman with the hair in curlers shouted rudely 'You after Charlie?' 'Mister Hawtrey,' I returned haughtily. 'We were seeking Mister Hawtrey!' 'Try the Saracen's Head,' she bawled and shut the window. Well we must have visited half the pubs in the neighbourhood, but eventually CH was found. Rather the worse for wear. Insisted on taking us to tea with these 'Wonderful friends of mine that have a little cafe where they make EVERYTHING with the[ir] own HOME stone ground flour.' After eating one of their cakes, I think I got the stone. Felt like a foundation stone. Just sank into the stomach relentlessly. Took a lot of bicarb & farting to shift it. O never again. As we walked along the front, fishermen eyed us warily. Charlie was in orange trousers, blue shirt and silk scarf at the neck. He was carrying his umbrella as a parasol. The day was quite fine. The rest of us were trying to look anonymous. 'Hallo lads!' he kept calling out to men painting their boats. 'They all adore me here,' he told us, 'brings a bit of glamour into their dull lives.' They smiled back uneasily, and certainly some returned his salutations, but I didn't get the impression of universal adoration. The house was awful. Everywhere you went there were these huge brass beds. 'They'll come back into fashion one day & I'll make a fortune!' he declared as he rubbed them affectionately. Then he recited an endless saga about some boys from the Royal Marines school of Music carousing with him round the local hostelries & all piling back to his place to stay the night: 'And just LOOK at what they gave me to show their appreciation!' he cried, thrusting a huge portfolio in front of us. Somebody asked nervously 'What is it?' and with extraordinary triumph CH announced 'The original score of THE BOHEMIAN GIRL.' He kept on about this being an original and repeating that it had 'the Vienna stamp on it' but the whole thing

---

[1]   KW had first appeared on 'Desert Island Discs' on 2 May 1961, interviewed by the originator of the programme, Roy Plomley.

smacked of fraudulence. What on earth has Balfe to do with Vienna, one asks oneself.

> yours,
> Kenneth

To JEFFERY KEMP

3 November 1987

Dear Jeff,
Very good of the postman to deliver your Plus Belle Lavande so promptly. I put some on straightway. Just so happens I'd only got some Greek stuff which wasn't v. good. Went to the Devonshire Hospital for the second gastroscopy on the 31st Oct. They said the recurrent ulcer had gone. But I'm left with the spastic colon. About which they can do nothing. So much for modern medicine. Heart transplants, kidney transplants, kidney replacements, plastic hips etc. but fuck all to cure the common cold. Off to TV Centre to do a programme called Cover to Cover. Got to talk about 3 books.[1] Two of 'em are lousy but the third is Ellmann's biog of Wilde which is superb. Getting slightly colder now & the leaves are falling & making a mess of the streets. All this rubbish about the hurricane smashing down our trees being tragic.[2] The more trees they smash down the better.

> Yours,
> Kenneth

To NICK LEWIS

6 November 1987

Dear Nick,
No, I didn't see the film.[3] I don't go to the cinema. Didn't see the play[4] either but I got a letter from the actor playing ME![5] saying he

---

[1] KW appeared with the writers Victoria Glendinning and Patricia Highsmith and the actor Jack Klaff, discussing Richard Ellmann's *Oscar Wilde*, Dan Jacobson's *Her Story*, and Highsmith's *Tales of Natural and Unnatural Catastrophes*.
[2] The small hours of the morning of 16 October had brought the 'storm of the century' to southern areas of England and Wales.
[3] *Prick Up Your Ears.*
[4] *Diary of a Somebody.*
[5] Philip Lowrie.

hoped I wouldn't be offended etc. Oh! I think they're all mad. Just had the 4th gastroscopy at the Devonshire Hospital – Oh! I'm sick of bloody doctors Nick!

> Yours,
> Kenneth

To JEFFERY KEMP

12 January 1988

Dear Jeff,

Got your letter of 6 January yesterday. I hope that the healing process continues & that it is no longer painful to use your hand. I remember when a fibroid neuroma was removed from my left hand, how agonising were the after effects (arm in sling etc.) and the pain which seemed to go on & on. I'm left handed. Still I could manage the Barclays Bank with the right so that was OK. Very interesting to read of your encounter in the forest. Sounds like something out of a novel. Almost unbelievable. A sort of too good to be true element. But I'm sure the account is accurate. Nearest I got to it was in Ceylon. A place called Kurunegala. He was a young Sikh and it was in a coconut grove. Only a Barclays or a J. Arthur Rank but at the time, extraordinarily exciting. O! no. I don't trust any of it. The sex urge is entirely animal. The bit left over in us from the apes. The intellectual life can only view it as pathetic, undignified & embarrassing. Understand exactly what Plato meant when he said that after the sexual compulsion vanished with age, he felt 'released from a demon.' Of course the animal hangover element in us is essential for reproduction. And man is supposed to reproduce. All the religious support the progenitive idea, sanctity of family life & so on, and therefore place TABOOS on any deviation hence the persecution of homosexuals, adulterers, incestuousness, lesbianism . . . all of 'em threats to the status quo. Religions are the biggest con tricks in the world. The money they make! From the orthodox to the moonies. It's a fortune. All done by kidding people they're immortal – you're not going to die, you're going to another place, Heaven, Nirvana, Happy Hunting Ground . . . you name it, they've got it. And the poor sods take it in, hook line & sinker. O! the gullibility of 'em! It's astonishing. Every time you hear that yet another bogus 'inspector' has conned a pensioner out of life savings you think 'O! they can't have fallen for THAT one!' but they did. And WHY are they so gullible? Because they HATE the idea of death. Can't accept mortality. Frightened to death of ANY mystery. Which is why crime writers do so well. It was a Tudor man who wrote 'And now we have our philosophical persons to make MODERN & FAMILIAR, things which are supernatural & causeless, hence it is that we make errors of trifles, ensconcing ourselves in seeming knowledge, when we SHOULD submit ourselves to an unknown fear.'[1] Odd really that Shakespeare should be thought of as a poet 'cos his prose is superb. No, I'm not going to do a Carry On film. Don't think such a project will EVER get off the ground. They float the rumour every so often in the hope that it will attract backers & money, but invariably nothing happens.

>   Yours,
>   Kenneth

To JEFFERY KEMP

26 January 1988

Dear Jeff,
Sorry to learn that such a precious member got black and blue. Happened to me once in Tangier & I had to visit a French Doctor in the Rue Goya. He examined it with telescopic spectacles. 'Ah yes . . . your friend has been over-enthusiastic . . . I will give you some cream to apply . . .' Later on, the skin was cascading like confetti every time I had a pee. Went to my own Doctor in London a week later. 'This ointment you've been using is too strong . . . it's taken a layer off the epidermis . . .' Very good photograph of Jean-Jacques,[2] the camera has captured a mood of such humanity. Yes, I expect I will be around on the date you mention when you're in London. Can't go away 'cos Lou is 86 & needs looking after. She's no good on the pins, so travel is out of the question. Hate the telephone with a pathological intensity, so you'll have to mention the day when you fix everything & we can meet at a restaurant. Off to the accountant now to find out what Norwich Union are going to shell out for my pension.

>   Yours,
>   Kenneth

---

[1] *All's Well That Ends Well*, II, iii. Lafew: 'They say miracles are past, and we have our philosophical persons, to make modern and familiar, things supernatural and causeless. Hence it is that we make trifles of terrors, ensconcing ourselves into seeming knowledge when we should submit ourselves to an unknown fear.'
[2] Jean-Jacques Front, a friend of Jeffery Kemp.

To NICK LEWIS

9 February 1988

Dear Nick,
Thank you for yr letter. No we don't want any cameras thank you very much. Good thing you sent the photograph so we can all recognise each other. You're right about meetings being a disappointment. They usually are. Looked at as a failure in ADVANCE, they're not so bad.

Yours,
Kenneth

To JEFFERY KEMP

19 February 1988

Dear Jeff,
Thank you for the Plus Belle Lavande. And for the birthday card. Since it was addressed in Jean-Jacques's hand I was misled at first. What a CHARMING gesture from him.

Went to the Ritz yesterday. It was a birthday party given by this millionaire for a chum. Gielgud at the next table, looking like the OAP being given the treatment. The food was rotten. They all said it was a LOVELY room. You can't eat architecture. Lobster cocktail 20 pounds!! I mean . . . who's got that sort of money?

One of the Royal Equerries was there & he made us laugh about the visiting foreign potentates. 'Ah well, another chimps' tea party you see . . .'

Yours
Kenneth

To NICK LEWIS

19 February 1988

Dear Nick,

. . . Got your letter today. Yes, I know what you mean about adolescence & the turbulent nature of burgeoning sex-urges. Just remember everyone else experiences much the same but few of 'em are articulate about it. You're both sophisticated and self-aware, so of course you feel it much more. You are right about Michael. He is a good friend. One in a million. This Edmund White book[1] is really v. repetitive. Seems to be endless fellatio. Amazing it got such good reviews! Perhaps we'd all better start talking about our auto-erotica!

> Yours,
> Kenneth

To NICK LEWIS

2 March 1988

Dear Nick,

You certainly write a good letter! It gave quite a fillip to the day. I'd had an awful night 'cos of the spastic colon – up at all hours – and telephoned this morning to cancel a dinner tonight 'cos I know late eating will result in pain. Interesting to read your comments on the play.[2] You're quite right, it wouldn't interest me in the least. Fell about when I read about the actor protesting his heterosexuality![3] As you know, I think the whole Orton saga has been turned into an industry by John Lahr; it's got a lot to do with his American background. It is extraordinary, the difference between the taste of the cultivated European & the Yanks. You can see it in Henry James as opposed to Virginia Woolf – weird, but it is always there. BBC rang up & asked if I would do a spot on 'The Spinners' as Rambling Syd!! I said 'Yes, well they don't mind that at all . . .' so I agreed. Consequently I have to go to the Paris to do it on Monday night. I'll have been there on Sunday as well – for 'Just A Minute'! Oh! I know that studio like the back of my hand. And I've looked at THAT quite a few times.

> Yours,
> Kenneth

---

[1] *The Beautiful Room is Empty*, the latest novel by Edmund White (b.1941).
[2] The touring production of *Diary of a Somebody*.
[3] Rob Heyland, a married man with children, playing Halliwell.

To JEFFERY KEMP

5 March 1988

Dear Jeff,

You say you are in England from April 1st to April 7th. So you must tell me what day you want to come up to London for lunch. Just tell me the day, and I'll fix the place. The week of 1st to 7th is free at the moment, so you can say what suits you.

The line about the Ritz was not right. I realise on reflection that the reply to 'what a beautiful room' should've been 'you can't eat the decor.' Oh, I don't know, the SHAPE of the room & the vast windows on to the park ARE architectural features. Perhaps it should stay as it is.

Freud said at 'Just A Minute' last week that he asked an American woman who'd get the Presidency & she said 'My heart tells me BUSH but my bush tells me HART . . .'[1]

       Yours,
       Kenneth

To JEFFERY KEMP

17 March 1988

Dear Jeff,

Got your letter this morning. I have put the 5th April in the engagement book. Suggest we meet at 12oc at Vecchia Milano in Welbeck St W1. That is a trattoria behind Debenham's in Oxford Street. I have asked a friend of mine, Michael Whittaker, to join us. Vecchia Milano is not hard to find. Dent (the publishers) in Welbeck Street introduced me to it 'cos it was so near to their offices. It is very nice & unpretentious. Trying a new thing for the spastic colon. It is called COLPERMIN & first indications are that it is helpful!

       Yours,
       Kenneth

---

[1] Michael Dukakis, not Gary Hart, was the eventual Democrat candidate defeated in the US Presidential elections by George Bush.

To JEFFERY KEMP

23 March 1988

Dear Jeff,
Just to warn you that our arrangement may well be in hazard. I go
into hospital for more tests etc. apropos this ulcer & spastic colon on
Friday 25th so may not be out of hospital by time we're supposed to
meet. Won't be doing any writing & won't be here to read letters so
everything will have to pile up till my return.

>   Yours
>   Kenneth

To PAUL RICHARDSON[1]

n.d. [approximately 23 March 1988]

Paul,
Murray Lyon[2] has got me into the Cromwell – go in about 2 o'c on
FRIDAY.
    Could you keep an eye on Lou? Her number is 387 3330.
    It's little things like changing the battery on her deaf aid she can't
cope with.

>   love,
>   Kenneth

To MICHAEL CODRON (by hand)

8 April 1988

My dear Michael,
Thought of you ALL DAY yesterday. Tried to phone but your office
no. which I have proved useless. Wanted to ask if you'd seen the
news about the death of Myra De Groot? It is extraordinary, 'cos she'd
written to me saying she was coming over to do Chat Shows here!!
apropos her part in NEIGHBOURS!! Must have been a very sudden
death.[3] She was 51.

---

[1] Paul Richardson writes: 'This would be the last note I would have received from
Ken.'
[2] Iain Murray-Lyon, physician/surgeon, who had first examined KW in 1986.
[3] She died of bone cancer. She had played Eileen Clarke in the Australian soap
opera.

Thanks for your card this morning. Yes – the ULCER is back with a vengeance. Made me give up the fags. Said if the Zantac doesn't work THIS time I'll have to be operated on & the surgeon added 'Sooner the better because let's face it, you're no chicken . . .' They kept me in the Cromwell for 2 days – tests etc. – Oh! How I HATE these places!

      Love,
      Kenneth

Kenneth Williams was found dead in bed on the morning of 15 April 1988. His papers include a delivery of mail he never saw.

MAIN CORRESPONDENTS OF KENNETH WILLIAMS

STANLEY BAXTER

Scottish actor, comedian and writer first known to KW as a fellow-member of the CSE troupe in Singapore ('Stan Baxter moved into my room', KW's diary, 1 January 1947). After demobilisation, Baxter returned to Scotland where he continued to base his activities for many years. This separation, and Baxter's marriage (to Moira), took some of the impetus out of the friendship, which was also troubled from time to time by feelings of rivalry, particularly on KW's side, once Baxter's career in films and, particularly, television, had begun to flourish. Nevertheless, KW admired Baxter deeply, and felt understood by him. At the time of KW's 'breakdown' at the end of 1965, it was the solace of Baxter's company that he sought in, of all places, Beirut.

HON. GEORGE BORWICK

Hon. George Sandbach Borwick, b.1922, of the 'Borwick's Baking Powder' family; half-brother and heir to the 4th Baron Borwick. A West End 'angel' who had backed KW's second revue success, *Pieces of Eight* (1959). They became close friends around the time of the death of KW's father, Charlie Williams, from carbon tetrachloride poisoning (October 1962), when Borwick offered assistance to Louie and Kenneth. By December 1971, KW was writing: 'I am ... gradually learning that one must expect nothing of anybody with the exception of G B. He is totally consistent with the years: and totally loyal.' Borwick travelled extensively, but corresponded diligently, while KW kept him in touch with London gossip. Borwick was an enthusiastic and supportive attender of KW's first nights, radio shows, TV cabarets, and even the set at Pinewood. He married (1981) Esther, Lady Ellerman; she died in 1985.

CARLETON CARPENTER

Vermont-born (1926) actor who made his Broadway debut in 1944, went into Hollywood films, and then returned to the stage. When Peter Glenville's 1956 translation/production of Feydeau's *Hotel Paradiso* transferred to New York, the part of Maxime, which had been played by K W in London, was taken by Carpenter, and this no doubt was their first point of contact. At the time of the correspondence preserved here, Carpenter, while still accepting theatrical engagements, had taken up a new and remarkably productive career in the writing of paperback thrillers and mysteries, all published under pseudonyms and difficult to trace. Some of the titles he mentions are *Deadhead*, *Sleight of Deadly Hand*, and *Only Her Hairdresser Knew*. Another title, *Pinecastle*, was certainly issued under the name 'Ivy Manchester'. Perhaps it was the notable fecundity of Carpenter the fictioneer that caused the slackness in the correspondence department which K W lost no opportunity to condemn.

MICHAEL CODRON

Perennially successful theatrical producer in the West End of London; produced five shows involving K W, starting with his first hit revue, *Share My Lettuce*, in 1957. All their collaborations were marked, to some degree, by K W's neuroses concerning scripts, rehearsals, directors, leading ladies, long runs, and other common features of theatrical life. Sensing Codron's sympathy, K W often complained to him directly, bitterly, and at length, by post and over the telephone. Reviewing *The Kenneth Williams Diaries* in 1993, Codron remarked: 'These diaries have enabled me to see in retrospect why so often our professional sorties, starting out with hope and optimism, ended in a state of stress. He realised that he did not seem to belong to any category of artist – "too good for tat, not good enough for the truly art-purposeful Theatre".'

BEVERLEY CROSS

Playwright, screenplay-writer and director: author of the musical *Half a Sixpence*, librettist of opera *The Mines of Sulphur*, etc. Known to K W in 1962 as partner of Maggie Smith, whom he much later married (1975). Married (1965) to Gayden Collins, a former model; K W was present at the wedding, and enjoyed the hospitality of the couple at Seillans in the south of France in 1972 (twice). The lack of sexual common ground seemed to leave K W unusually relaxed in Cross's company. They took 'cultural' cruises in the eastern Mediterranean together in both 1963 and 1965 – rare instances of holidays appropriate to KW's historically enquiring temperament. Cross directed KW (1965) in *The Platinum Cat*: rehearsals were less troubled than usual, but the play failed badly, causing KW what he called his 'breakdown'. 'Mags and Bev', reunited in the seventies, represented an ideal combination of his best friends.

RAE HAMMOND

CSE troupe member, known at that stage for conjuring. A witness to the suicide of ex-Sergeant Major Hank Marriott (in 1947), the means being prussic acid, according to KW: this event and the funeral that followed numbered among his favourite anecdotes. Hammond later became General Manager of the Everyman Theatre, Cheltenham, and an energetic correspondence among former CSE members resumed when Peter Nichols, the playwright, began to assemble material for what became his reminiscent stage-play, *Privates On Parade*. Hammond's memory seems, by all accounts, to have been more retentive than most.

ANDREW HATHAWAY

Penfriend from Beachwood, New Jersey, who took an interest in British comedy films and shows. First wrote KW a fan letter about the Carry On films on 2 September 1971 (though he was under the impression that the series had come to an end in 1964). Later offered to write 'semi-regularly', on which basis the correspondence developed. On his side, KW seems to have enjoyed explaining British institutions and idioms, and taking up extreme monarchist and jingoistic positions in matters of historical debate. The latest-dated of Hathaway's own tightly packed, inaccurately typed air-letters is marked 30 August 1978, at which time the writer was thirty-two, in the 'appliance business' (repairs etc.), and trying 'to get training for theatre and films'.

ERICH HELLER

Distinguished Germanist, born 1911 in Bohemia. Educated in Prague and Cambridge (Ph.D); in England from 1939. University posts at the London School of Economics, Cambridge, and the University of Wales (Swansea), where he held the Chair of German. Wrote to KW 17 November 1950 after seeing him play Hugo in Sartre's *Crime Passionel*; they met for dinner two days later. 'Gay of course. Charming and wholly delightful but I must [not] get too embroiled' (KW's diary, 19 November 1950). This remained roughly KW's attitude throughout their long friendship, which Heller would have liked to see develop into a greater intimacy. KW's letter to Heller of 20 October 1951 (p. 15) contains a remarkable analysis of his reasons for resisting this. Heller remained his friend's intellectual mentor, and his famous book *The Disinherited Mind* provided the basis of many of KW's moral and ethical beliefs. Heller passed the last thirty years of his life teaching at Northwestern University, Evanston, Illinois. He died in 1990.

MICHAEL HITCHMAN

Actor, poet. Another member of the small circle of young actors to which KW belonged in the early fifties. Of all the group, Hitchman seems to have been the one most cast down by lack of work, and KW's diary often describes him as 'depressed'. He died in October 1960. Annette Kerr writes: 'I was the last person to see Michael Hitchman alive. I was living quite near him and went to tea. He was out of work and low but not suicidal. He walked to the bus with me and mentioned he had a severe headache coming on. He died, alone, a few hours later of a brain haemorrhage.' KW wrote in his diary: 'I really loved M. I know I was better for knowing him' (29 October 1960). Later, recording an LP of songs: 'I did the "Boiled Egg" of Michael Hitchman. I felt a particular delight in this, because it's my small way of [paying] a tribute to him, and a way of perpetuating his poem' (30 December 1966). And again, entertaining his friends Tom and Clive at home: 'Afterwards I read them a lot of Hitchmania – how that good man lives *on* in my life' (13 July 1968).

JOHN HUSSEY

Actor, first known to KW at Eastbourne Rep in early 1950: 'John Hussey . . . played piano in the evening very enjoyably' (KW's diary, 7 February 1950). For several years Hussey, KW, Annette Kerr, Richard West and others made up an informal self-supporting group, appearing together in various combinations around the Home Counties repertory companies. In October 1959, KW took a room in Hussey's flat in Hastings Street, London WC1, a unique (and brief) instance of his agreeing to share living-space. Though Hussey appeared with the RSC during the sixties, it was not until he moved to South Africa that he achieved a satisfactory continuity of work, and finally a degree of fame in the serial 'The Dingleys' in 1979. A combination of distance and Hussey's frequent money troubles (with which KW was sometimes asked to help) caused a cooling of the friendship in later years.

ANNETTE KERR

Actress, who first worked with KW in the summer of 1949, during his second season at Newquay Rep in Cornwall. She made an immediate impression on him ('I love Annette Kerr. She's quite the sweetest person I ever knew' — KW's diary, 10 July 1949), and they remained fast friends through several further periods of work, on the south coast (Eastbourne, Margate), in south Wales (Cardiff, Swansea), in the London area and elsewhere. Their friendship survived KW's rise to fame; he even informally proposed marriage in 1961, and a flat-sharing arrangement the following year. Her response was typically sensible: 'she said it would never work out — her smalls in the bathroom, she said, were inevitable . . .' (KW's diary, 7 October 1962). Their meetings became rare in later years, but 'She doesn't change one iota' (diary, 4 May 1979).

ANDREW RAY

Actor (b.1939), son of Ted Ray (Olden), the comedian. Appeared with KW in *Twice Round the Daffodils* (1962), a Carry On-style comedy set in a hospital. They remained friends through the sixties and beyond, sometimes attending films together, sometimes indulging in KW's new habit of observing court proceedings at the Old Bailey. Ray later toured widely, e.g. in India and Africa, during which time KW took on his increasingly-practised role of epistolary mentor — a service he also offered to Ray's wife Susan (Burnet), of whom he was equally fond. This was a turbulent and sometimes unhappy period in Ray's life, however, and KW eventually wound down the friendship, reasoning that the depressions suffered by the two parties tended to mirror each other, unhelpfully to both.

MAGGIE SMITH

Actress, made DBE 1990, now probably the most sought-after actress in the English-speaking theatre, especially in comedy. Raised in Oxford, first acted in OUDS production of *Twelfth Night* in 1952. First worked with KW in the revue *Share My Lettuce* (1957): 'I know nobody except Margaret Smith whom I like v. much' (KW's diary, 13 July 1957). This reciprocated liking persisted through their work in Peter Shaffer's *The Private Ear* and *The Public Eye* (1962), and thereafter through their many backstage encounters while working in adjacent Shaftesbury Avenue theatres. Though critics (and her biographer) have tended to scorn the idea, KW liked to think that he had contributed to Maggie Smith's remarkable technique, and on one occasion she gave him to understand that he had (see *The Kenneth Williams Diaries*, 31 January 1973, p.443). KW was more at ease with Beverley Cross, whom she married in 1975, than with her first husband (1967), Robert Stephens, as is reflected in the correspondence.

NOEL WILLMAN

Actor and director, b. Londonderry, 1918, whom KW first met at Robert Bolt's house (July 1963) when Bolt was preparing his play *Gentle Jack*, to feature KW as the Pan-like sprite Jack. Willman directed the play, and though it turned out a painful failure, their friendship survived. Willman had trained with Michel St Denis at the London Theatre Studio. Without achieving great fame, he worked internationally for many years, appearing in films as various as *Kiss of the Vampire* and *Doctor Zhivago*. His speciality was cold-hearted villains. When KW suffered a virtual nervous breakdown in December 1969 over the noises in his Farley Court flat, Willman put him up; the subject of their sharing accommodation seems to have been broached semi-seriously later, by Willman (see KW's letter of 20 November 1967, p. 72). They fell out later over KW's refusal to do a play which Willman had either written or was proposing to direct (see letter to George Borwick of 2 January 1972, p. 148).

JOHN WINDEATT

A shadowy figure whose name pops up obstinately in the mid-sixties. Described by Sarah Miles as 'one of those divine chaps, a homosexual, a landscape gardener, and a procurer of young boys to the rich'. Miles met him in a park, and rented him her house. He did not, however, pay, for he had quickly acquired bad memories of the house (see the sundered love-affair referred to in KW's letter of 20 November 1967, p. 70), and was in any case largely absent on the Sicilian landscape-gardening project that forms the background to the correspondence here. On his return to London, Windeatt was seen in a Rolls-Royce, which caused Miles's husband, Robert Bolt, to ask her whether he had paid any rent yet. She rang him, and he undertook to pay. The day before the due date, another voice rang to tell Sarah Miles, 'I'm sorry to tell you that a Johnny Windeatt has just put his head in your gas oven.' Windeatt left a note asserting 'All I have belongs to Sarah Miles.' 'All that turned out to be was a fucking Pyrenean mountain dog,' she recalled. The *Guardian Weekend Magazine*, 16 October 1993, places the above story in its fuller domestic context (see 'Being Mrs Bolt', article by Susie McKenzie).

INDEX

INDEX

Page numbers in **bold** refer to letters from KW.